Survival

GLOBAL POLITICS AND STRATEGY

Volume 63 Number 4 | August–September 2021

'American international success depended not just on raw American power but on the combination of power, liberal-democratic ideas and liberal-internationalist projects. The United States was ascendant in part because the liberal-democratic ideal, as manifested in modern America, was profoundly appealing to people all over the world.'

Daniel Deudney and G. John Ikenberry, Misplaced Restraint: The Quincy Coalition Versus Liberal Internationalism, p. 25.

'For all the handwringing about "forever wars" over the past several years, the United States has arrived at a reasonably effective, reasonably sustainable strategy for managing a terrorism problem that will not be solved anytime soon.'

Hal Brands and Michael O'Hanlon, The War on Terror Has Not Yet Failed: A Net Assessment After 20 Years, pp. 47–8.

'Trump himself would never admit that there had been Russian interference, because he understood that this would cast doubt on his right to occupy the White House. A wiser course might have been to acknowledge possible interference, appoint a commission and move on.'

Angela Stent, Trump's Russia Legacy and Biden's Response, p. 57.

T0191098

Survival
GLOBAL POLITICS AND STRATEGY
Volume 63 Number 4 | August–September 2021

Contents

Survival GLOBAL POLITICS AND STRATEGY

Debating US foreign policy

On the cover
US Secretary of State
Antony Blinken speaks
at a press conference in
Amman, Jordan, on 26
May 2021.

On the web
Visit www.iiss.org/
publications/survival
for brief notices on new
books on Politics and
International Relations,
Asia-Pacific, and Russia
and Eurasia.

***Survival* editors' blog**
For ideas and
commentary from
Survival editors and
contributors, visit
www.iiss.org/blogs/
survival-blog.

Cover: Alex Brandon/POOL/AFP via Getty Images

Survival
GLOBAL POLITICS AND STRATEGY

The International Institute for Strategic Studies

2121 K Street, NW | Suite 600 | Washington DC 20037 | USA
Tel +1 202 659 1490   Fax +1 202 659 1499   E-mail survival@iiss.org   Web www.iiss.org

Arundel House | 6 Temple Place | London | WC2R 2PG | UK
Tel +44 (0)20 7379 7676   Fax +44 (0)20 7836 3108   E-mail iiss@iiss.org

14th Floor, GBCorp Tower | Bahrain Financial Harbour | Manama | Kingdom of Bahrain
Tel +973 1718 1155   Fax +973 1710 0155   E-mail iiss-middleeast@iiss.org

9 Raffles Place | #49-01 Republic Plaza | Singapore 048619
Tel +65 6499 0055   Fax +65 6499 0059   E-mail iiss-asia@iiss.org

Pariser Platz 6A | 10117 Berlin | Germany
Tel +49 30 311 99 300   E-mail iiss-europe@iiss.org

Survival Online www.tandfonline.com/survival and www.iiss.org/publications/survival

Aims and Scope *Survival* is one of the world's leading forums for analysis and debate of international and strategic affairs. Shaped by its editors to be both timely and forward thinking, the journal encourages writers to challenge conventional wisdom and bring fresh, often controversial, perspectives to bear on the strategic issues of the moment. With a diverse range of authors, *Survival* aims to be scholarly in depth while vivid, well written and policy-relevant in approach. Through commentary, analytical articles, case studies, forums, review essays, reviews and letters to the editor, the journal promotes lively, critical debate on issues of international politics and strategy.

Editor **Dana Allin**
Managing Editor **Jonathan Stevenson**
Associate Editor **Carolyn West**
Assistant Editor **Jessica Watson**
Production and Cartography **John Buck, Kelly Verity**

Contributing Editors

Ian Bremmer	**Toby Dodge**	**Melissa Griffith**	**Hanns W. Maull**	**Steven Simon**
Rosa Brooks	**Bill Emmott**	**John L. Harper**	**Jeffrey Mazo**	**Angela Stent**
David P. Calleo	**Mark Fitzpatrick**	**Matthew Harries**	**'Funmi Olonisakin**	**Ray Takeyh**
Russell Crandall	**John A. Gans, Jr**	**Erik Jones**	**Teresita C. Schaffer**	**David C. Unger**
				Lanxin Xiang

Published for the IISS by
Routledge Journals, an imprint of Taylor & Francis, an Informa business.

About the IISS The IISS, a registered charity with offices in Washington, London, Manama and Singapore, is the world's leading authority on political–military conflict. It is the primary independent source of accurate, objective information on international strategic issues. Publications include *The Military Balance*, an annual reference work on each nation's defence capabilities; *Strategic Survey*, an annual review of world affairs; *Survival*, a bimonthly journal on international affairs; *Strategic Comments*, an online analysis of topical issues in international affairs; and the *Adelphi* series of books on issues of international security.

SUBMISSIONS

To submit an article, authors are advised to follow these guidelines:

- *Survival* articles are around 4,000–10,000 words long including endnotes. A word count should be included with a draft.
- All text, including endnotes, should be double-spaced with wide margins.
- Any tables or artwork should be supplied in separate files, ideally not embedded in the document or linked to text around it.
- All *Survival* articles are expected to include endnote references. These should be complete and include first and last names of authors, titles of articles (even from newspapers), place of publication, publisher, exact publication dates, volume and issue number (if from a journal) and page numbers. Web sources should include complete URLs and DOIs if available.
- A summary of up to 150 words should be included with the article. The summary should state the main argument clearly and concisely, not simply say what the article is about.

- A short author's biography of one or two lines should also be included. This information will appear at the foot of the first page of the article.

Please note that *Survival* has a strict policy of listing multiple authors in alphabetical order.

Submissions should be made by email, in Microsoft Word format, to survival@iiss.org. Alternatively, hard copies may be sent to *Survival*, IISS–US, 2121 K Street NW, Suite 801, Washington, DC 20037, USA.

The editorial review process can take up to three months. *Survival*'s acceptance rate for unsolicited manuscripts is less than 20%. *Survival* does not normally provide referees' comments in the event of rejection. Authors are permitted to submit simultaneously elsewhere so long as this is consistent with the policy of the other publication and the Editors of *Survival* are informed of the dual submission.

Readers are encouraged to comment on articles from the previous issue. Letters should be concise, no longer than 750 words and relate directly to the argument or points made in the original article.

ADVERTISING AND PERMISSIONS
For advertising rates and schedules

USA/Canada: The Advertising Manager, Taylor & Francis Inc., 530 Walnut Street, Suite 850, Philadelphia, PA 19106, USA Tel +1 (800) 354 1420 Fax +1 (215) 207 0050.

UK/Europe/Rest of World: The Advertising Manager, Routledge Journals, Taylor & Francis, 4 Park Square, Milton Park, Abingdon, Oxfordshire OX14 4RN, UK Tel +44 (0) 207 017 6000 Fax +44 (0) 207 017 6336.

SUBSCRIPTIONS

Survival is published bimonthly in February, April, June, August, October and December by Routledge Journals, an imprint of Taylor & Francis, an Informa Business.

Annual Subscription 2021

	UK, RoI	US, Canada Mexico	Europe	Rest of world
Individual	£172	$290	€ 233	$290
Institution (print and online)	£620	$1,085	€ 909	$1,142
Institution (online only)	£527	$922	€ 773	$971

Taylor & Francis has a flexible approach to subscriptions, enabling us to match individual libraries' requirements. This journal is available via a traditional institutional subscription (either print with online access, or online only at a discount) or as part of our libraries, subject collections or archives. For more information on our sales packages please visit http://www.tandfonline.com/page/librarians.

All current institutional subscriptions include online access for any number of concurrent users across a local area network to the currently available backfile and articles posted online ahead of publication.

Subscriptions purchased at the personal rate are strictly for personal, non-commercial use only. The reselling of personal subscriptions is prohibited. Personal subscriptions must be purchased with a personal cheque or credit card. Proof of personal status may be requested.

Dollar rates apply to all subscribers outside Europe. Euro rates apply to all subscribers in Europe, except the UK and the Republic of Ireland where the pound sterling rate applies. If you are unsure which rate applies to you please contact Customer Services in the UK. All subscriptions are payable in advance and all rates include postage. Journals are sent by air to the USA, Canada, Mexico, India, Japan and Australasia. Subscriptions are entered on an annual basis, i.e. January to December. Payment may be made by sterling cheque, dollar cheque, euro cheque, international money order, National Giro or credit cards (Amex, Visa and Mastercard).

Survival (USPS 013095) is published bimonthly (in Feb, Apr, Jun, Aug, Oct and Dec) by Routledge Journals, Taylor & Francis, 4 Park Square, Milton Park, Abingdon, OX14 4RN, United Kingdom.

The US annual subscription price is $1,023. Airfreight and mailing in the USA by agent named WN Shipping USA, 156-15, 146th Avenue, 2nd Floor, Jamaica, NY 11434, USA. Periodicals postage paid at Jamaica NY 11431.

US Postmaster: Send address changes to Survival, C/O Air Business Ltd / 156-15 146th Avenue, Jamaica, New York, NY11434.

Subscription records are maintained at Taylor & Francis Group, 4 Park Square, Milton Park, Abingdon, OX14 4RN, United Kingdom.

ORDERING INFORMATION

Please contact your local Customer Service Department to take out a subscription to the Journal: **USA, Canada:** Taylor & Francis, Inc., 530 Walnut Street, Suite 850, Philadelphia, PA 19106, USA. Tel: +1 800 354 1420; Fax: +1 215 207 0050. **UK/Europe/Rest of World:** T&F Customer Services, Informa UK Ltd, Sheepen Place, Colchester, Essex, CO3 3LP, United Kingdom. Tel: +44 (0) 20 7017 5544; Fax: +44 (0) 20 7017 5198; Email: subscriptions@tandf.co.uk.

Back issues: Taylor & Francis retains a two-year back issue stock of journals. Older volumes are held by our official stockists: Periodicals Service Company, 351 Fairview Ave., Suite 300, Hudson, New York 12534, USA to whom all orders and enquiries should be addressed. *Tel* +1 518 537 4700 *Fax* +1 518 537 5899 *e-mail* psc@periodicals.com *web* http://www.periodicals.com/tandf.html.

The International Institute for Strategic Studies (IISS) and our publisher Taylor & Francis make every effort to ensure the accuracy of all the information (the "Content") contained in our publications. However, the IISS and our publisher Taylor & Francis, our agents, and our licensors make no representations or warranties whatsoever as to the accuracy, completeness, or suitability for any purpose of the Content. Any opinions and views expressed in this publication are the opinions and views of the authors, and are not the views of or endorsed by the IISS and our publisher Taylor & Francis. The accuracy of the Content should not be relied upon and should be independently verified with primary sources of information. The IISS and our publisher Taylor & Francis shall not be liable for any losses, actions, claims, proceedings, demands, costs, expenses, damages, and other liabilities whatsoever or howsoever caused arising directly or indirectly in connection with, in relation to or arising out of the use of the Content. Terms & Conditions of access and use can be found at http://www.tandfonline.com/page/terms-and-conditions.

The issue date is August–September 2021.

The print edition of this journal is printed on ANSI-conforming acid-free paper.

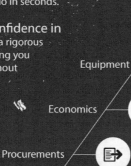

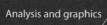

Misplaced Restraint: The Quincy Coalition Versus Liberal Internationalism

Daniel Deudney and G. John Ikenberry

Ideas matter. American foreign policy has always been, and remains, ideologically contested. It has been shaped by a mixture of intellectual legacies, historical institutional commitments and shifting circumstances. Historians have repeatedly noted that ideological and intellectual movements – schools of thought – often play an important role in forming American foreign policy, particularly in periods where uncertainty about priorities reigns. Whether it is the progressivism and reformism of the early years of the twentieth century, giving rise to Wilsonian internationalism, or the realism of Reinhold Niebuhr and Hans Morgenthau during the early Cold War, public intellectuals and theorists have often provided powerful interpretive crystallisations of current world realities, their relation to basic American interests and agendas for action. Sometimes these intellectual influences come from lone individuals, but over recent decades, competing schools of thought about American grand strategy have increasingly been institutionalised in think tanks and policy-research centres. They are often well funded, perpetually prolific and deeply engaged in day-to-day commentary on current events and policies.

One proven formula for persuasiveness is to couple powerful domestic ideological and political movements with a foreign-policy vision and agenda. Successful foreign policy does not begin at the water's edge; it

Daniel Deudney is a Professor of Political Science at Johns Hopkins University. **G. John Ikenberry** is the Albert G. Milbank Professor of Politics and International Affairs at Princeton University.

Survival | vol. 63 no. 4 | August–September 2021 | pp. 7–32   https://doi.org/10.1080/00396338.2021.1956187

projects domestic forces across the water. The rise and fall of foreign-policy projects are also powerfully determined by major events, often unexpected, which suddenly transform the landscape of threat, interest and possibility. The Pearl Harbor attack, the Cuban Missile Crisis, 9/11 and now the COVID-19 pandemic instantly redefined the landscape, rendering some agendas obsolete and others more viable.

The discursive battlefield between ideologies and agendas also features narratives of major foreign-policy failures, such as appeasement in the 1930s, the Vietnam War and, most recently, the Iraq War. To the extent that foreign-policy schools are – or can be – associated and implicated in costly failures, they are discredited. And foreign-policy schools offering compelling diagnoses of the sources of these failures and policies to avoid their recurrence gain credibility and influence. Appeasement was blamed on the interwar idealists. Realpolitik, previously an outlier, became influential by providing a guidebook for avoiding another Munich and the vulnerability of military unpreparedness.[1] Later, the Cuban Missile Crisis punctured the dominant early Cold War thinking about nuclear risks and elevated the need for mutual superpower restraint and institutionalised arms control. More recently, the debacle of the American invasion and occupation of Iraq in 2003 has fuelled far-reaching doubts about the desirability of America's global commitments and the expansive use of force against perceived threats virtually everywhere. While understandable, unavoidable and to an extent desirable, of course, an undue focus on avoiding repeats of past failures risks not giving adequate attention to emergent problems and new threats.

The Quincy coalition

Over the last decade, as the Iraq disaster has haunted US foreign policy, the Quincy coalition, a new school of thought emphasising 'restraint', has emerged and quickly become a major voice in the conversation about American foreign policy. It sprung from the ostensibly odd alliance of domestic libertarians, balance-of-power realists and the anti-imperialist liberal left. Despite their common foreign-policy critique, each has a distinct world view and lineage. American libertarianism seeks to shrink the size, cost and powers of government, which it deems an inherent threat to liberty, and views foreign wars, alliances and international institutions as reinforc-ing and extending a menacing American Leviathan. Realism comes in many varieties, but particularly prominent among American realists is a view of the world stressing the balance of power as the necessary and sufficient basis for international order, along with an antipathy to foreign military intervention, over-extension by alliance commitment and the international liberal project of moderating anarchy with institutions. The progressive-left partners in the new Quincy coalition are anti-imperialist, and view Pax Americana as coer-cive, exploitative and corrosive of domestic democracy, as it empowers the national security state. Each of these coalition partners in the new 'restraint' school has a deep domestic history and intellectual foundation. Prior to this alliance, they had been as much adversaries as allies. Their unifying objective is avoiding another Iraq War and curtailing American military interventions. More generally, they are united in opposing the project of American liberal internationalism, manifest in a system of rules, institutions and partnerships that the United States has built and led over the last 70 years. Overall, the new restraint coalition poses a radical challenge to the main course of American foreign policy in the post-war global era.

In part, the new restraint school has gained influence because of gen-erous funding provided by libertarian philanthropists Charles and David Koch, and liberal philanthropist George Soros. A new think tank – the Quincy Institute for Responsible Statecraft, headed by Andrew Bacevich – affords it a base with the resources to weigh in assertively and authori-tatively on American foreign-policy choices.[2] The Quincy Institute and the restraint school have gathered a wide array of formidable foreign-policy scholars and commentators. The libertarians – crucially represented by the Cato Institute, long a beneficiary of the Koch brothers – include Christopher Preble and Ted Carpenter. The leading neo-realists are John Mearsheimer, Stephen Walt, Barry Posen, Patrick Porter and Michael Desch. From the pro-gressive left are Samuel Moyn, Jeanne Morefield, Stephen Wertheim and Gordon Adams. Given its abundant resources in people, ideas and money, and the salience of its pledge to avoid another Iraq War, the Quincy coali-tion has appeared well positioned to help shape US foreign policy and, by extension, the world order. Indeed, President Joe Biden's withdrawal from

Afghanistan – and Donald Trump's earlier plan to do so as well – appear to be following the Quincy playbook.[3]

In many ways, the unexpected rise of Trump to the presidency seemed to be a breakthrough moment for the restraint school. Like the restrainers, Trump condemned the Iraq War and American interventionism in distant countries. Like them, Trump rejected alliance commitments, calling into question NATO and the security pacts with Japan and South Korea. Like them, he rejected international institutions, withdrawing from numerous arms-control accords and free-trade agreements and even pulling out of the World Health Organization in the middle of a global pandemic. Trump withdrew from the Paris agreement on climate change, deeming it a threat to American sovereignty and prosperity. He was indifferent to democracy promotion and human rights. Trump's foreign policy was also purely transactional and fundamentally hostile to institutionalised restraint and cooperation.[4] While the new restraint coalition did not commend Trump's reckless conduct and administrative incompetence, it is hard to escape the conclusion that the basic thrust of his 'America First' foreign policy was a bold – if crude – implementation of the Quincy coalition's core vision.

Despite its rising clout, the Quincy coalition has not received the critical scrutiny it warrants. Its visions and agendas are fatally flawed. It is profoundly deficient in its understanding of the wellsprings of American success in the twentieth century. It is largely blind to domestic and international realities, a blindness deeply rooted in the basic world views that animate it. It incorporates regressive tendencies, undermining important American accomplishments both domestic and international. More particularly, its foreign-policy agenda is profoundly outmoded. If pursued, it would harm fundamental American interests, standing and influence. It would do grave damage to important international institutions and global capacities to address significant and rapidly growing global problems, ranging from nuclear proliferation and climate change to cyber governance and pandemic-disease response. It would also diminish the prospects for liberal democracy and human rights globally. And it offers a woefully weak response to the undeniable reality of China's expansion and hegemonic aspirations. A critique of the Iraq blunder during the post-Cold

War unipolar moment provides little guidance for conducting American foreign policy in response to cascading global interdependence, democratic backsliding and a historic strategic challenge from an illiberal great power.

Modern liberalism and internationalism

The prime target of the three Quincy schools – usually explicit but always implicit – is the modern liberal and internationalist thinking that emerged in the early twentieth century. The real essence of this variant of liberal-democratic theory and practice is often mischaracterised by its adversaries. Modern liberals and internationalists do hold strong versions of basic liberal values and goals. But they are distinctive in attempting to link these core liberal commitments to a fundamentally new set of world developments that have sprung from the Industrial Revolution and its consequences.[5] The basic insight of modern liberalism and internationalism is that much higher levels of interdependence at larger scales than existed in previous eras, due to radically changed industrial circumstances, necessitate new and extraordinary measures to secure and realise those basic liberal values and goals.[6]

Building on the liberalism of Montesquieu, Adam Smith, James Madison and John Stuart Mill, twentieth-century liberals such as Leonard Hobhouse, John Dewey and Jane Addams sought to reinvent the liberal state in ways that were responsive to the new industrial world of immense cities, extreme economic stratification and multinational corporations, and the complexities of societies increasingly dependent on a cascade of new technologies, from the automobile and radio to the jet aeroplane and internet. The essence of the new approach is contained in Dewey's concept of the public as an interdependence group whose scope changes as technology changes, thus requiring new forms of government and community.[7] At every step of reform, old liberals and libertarians argued that extensions of democratic government were essentially erosions of freedom.

Modern liberals argue that the new arrangements serve both freedom and the public interest in new circumstances.[8] To their way of thinking, the mixed economy – which combines capitalism with extensive but carefully crafted governmental regulation – is necessary for capitalism to flourish and for other core liberal-democratic values and goals to be preserved. The modern regulatory state has evolved to curtail the negative externalities – such as noise, air and water pollution, and resource degradation – that modern technology has produced, and which threaten human health and erode the foundations of prosperity. The essential task of the modern liberal state is to protect the health of its citizens by harnessing the fruits of science and technology. A simultaneous commitment to universal education and the creation of skilled labour would ensure that the people remain capable of self-government and able to flourish economically.

Theodore Roosevelt's New Nationalism, Woodrow Wilson's New Freedom, Franklin Delano Roosevelt and Harry Truman's New Deal and Lyndon Johnson's Great Society were all attempts to extend core liberal-democratic values in a new world marked by the intensification of industrialism and the rise of interdependence. This tradition of modern liberalism gave birth to pragmatism as a philosophy, and it is highly experimental and adaptive. It looks to modern science and engineering as a source of new wealth and power, as well as authority. Had the modern regulatory state not developed, the negative effects of industrialism would likely have overshadowed its positive ones.[9]

Modern liberals also contend that the Industrial Revolution profoundly altered the world of international politics in revolutionary ways. Early proto-liberals and nineteenth-century liberals looked to international law to moderate international conflict and reduce the severity and frequency of war. With the coming of industrial warfare and its great amplification in levels of violence, modern liberals increasingly argued that further international steps were necessary to restrain violence and war, and prevent civilisational cataclysm. With the advent of the titanic destructive power of nuclear weapons, the avoidance of major war and creation of new architectures of restraint – in particular, arms-control regimes – became central to the liberal-international project. The League of Nations, the United Nations and arms-control projects that have been such a distinctive feature of global politics in the twentieth century are all attempts by liberals to adapt to these new realities.[10]

The Industrial Revolution and the global spread of capitalist exchange and production also brought new forms of interdependence, which liberal internationalists believed required new international economic institutions.

The world economy, like domestic economies, required carefully designed supports and restraints. In the wake of the mass disruption and impoverishment caused by the Great Depression, modern liberals laid out an evolving programme to channel and bolster international trade and finance. Following the Second World War, they designed and implemented the International Monetary Fund, the World Bank and the General Agreement on Tariffs and Trade. These international institutions provided a framework for reopening the world economy, paving the way for a 'golden era' of sustained global economic growth, and extending capitalism and its attendant prosperity to previously very poor societies all over the world.[11]

In turn, the spread of industrial production and the acceleration of economic growth created major new problems of environmental degradation. But in the 1960s, awareness of the limited capacities of the planetary biosphere to withstand the demands of resource extraction and mounting pollution triggered another wave of institution-building that was typically spearheaded by American liberals and the US government.[12] Perhaps the signature development was the depletion of the ozone layer of the upper atmosphere by industrial chemicals, which posed a major threat to human health and the operation of the biosphere. The paradigmatic liberal-internationalist response was the highly effective global regime to restrain and eliminate chlorofluorocarbons globally. Most recently, atmospheric alterations caused by carbon-dioxide and methane emissions have seriously affected the planetary climate system. Scientific evidence indicates that rising emissions are bringing severe storms, widening drought, increased sea levels and ocean acidification, which in combination will produce a global catastrophe unless they are curtailed. To grapple with these new realities, the restraints offered by the Quincy coalition are thoroughly outmoded. And it is the restraints offered by modern liberalism and its globalist internationalism that are needed now.

Strange bedfellows

At first glance, the three schools in the Quincy coalition seem to be unlikely alliance partners. Realists of all varieties, and particularly in American foreign-policy debates, have been harsh critics of liberalism, seeing it either as unworldly and idealistic or crusading and imperial. Realism incorporates a profound commitment to the state as a vital source of order, and has a hallowed tradition of building and strengthening the state. Libertarianism is an extreme version of domestic liberalism and a radical form of individualism, hostile to claims of society, community and nationality. Realists not only embrace statism; they cultivate national commonality as a source of domestic order and strength for defence and war-making. Libertarians are hostile to the state, seeking to minimise it to the greatest degree compatible with public order. They want to thoroughly diminish claims of government and community on the individual, while realists want the individual to sacrifice for the state and nation. During the Cold War, the libertarians were a domestic outlier in questioning NATO and American alliances; Cold War realists supported such measures as central to their foreign-policy agenda.

An even wider chasm divides libertarians from the progressive left, which lies at the opposite end of the political spectrum of liberalism. The progressive agenda seeks to diminish economic inequality, regulate market activity for the common good and make institutions at all levels demo-cratically accountable. Libertarians are indifferent to inequality, hostile to the regulation of capital and markets, and have no fundamental commit-ment to democracy, except as a possible restraint on state power. In the American context, the Koch-backed libertarian movement has staunchly opposed economic and environmental regulation, progressive taxation and expanded government healthcare policies, promotion of which has been at the top of the progressive agenda. The libertarian domestic agenda is to dismantle the institutions of the New Deal, while American progressives seek to preserve and extend them. Like the alliance between the Soviet Union and the liberal democracies against fascism, the Quincy coalition is driven almost entirely by common adversaries rather than a shared vision of political order and society.

To understand the limitations of the new Quincy coalition, it is neces-sary to look at the basic ideas, agendas and deficiencies of each of the three alliance partners. Once these points have been laid out, it will be possible to see a deeper affinity connecting the libertarians and the realists, and the actual affinities that the left-liberal foreign-policy thinkers have with liberal internationalism. Once these anatomies and catalogues of deficiencies have been exposed, we explore the ways in which liberal internationalism offers a programme of commitments and restraints appropriate to contemporary global realities.

Libertarianism at home and abroad

Over the several centuries of its development, Western liberalism has been marked by an incredible diversity of variations, and much of the internal life of liberal democracies has been shaped by their rivalries and alliances. A strong emphasis on the rights of the individual has been a defining feature of Western liberalism from its inception, but in the nineteenth and twentieth centuries, libertarianism crystallised as a highly self-conscious intellectual and political project. It aimed to combat the rise of popular democracy and the development of governmental capacity to serve the public interest in industrial societies. Libertarianism has also been closely attached to concepts of private property and free-market exchange, making it the ideology of property and capital. And in the face of totalitarian, anti-liberal movements on both the left and the right, libertarians came to view the liberal-democratic welfare state as a slippery slope to totalitarianism. In the classic statement by Friedrich Hayek, the democratic welfare state is on the 'road to serfdom' – an ominous return to pre-liberal and pre-capitalist formations rather that a realisation of democratic interests.[13]

In the Anglo-American world, Hayek and University of Chicago economist Milton Friedman launched multi-sided attacks on the New Deal and British social democracy. In response to the Keynesian programme of state power for macroeconomic stabilisation and growth, the neoliberals, as they came to call themselves, saw inefficiency, stagnation and the creeping death of individual liberty.[14] The novels of Ayn Rand furnished the libertarian world view with inspiring heroic exemplars, a new mythology of the entrepreneurial elite and a winner-take-all ethos.[15] Libertarianism has been particularly strong in the United States because it rhetorically connects with the founding 'don't tread on me' American narrative of freedom and suspicion of government, as well as a commitment to widespread gun ownership.

Under the leadership of Ronald Reagan in the United States and Margaret Thatcher in the United Kingdom, libertarianism and the neoliberal movement, paradoxically portrayed in both countries as conservative, rapidly began undermining labour unions, dialling back progressive taxation, deregulating market activity and cutting social-welfare services. Against rising concern over environmental degradation, libertarians led resistance to environmental regulation, casting it as an infringement on private property and individual liberty.[16]

The libertarian agenda for the international order is modest and almost entirely negative. Classical free-market theory, as laid out by Smith in *The Wealth of Nations* in 1776, sought to dismantle mercantilism and tariffs in order to encourage market transactions across international borders. Instead of state power, the 'hidden hand' of the market would operate, and order would emerge spontaneously. By the middle of the nineteenth century, the vision of a world order centred on market exchange was well developed and widely held. As rising interdependence prompted liberals to build international legal systems to restrain states and international organisations to provide global public services, some capitalists joined in support, while others adopted the libertarian stance of opposition. Libertarians reasoned that just as the individual in domestic society should be protected from regulation and restraint, the state in the international system should not be abridged or encumbered.

The libertarian agenda is modest and negative

Such thinking led American libertarians to oppose the League of Nations and the United Nations. As decolonisation proceeded, they resisted the international effort to develop what came to be called the Third World and objected to development aid and efforts to build a new international economic order that would regulate international trade to help developing societies advance. During the Cold War and thereafter, American libertarians vociferously opposed binding international arms-control agreements, seeing them as both unnecessary and dangerous. Although strong anti-communist convictions had led many libertarians to grudgingly support the American alliance system and NATO during the Cold War, they considered

NATO expendable once the threat of global communism was extinguished. The European Union, championed by liberal internationalists, became a new target.[17] By the late twentieth century, American libertarianism had gelled into wholesale opposition to international law and organisations of virtually all varieties.

Libertarianism has deeply shaped – largely for the worse – American society and the capacity of the American government to address problems, both domestically and internationally. Its understanding of social reality is fundamentally deficient because it ignores the reality of rising levels of domestic and international interdependence. Many of the central problems in world politics, ranging from nuclear proliferation and climate change to transnational border flows and pandemic management, spill across borders. They arise because individuals, corporations and states are doing things, intentionally and unintentionally, that have significant negative effects on other actors at increasing distance. To address these problems, as liberal internationalists argue, cooperation and institutions are required.

The libertarian world view also does not recognise extreme inequality in wealth as a problem. While the pursuit of complete equality would indeed be stifling and coercive, extreme wealth inequality curtails freedom by affording a rich elite inordinate political and economic power. Left unregulated, capitalist societies stratify, with great privilege accruing to the few and diminished circumstances and opportunities afflicting the many.[18] Internationally, a chasm of inequality between the wealthiest and poorest states produces an international hierarchy, not an order of freedom. The wealthy few will prevail and the poorest many must submit. The ability to solve collective problems, such as climate change, is severely hampered, as the poor lack the resources to address their own problems. Redistribution by government on behalf of a large majority is not a threat to free societies but necessary to sustain them.

With the COVID-19 pandemic, the costs of libertarian success in restraining government have become all too clear. While the United States leads the world in science and innovation, it has substantially failed in implementing simple public-health measures, such as mask-wearing. As of May 2021, America led the world in COVID-19 deaths by a significant margin.[19]

The pandemic is a global phenomenon, inevitably spilling across borders. If the majority of the world population cannot be vaccinated soon, the potential for new, more lethal viral mutations will again place the successfully vaccinated in jeopardy. By opposing international aid and the development of minimal healthcare services globally, libertarians have left America – and humanity – more vulnerable than it has to be. While libertarians are concerned about compromising the absolute freedom of the American body politic, the health of human bodies everywhere requires globally coordinated minimum healthcare.

Restraint-realism, the Iraq War and world order

Realists are extremely conscious of themselves as a tradition of thinking about international politics, ancient in its lineage and espoused by leading stars of the Western canon, including Thucydides, Niccolò Machiavelli, Thomas Hobbes and Jean-Jacques Rousseau. Realists also believe that their approach to politics and international order is certified by long practical experience, across millennia of wars and diplomatic rivalries.[20] But realism is a broad tent in which many variations on the basic theme, some quite antagonistic to one another, find a common home. Some realists of the hegemonic-order school argue that order arises only from concentrations of power. Other realists argue essentially the opposite: that order stems from opposition to concentration and from distributed and balanced configurations of power in equilibrium.[21] The hegemonic school includes Thucydides, E.H. Carr and, most recently, Robert Gilpin and William Wohlforth.[22] The balance-of-power school includes Machiavelli, Rousseau and, most recently, Kenneth Waltz, Posen and Walt. Another prominent realist, John J. Mearsheimer, straddles the two camps.[23]

Restraint is central to both realist visions of order, but in contrary ways. For hegemonic realists, subordinate powers and the dynamics of anarchy are restrained by the most powerful state. For balance theorists, the emergence of hegemons is restrained by the balance of power, which also moderates anarchy. Realists differ significantly on international institutions, which hegemonic theorists value as expressions of dominance, but balance theorists view sceptically as constraints on state freedom of action. Realism seems to be a cat with nine lives, always prepared for any eventuality. But on closer examination, it is more like nine cats, often quarrelsome and each suited to different circumstances. Even so, most realists do not attach much importance to differences in domestic regime type, focusing instead on the dynamics of anarchy, which impose restraints on states regardless of type of government.

While American realists chronically complain about their marginalisation in US foreign policy, in fact they have had a major impact on grand strategy and foreign policy. Realism's most central insights focus on the conduct of enduring great-power rivalries. Particularly during the Cold War, realists such as George Kennan, Morgenthau, Robert Tucker and Henry Kissinger were extraordinarily influential in guiding US strategy. They shared deep scepticism of liberal crusades to transform the world and American interventions to democratise foreign governments.[24] But they have often sharply disagreed about important policy issues, from the Vietnam War to nuclear arms control.

After the Cold War ended and the Soviet Union collapsed, realism seemed to be obsolete. American foreign-policy thinking gravitated towards liberal agendas. But American realists soon found a new role as critics. As the United States expanded NATO into the former Soviet Union and deployed forces for humanitarian and peacekeeping missions in the Balkans, Somalia, Haiti and West Africa, American realists vigorously objected to the use of American power when fundamental national interests were not at stake. After the 9/11 attacks and the focus of American foreign policy on aggressive counter-terrorism and coercive counter-proliferation, many American realists warned against overreach. With the Bush administration's invasion of Iraq in 2003, American restraint-realists' critique regained traction. The United States found itself in a quagmire, sustaining high casualties but unable to achieve its goals. For realist critics, the Iraq War was a textbook case of disaster resulting from unchecked power and expansive liberal agendas.[25]

Restraint-realists' standard interpretation of the Iraq War, however, is inaccurate. They fail to recognise that hegemonic realists – their doctrinal cousins – and not liberal internationalists were the main drivers of the war.

While the Bush administration did articulate the democratisation of Iraq as a goal, this was not its main motive and was presented as a primary rationale mainly for domestic American consumption. The key architects of the war – Richard Cheney, Donald Rumsfeld and Paul Wolfowitz – were not liberals or liberal internationalists but hegemonic realists seeking to preserve and extend American primacy in the Middle East in the face of a revisionist challenge. The Iraq War was a realist war far more than a liberal one, which many American as well as European liberal internationalists vigorously opposed.[26]

As debate about the real motivations of the Iraq War has faded, restraint-realists have generalised their argument, and called for far-reaching American retrenchment. Withdrawing from the Middle East and terminating the war on terrorism are their prime objectives. But they also advise the United States to dismantle much of its global presence of alliances and bases. NATO, they argue, has outlived its purposes, and the United States should make an orderly withdrawal to a posture of what they call 'off-shore balancing'. They observe that the Europeans are wealthy enough to defend themselves, as are the Japanese and the South Koreans.[27] The global American military footprint is exorbitantly costly in resources better spent for domestic purposes, and repeatedly draws the United States into conflicts that have little to do with core American national interests or security.[28]

Quite aside from their misreading of the Iraq War, the equilibrium realists have a seriously incomplete understanding of the major forces at play in world politics. The greatest deficiency is an underappreciation of interdependence and the imperatives it creates for achieving security and basic national interests. Because of the industrial and subsequent revolutions in the power of human actors, the contemporary world is quite unlike the great sweep of previous history. It is marked by large and growing spillovers, externalities and unintended consequences. The equilibrium-realist approach, focusing on relative power, fails to register the epochal shift in the absolute levels of power generated by industrial modernity. In a world of intense interdependences in terms of violence, economics and ecology, the anarchic system is simply unable to provide appropriate and adequate restraints. In this world, self-generating equilibrium is not a sufficient basis for world order. A tradition that arose and thrived in a low-interdependence world is utterly ill-suited for providing insight and guidance in a highly interdependent world.

Hidden affinities

Once the deeper logics of libertarianism and equilibrium realism are brought into view, they seem less like strange bedfellows and more like natural allies. Both cast politics and society as atomistic. For libertarians, the individual or the corporation is the sole legitimate actor, and anything – such as society and community – that would restrain them is suspect. Similarly, equilibrium realists elevate the autonomous sovereign state and view binding international commitments, law and institutions as violative of appropriate order and threatening to sovereignty, as well as ultimately ineffective. Thus, in their fundamentals, realism is state libertarianism and libertarianism is domestic realism. Both rely on the spontaneous emergence of order – realism via the 'balance of power', libertarianism by the 'hidden hand'. Libertarians see domestic government beyond the bare minimum as a potentially despotic leviathan, and any governmental authority or capacity to meet public needs as an aggregation of power that threatens freedom. At the international level, equilibrium realists are similarly wary of any accretion of power, whether by empire or international organisation, as intrinsically threatening to the freedom of states.[29] Given these kindred biases, it is quite understandable that libertarians and equilibrium realists would join forces in seeking to constrain NATO, the EU and other significant international organisations.

When these deficiencies are combined with the severe underappreciation of interdependence, the unifying theme in the libertarian–realist alliance of restraint is revealed to be deeply flawed. The restraints they advocate are misplaced and inadequate, and any domestic and international world order following these guidelines would be marked not by restraint, but by a significant and dangerous lack of restraint. The libertarian agenda of shrinking the state to the size where 'we can drown it in the bathtub', as the Washington libertarian activist Grover Norquist memorably put it,[30] would leave the concentrated power of corporations and the extremely wealthy unrestrained to the detriment of the larger public. In contrast, modern liberals claim that perennial problems, ranging from pollution to pandemics, require carefully organised government capacities and actions, ones which invariably restrain the freedom of everyone to some degree. The realisation of the public interest and the successful functioning of modern industrial societies requires not fewer restraints, but appropriately configured ones.

In an increasingly interdependent world, basic security and welfare interests demand thicker restraints, configured in ways that are completely alien to the realist approach. With the hypertrophy of violent capacity produced by the nuclear revolution, simple attention to the relative distribution of power is grossly inadequate. Security requires architectures of restraint – such as strategic arms-control agreements – that cut deeply into the core traditional prerogatives of sovereign war-making states. As the globalised world faces pandemic disease and climate change, restraining arrangements must now extend to the micro-level of widely dispersed individual activities in ways that are incomprehensible to the state-centric, bordered world of realism. The libertarian–realist programme would leave unrestrained precisely those actors and behaviours that must be restrained to achieve basic human interests in security and survival. Modern liberals assess that problems such as pollution and pandemics call for carefully organised government capacities and actions that invariably inhibit individual freedom to some degree. It is not minimal restraints, but rather appropriately distributed and calibrated ones, that enable modern industrial societies facing these challenges to function in the public interest.

Progressive anti-imperialism and anti-interventionism

The third member of the Quincy restraint coalition consists of progressive democrats who oppose imperialism and military interventionism – and tend to see it everywhere.[31] The roots of this tradition too run deep in republican and democratic thought. Opposition to empire and imperialism was a defining goal of early-modern republicans and liberal democrats. Enlightenment voices condemned the domination of one people by another.[32] While Machiavelli and John Locke embraced imperial expansion, Montesquieu laid the foundations for anti-imperialism, which was coupled with a critique of militarism and slavery. The political theory underpinning the American Revolution was profoundly anti-imperial. The revolution was an anti-colonial independence movement, and the founders rejected any imperial project as corrosive of limited government and constitutionalism. In the nineteenth and early twentieth centuries, opponents of the Mexican War, Cuban annexation and the occupation of the Philippines echoed these themes. In light of American economic dominance and the inequalities of the Gilded Age, Charles Beard and other progressives and populists identified mercantile capitalism as the key force behind American state development and territorial and imperial expansion.[33] These strands of thinking converged with those on the libertarian right and socialist left, which reinforced the United States' strong isolationist tendencies and its disinclination to maximise its territorial expansion to the extent that its relative power in the early twentieth century would have allowed.

As the United States became the 'arsenal of democracy', first against the fascist powers in the Second World War and then against the Soviet Union and international communism, the critics of American militarism and imperialism were initially pushed to the margins. But by the 1960s, with the Vietnam War and other American military interventions against communist revolutions under way, earlier lines of criticism were revived and extended. Some saw Pax Americana as a new type of empire, propelled by American corporations seeking resources and markets.[34] Others saw the United States leading global opposition to agrarian populist revolutions and to democratisation in the deeply oppressive and unequal societies that emerged in the wake of decolonisation.[35] With the rise in global dependence on Middle Eastern oil and the expansion of American military alliances in the region, updated versions of the Beardian critique formed the basis for running opposition to American commitments.[36]

Over the last 50 years, left-leaning revisionist historians have constructed a compelling narrative of the trajectory of American growth and change, a kind of mirror-image of the mainstream liberal storyline of the advance of freedom. In the revisionist-left view, the United States was built through the domination of indigenous peoples, African slaves and workers, and is thus an 'empire all the way down'.[37] In this view, the American liberal order amounts to an ideological fig leaf for the most successful of modern global empires, made stronger and less restrained by its apparent invisibility and seamless alignment with capital.[38]

After the Cold War, leftist critics of the American order redirected their energies, questioning US peacekeeping, humanitarian interventionism and democracy promotion as neo-colonial. They also renewed the assessment of American power as largely a servant of capital. And they led transnational coalitions against neoliberal globalisation, which they viewed as profoundly harmful to local economies, indigenous groups and the environment. For figures like Noam Chomsky, the United States was an oppressive and violent global problem, having morphed from the leader and protector of liberal democracy into a globally extended and over-militarised guarantor of the status quo. America had become an empire, and the giant national-security state created to service it a menace to democracy and republican institutions at home.

The politics of the left-revisionists combines hyper-liberalism and anti-liberalism. Many of the left-revisionists' indictments of America and American foreign policy are straightforwardly liberal-democratic in their character. Modern liberalism and left-revisionism share a hostility to imperialism, militarism and armed intervention. Left-revisionists employ strong liberal-democratic values to judge the failings and insufficiencies of actual American institutions and conduct. But left-revisionists also harbour a resolute hostility to capitalism and market economics that separates them from the modern liberal embrace of modified market capitalism, cast not just as a necessary evil for the generation of wealth but as an essential part of the freedom programme. They commonly link their antipathy to capitalism with various types of communalism and collectivism, which compromise individual freedom. They fail to realise that popular democracy and revolutionary movements are often the enemies of limited government constitutionalism and the protection of minority rights. And they fail to recognise that the hard-fought struggle against the greater evils of fascism and communism required the toleration of lesser evils, such as situational support for anti-communist dictatorships.

Modern liberal wellsprings of American success

While all three intellectual traditions make insightful historical arguments, their overall narrative of America, American success and contemporary realities is selective and blinkered. Modern liberals provide a more accurate and constructive historical account of the American project and its success.

The traditional modern liberal narrative insists that the twentieth-century realisation of its vision at home and abroad largely explains the expansion of American liberty and the United States' success in the world. Libertarians seem to have forgotten that the America that won the Second World War, prevailed in the Cold War and brought unprecedented peace, prosperity and security to the international system was the America brought into existence by what many historians refer to as the 'Third Founding': the New Deal.[39] Progressive liberal foundations are what ultimately made America great.[40] Had libertarian opposition to the New Deal, NATO, the UN and other international organisations been successful, the United States might well not have sought or been able to play its pivotal role in the great struggles against fascism and communism.

American international success depended not just on raw American power but on the combination of power, liberal-democratic ideas and liberal-internationalist projects. The United States was ascendant in part because the liberal-democratic ideal, as manifested in modern America, was profoundly appealing to people all over the world. American leadership in solving global problems and building international institutions to advance liberal-democratic and capitalist goals was a multifaceted effort to make the world safe for democracy.[41] The alliances of the Second World War and the Cold War were more than mere expedients. They arose from the superior capacity of modern liberal democracies to solve the problems of global interdependence, and of modernity itself.

The left-revisionists, for their part, offer an account of liberal America's rise and impact that is just as truncated and unbalanced as the libertarian view. On the one hand, left-revisionists promote liberal values of freedom, equality and democracy, helping to provide a liberal autocritique and partially advancing the liberal programme. On the other hand, the revisionist left is blind to the many ways in which liberal democrats and their movement have over two centuries of often difficult struggle expanded freedom, human rights and mass prosperity in ways that are cumulatively revolutionary. To be sure, America was born with slavery. But liberal abolitionists spearheaded a costly struggle that accomplished its abolition. While left-revisionists have shown that the glass of freedom has never been full, they fail to acknowledge that it has become steadily fuller, and that the United States has played a key role in filling it. The reanimation of American racism and other forms of illiberalism under Trump has partially drained the metaphorical glass. But this admittedly retrograde development does not vitiate the United States' liberal advances, and indeed has prompted vigorous efforts to preserve and extend them.

Liberal renewal and the Biden agenda

The Quincy-coalition agenda points towards a foreign policy that is roughly Trumpian, while modern liberalism and internationalism underwrite the Biden administration's strategy. It has laid out a comprehensive agenda for change that aims to put the United States back at the centre of progressive liberal leadership to address twenty-first-century problems. Whether the American political system can realise this agenda is open to question. Doing so would be a logical next step in the evolution of modern liberalism and internationalism. The Biden programme proposes an array of new restraints, to be sure, but unlike the Quincy coalition's programme, it will advance rather than impede the realisation of basic liberal-democratic goals and values.

The problems that the Biden administration has elevated to strategic importance are both familiar and novel. Like Barack Obama and Trump, Biden has framed the rise of China as a key focus. Biden's emphasis on rebuilding alliances, championing democracy and human rights, and promoting national industrial policy is strategically preferable to the libertarian project of coming home and dismantling the modern American state. The Biden strategy rests on the assumption that China – with its strong autocratic government, booming capitalist economy and revisionist foreign policy – poses a comprehensive threat that will require a comprehensive response. The Biden programme dismisses the libertarian faith that capitalism alone will propel American growth and power as simplistic and inadequate. The new administration also believes that the libertarian and restraint-realist prescription of offshore balancing, alliance-shedding and marginalising international organisations deprives the United States of some of its most important global assets at a time when they are needed more than ever. Likewise, they see the left-revisionists' aspiration to reduce American power and impact in the world when the global balance of power between liberal democracy and autocracy is unfavourably shifting as distinctly out of phase. In the face of China's potent autocratic challenge, the task for America, as Biden has succinctly captured it, is to show the world that democracy works at solving problems.

Throughout the twentieth century, liberals advanced a wide array of projects to respond to problems related to growing interdependence, such as public health and environmental protection. But, while often effectively pursued, they always had second-tier status as American strategic interests, leaving them more vulnerable to libertarian attack. In turn, libertarians have impoverished America's public healthcare system and hobbled the creation of international capabilities of disease response. They have embraced the absurd notion that mask-wearing to curb the spread of disease somehow abridges fundamental freedoms. On climate change, libertarians have adopted climate denialism to support cut-to-the-bone deregulation and opposition to the Paris agreement. In response, Biden's new vision and strategy accord high priority to pandemic disease in light of COVID-19, and decarbonisation to fight global warming.

*   *   *

Given the Quincy agenda's serious defects, it is perhaps not surprising that liberal global internationalism has rebounded relatively fast. An essential assumption of the Biden programme is that achieving basic national inter-ests requires domestic change in response to global conditions. The Biden administration recognises that an effective response to the planetary climate emergency requires major domestic reforms and initiatives. Just as the social and industrial mobilisation required to defeat the Axis Powers and then the

Soviet Union left no aspect of American life untouched, so too will tackling the climate crisis remake the nation. To the extent that this reconstruction is in the service of liberal-democratic values and standards, it will make America stronger, more capable and more democratic.

The Biden administration also understands that increasing the United States' capacity to compete with China must occur alongside efforts to work cooperatively with Beijing on climate change and the threat of pandemics. Again, the appropriate model is post-war liberal and internationalist US foreign policy. On the basis of that policy, the United States not only confronted the Soviet Union, but also found common ground with it to control nuclear weaponry and stamp out smallpox.

Both the Quincy coalition and the new liberalism offer packages of restraint. But the Quincy restraints are for a different time and place, while the restraints proposed by the new liberalism are tailor-made to address the central domestic and international problems of the present and future. Unlike those of its rivals, the Biden world view and programme build on the successes of earlier American liberal and internationalist projects. The success of the free world, and of America in that world, still depends on the implementation of a progressive liberal agenda.

Notes

[1] See Yuen Foong Khong, *Analogies at War: Korea, Munich, Dien Bien Phu, and the Vietnam Decisions of 1965* (Princeton, NJ: Princeton University Press, 1992); and Michael Roskin, 'From Pearl Harbor to Vietnam: Shifting Generational Paradigms and Foreign Policy', *Political Science Quarterly*, vol. 89, no. 3, Fall 1974, pp. 563–88.

[2] See Greg Jaffe, 'Libertarian Billionaire, Charles Koch, Is Making a Big Bet on Foreign Policy', *Washington Post*, 11 November 2017, https://www.washingtonpost.com/world/national-security/libertarian-billionaire-charles-koch-is-making-a-big-bet-on-foreign-policy/2017/11/10/f537b700-c639-11e7-84bc-5e285c7f4512_story.html; and William Ruger, 'With US Strategy on the Rocks, We Are Supporting Fresh Perspectives in Foreign Policy', *War on the Rocks*, 10 November 2017, https://warontherocks.com/2017/11/u-s-strategy-rocks-supporting-fresh-perspectives-foreign-policy/. See also Armin Rosen, 'Washington's Weirdest Think Tank', *Tablet*, 28 April 2021, https://www.tabletmag.com/sections/news/articles/quincy-trita-parsi-soros-koch-armin-rosen. For a critique of the restraint school of foreign policy,

see Michael J. Mazarr, 'Rethinking Restraint: Why It Fails in Practice', *Washington Quarterly*, vol. 42, no. 2, Summer 2020, pp. 7–32.

3   See, for example, Quincy Institute for Responsible Statecraft, 'Quincy Institute Experts Applaud Biden for Ending America's "Forever" War in Afghanistan', 21 April 2021, https://quincyinst.org/press/quincy-institute-experts-applaud-biden-for-ending-americas-forever-war-in-afghanistan/.

4   See Thomas Wright, 'Trump's 19th Century Foreign Policy', *Politico*, 20 January 2016, https://www.politico.com/magazine/story/2016/01/donald-trump-foreign-policy-213546/.

5   See Barry Buzan and George Lawson, *The Global Transformation: History, Modernity, and the Making of International Relations* (Cambridge: Cambridge University Press, 2015); and Daniel Deudney, *Bounding Power: Republican Security Theory from the Polis to the Global Village* (Princeton, NJ: Princeton University Press, 2007).

6   See Paul Starr, *Freedom's Power: The History and Promise of Liberalism* (New York: Basic Books, 2007). On the lineages of Western liberalism, see Anthony Arblaster, *The Rise and Decline of Western Liberalism* (New York: Basil Blackwell, 1984); and Helena Rosenblatt, *The Lost History of Liberalism: From Ancient Rome to the Twenty-first Century* (Princeton, NJ: Princeton University Press, 2018).

7   See John Dewey, *The Public and Its Problems* (New York: Swallow Press, 1927).

8   See Daniel T. Rogers, *Transatlantic Crossings: Social Politics in a Progressive Age* (Cambridge, MA: Harvard University Press, 1998).

9   On the rise of the modern liberal-democratic state, see Alan Brinkley, *The End of Reform: New Deal Liberalism in Recession and War* (New York: Alfred A. Knopf, 1995); and Ira Katznelson, *Fear Itself: The New Deal and the Origins of Our Times* (New York: W. W. Norton & Co., 2013).

10 See Deudney, *Bounding Power*, chapters 8 and 9.

11 See Elizabeth Borgwardt, *A New Deal for the World: America's Vision for Human Rights* (Cambridge, MA; Harvard University Press, 2005); and G. John Ikenberry, *Liberal Leviathan: The Origins, Crisis and Transformation of the American World System* (Princeton, NJ: Princeton University Press, 2011).

12 See Perrin Selcer, *The Postwar Origins of the Global Environment: How the United Nations Built Spaceship Earth* (New York: Columbia University Press, 2018).

13 See Friedrich Hayek, *The Road to Serfdom* (London: Routledge, 1944).

14 On the twentieth-century origins of neoliberalism, see Alan Ebenstein, *Friedrich Hayek: A Biography* (New York: St. Martin's Press, 2001); Daniel Stedman Jones, *Masters of the University: Hayek, Friedman, and the Birth of Neoliberal Politics* (Princeton, NJ: Princeton University Press, 2012); and Quinn Slobodian, *Globalists: The End of Empire and the Birth of Neoliberalism* (Cambridge, MA: Harvard University Press, 2018).

15 See David Boaz, *The Libertarian Mind: A Manifesto for Freedom* (New York: Simon & Schuster, 2015); and Anne C. Heller, *Ayn Rand and the World She Made* (New York: Doubleday, 2009).

16 For a sweeping account of the 1970s and the rise of neoliberalism in the Reagan–Thatcher era, see Simon Reid-Henry, *Empire of Democracy: The Remaking of the West Since the Cold War, 1971–2015* (New York: Simon & Schuster, 2019).

17 See Jeremy Rabkin, *The Case for Sovereignty: Why the World Should Welcome American Independence* (Washington DC: American Enterprise Institute, 2004); Jeremy Rabkin, *Law Without Nations? Why Constitutional Government Requires Sovereign States* (Princeton, NJ: Princeton University Press, 2005); and Christopher Preble, *The Power Problem: How American Military Dominance Makes Us Less Safe, Less Prosperous, and Less Free* (Ithaca, NY: Cornell University Press, 2009).

18 For the definitive account, see Thomas Piketty, *Capital in the Twenty-first Century* (Cambridge, MA: Harvard University Press, 2007).

19 Statista, 'Number of Novel Coronavirus (COVID-19) Deaths Worldwide as of May 31, 2021, by Country', 31 May 2021, https://www.statista.com/statistics/1093256/novel-coronavirus-2019ncov-deaths-worldwide-by-country/.

20 Among many formulations, see Jonathan Haslam, *No Virtue Like Necessity: Realist Thought in International Relations Since Machiavelli* (New Haven, CT: Yale University Press, 2002).

21 See, for example, William C. Wohlforth, 'Gilpinian Realism and International Relations', *International Relations*, vol. 24, no. 1, December 2011, pp. 499–511.

22 See E.H. Carr, *The Twenty Years' Crisis: 1919–1939: An Introduction to the Study of International Relations* (New York: Macmillan, 1939); Robert Gilpin, *War and Change in World Politics* (Cambridge: Cambridge University Press, 1981); and William C. Wohlforth, 'The Stability of a Unipolar World', *International Security*, vol. 24, no. 1, Summer 1999, pp. 5–41.

23 See John J. Mearsheimer, *The Tragedy of Great Power Politics* (New York: W. W. Norton & Co., 2001).

24 See Walter McDougal, *Promised Land, Crusader State: The American Encounter with the World Since 1776* (New York: Houghton Mifflin, 1997); and John J. Mearsheimer, *The Great Delusion: Liberal Dreams and International Realities* (New Haven, CT: Yale University Press, 2018).

25 See Andrew Bacevich, *American Empire: The Realities and Consequences of US Diplomacy* (Cambridge, MA: Harvard University Press, 2002).

26 See Daniel Deudney and G. John Ikenberry, 'Realism, Liberalism, and the Iraq War', *Survival*, vol. 59, no. 4, August–September 2017, pp. 7–26; and Elizabeth Drew, *Fear and Loathing in George W. Bush's Washington* (New York: New York Review of Books, 2004).

27 See, for example, Barry R. Posen, 'Europe Can Defend Itself', *Survival*, vol. 62, no. 6, December 2020–January 2021, pp. 7–34.

28 See Michael C. Desch, 'America's Liberal Illiberalism: The Ideological Origins of Overreaction in US Foreign Policy', *International Security*, vol. 32, no. 3, Winter 2007/08, pp. 7–43; and Barry Posen, *Restraint: A New Foundation for US Grand Strategy* (Ithaca, NY: Cornell University Press, 2014). For an early statement

of the restraint thesis, see Eugene Gholtz, Daryl G. Press and Harvey M. Sapolsky, 'Come Home, America: The Strategy of Restraint in the Face of Temptation', *International Security*, vol. 21, no. 4, Spring 1997, pp. 5–48.

29 The foundational role of state freedom in the international system was registered more clearly in the beginning, when early-modern European thinkers referred to the European state system as a whole as a 'republic' to distinguish it from Roman-inherited versions of empire. See Deudney, *Bounding Power,* chapter 4.

30 NPR, 'Conservative Advocate', *Morning Edition,* 25 May 2001, https://www.npr.org/templates/story/story.php?storyId=1123439.

31 See Jeanne Morefield, 'Trump Foreign Policy Isn't the Problem', *Boston Review*, Fall 2018.

32 See Jennifer Pitts, *A Turn to Empire: The Rise of Imperial Liberalism in Britain and France* (Princeton, NJ: Princeton University Press, 2005).

33 See Charles A. Beard, *The Economic Interpretation of the Constitution of the United States* (New York: Macmillan, 1913); and Charles A. Beard, *The Idea of National Interest: An Analytical Study in American Foreign Policy* (New York: Macmillan, 1934). The Wisconsin School of diplomatic history, led by William Appleman Williams and his students, has generated many rich and illuminating studies of the domestic sources of American foreign policy, emphasising economic interests and expansionist ideology. See William Appleman Williams, *The Tragedy of American Foreign Policy* (New York: World Publishing Co., 1959). See also Lloyd C. Gardner, *Economic Aspects of New Deal Diplomacy* (Boston, MA: Beacon Press, 1964); Lloyd C. Gardner, *Imperial America: American Foreign Policy Since 1898* (New York: Harcourt Brace Jovanovich, 1976); Lloyd C. Gardner, *Safe for Democracy: The Anglo-American Response to Revolution, 1813–1923* (Oxford: Oxford University Press, 1984); and Walter LaFeber, *The New Empire: An Interpretation of American Expansion, 1860–1898* (Ithaca, NY: Cornell University Press, 1963).

34 See Gabriel Kolko, *The Roots of American Foreign Policy: An Analysis of Power and Purpose* (Boston, MA: Beacon Press, 1969); and Gabriel Kolko and Joyce Kolko, *The Limits of Power: The World and United States Foreign Policy, 1945–1954* (New York: Harper & Row, 1972).

35 See, for example, Richard Barnet, *Intervention and Revolution: The United States and the Third World* (New York: World Publishing Co., 1968); and Noam Chomsky, *American Power and the New Mandarins* (New York: Random House, 1969).

36 See Bacevich, *American Empire;* and Chalmers Johnson, *The Sorrows of Empire: Militarism, Secrecy, and the End of the Republic* (New York: Metropolitan Books, 2004).

37 See Howard Zinn, *A People's History of the United States* (New York: Harper, 2017).

38 See Daniel Immerwahr, *How to Hide an Empire: A History of the Greater United States* (New York: Vintage, 2020); and Jeanne Morefield, *Empire Without Imperialism: Anglo-American Decline and the Politics of Deflection* (Oxford: Oxford University Press, 2014).

39 See Timothy Garton Ash, *Free World:*

America, Europe, and the Surprising Future of the West (New York: Random House, 2004); Ikenberry, *Liberal Leviathan*; Stewart Patrick, *The Best Laid Plans: The Origins of American Multilateralism and the Dawn of the Cold War* (Lanham, MD: Rowman & Littlefield, 2009); and Wesley Wooley, *Beyond Anarchy: American Supranationalism after World War II* (Bloomington, IN: University of Indiana Press, 1988).

40 See Daniel Deudney and G. John Ikenberry, 'Unraveling America the Great', *American Interest*, vol. 11, no. 5, Summer 2016, pp. 7–17.

41 See G. John Ikenberry, *A World Safe for Democracy: Liberal Internationalism and the Crises of Global Order* (New Haven, CT: Yale University Press, 2020).

The War on Terror Has Not Yet Failed: A Net Assessment After 20 Years

Hal Brands and Michael O'Hanlon

A generational struggle has reached a sobering milestone: this year marks two decades since the 11 September 2001 terrorist attacks. The result of those attacks was what the George W. Bush administration called the 'global war on terror', or GWOT. Though the name and tactics have varied, the basic goal of using all forms of American power to prevent major terrorist attacks on the United States and its key interests and allies has persisted. With the advent of the Biden administration, the campaign against transnational violent extremism – and particularly Salafist extremism, a movement based on a perverted interpretation of Sunni Islam – has now continued into its fourth US presidency. Yet it is hard to find many observers who would declare that campaign a strategic success.

During the 2016 campaign and throughout his presidency, Donald Trump argued that America had failed to wage counter-terrorism aggressively enough, while also mocking as pointless the country's open-ended military operations in the greater Middle East. Today, many Democrats and some conservatives call for 'ending endless wars'. The war in Iraq is seen as the exemplar of misguided and mishandled military intervention.[1] Two successive presidents, one from each major party, tried to withdraw

Hal Brands is the Henry A. Kissinger Distinguished Professor of Global Affairs at the Johns Hopkins School of Advanced International Studies (SAIS), a senior fellow at the American Enterprise Institute and a Bloomberg Opinion columnist. **Michael O'Hanlon** is a senior fellow and the director of research in the Foreign Policy Program at the Brookings Institution, and author of *The Art of War in an Age of Peace: U.S. Grand Strategy and Resolute Restraint* (Yale University Press, 2021).

Survival | vol. 63 no. 4 | August–September 2021 | pp. 33–54   https://doi.org/10.1080/00396338.2021.1956194

from Afghanistan. A third, President Joe Biden, has now done so, more out of sadness, resignation and frustration than any real sense of accomplishment. Some charge that the war on terror has come home in ugly ways, through high rates of veteran suicide, militarised policing and a flourishing of white-nationalist movements and right-wing domestic terrorism. From this perspective, the war on terror could certainly seem like a case of strategic backfire.

There is no question that the GWOT has not gone as planned. Few analysts or policymakers envisioned that, after 9/11, the United States would spend the next 20 years fighting in Afghanistan, much less that it would then withdraw with the Taliban on the march. Or that it would send troops back to Iraq in 2014 to destroy a terrorist caliphate that the American invasion – and subsequent withdrawal – had helped produce. Or that America would have spent trillions of dollars and lost thousands of lives in a struggle that still lacks a clear endpoint. Or that the greater Middle East would be a nastier, more violent place now than it was in 2001. Or that rates of global terrorism, measured in terms of violence and loss of life, would be higher today than at the start of America's war on terror.

Yet it would still be wrong – and rash – simply to discard the GWOT as a strategic failure. The fact that consecutive presidents have found it so difficult to extricate the United States from ongoing operations in the greater Middle East reflects the reality of a persistent threat from extremist organisations and their allies. Opinion polling consistently shows that the American people fear terrorism as much as any other security challenge. And the GWOT has been considerably more fruitful than it might first appear.

There are six key criteria on which analysts can assess the success or failure of that endeavour. On three of those criteria – protecting the American homeland from another catastrophic attack, denying or destroying terrorist sanctuaries, and decapitating and otherwise dismantling terrorist organisations – the GWOT has been a relatively clear success. On two more, improving regional stability and decreasing overall levels of terrorism worldwide, it has been a relatively clear failure, which is why the threat will not disappear anytime soon. On a final criterion, cost, the verdict is mixed. The GWOT has taken a human, financial and geopolitical toll higher than all but the most pessimistic analysts initially predicted, but that price has fallen dramatically as the United States has quietly adopted a cost-conscious, limited-liability approach to keeping the most dangerous threats at bay. Today, the error that American policymakers are most likely to make is abandoning, out of undue pessimism, a struggle that the United States has now developed a reasonably efficient approach to waging – and that will require strategic persistence for years to come.

More success than failure

From the beginning, the most important objective of the GWOT was protecting the homeland from mass-casualty terrorism that might fundamentally disrupt the American way of life. Achieving that goal, in turn, required preventing or disrupting any major Salafist safe havens, while pummelling the terrorist organisations and leaders aiming to conduct such attacks. By these measures, the United States has enjoyed far more success than failure.

Homeland security

Most obviously, the United States has not suffered another catastrophic terrorist attack since 9/11. Nor have its major European and Asian allies suffered spectacular events on the scale of 9/11, although some have absorbed larger attacks than the United States has. The world did experience, in the four years after 9/11, significant attacks in Bali, Saudi Arabia, Spain and London, each claiming from dozens to hundreds of lives. Europe was hit by a slew of Islamic State and al-Qaeda attacks between 2014 and 2017. There were many other attempts – shoe bombers, underwear bombers, Times Square bombers – to carry off mass-casualty attacks in America and other countries.[2] But since 9/11, there have been just over 100 Americans killed on US soil by those with Salafist leanings or connections – far fewer than the number of fatalities caused by right-wing extremists over the same period, and only a tiny fraction the nation's overall murder total.[3]

It could have been far worse. After 9/11, the threat-stream reporting that reached the White House was terrifying. There were widespread fears, fuelled by the anthrax attacks of late 2001, that 9/11 might presage repeated mass-casualty attacks, perhaps involving weapons of mass destruction. One need not agree with vice president Dick Cheney's infamous '1% doctrine' – the idea that if there were even a 1% chance of a terrorist attack using nuclear weapons, the risk had to be treated as a near-certainty – to understand why he and his colleagues were so alarmed.[4] Indeed, the Bush administration's greatest fear was that sustained, catastrophic terrorism might force the United States to dramatically change its democratic way of life by accepting harsher restrictions on privacy, movement, public gatherings and other civil liberties as the price of safety.[5]

The reasons America has so far avoided that outcome are still subject to debate. Luck has played a role in frustrating attackers, as in the case of the individual who, having slipped through American defences, sought but failed to bring down an airliner over Detroit in 2009 using a bomb concealed in his underwear. And most attacks in the West since 9/11 have seemed relatively modest in scale partly because 9/11 set the bar so high that subsequent jihadists struggled to approach it. The projection of US military power into the Middle East also gave Salafists a chance to kill Americans 'over there' rather than killing them 'over here'. Finally, ongoing instability in the Middle East has made it more attractive to attack the 'near enemy' (Middle Eastern governments and polities) or the 'intermediate enemy' (certain less vigilant, or more accessible, European countries) rather than an increasingly hardened 'far enemy' (the United States) – though American strategists should of course hesitate before interpreting these facts as proof of any success.

But clearly, US policies have played a role. Integration of terrorist watch lists, advance screening of cargo headed for the United States, better technology at border-crossing sites, good police work on America's streets, and fuller funding for intelligence and homeland security since 9/11 have all helped.[6] Increasingly precise financial sanctions have made it far harder for terrorist groups to move money via the international banking system. Improved cooperation with law-enforcement and intelligence agencies in other countries, from Southeast Asia to the Arabian Peninsula to Western Europe, has resulted in the detention or killing of untold numbers of terrorist operators. Covert action, paramilitary strikes and sustained military operations have put extreme pressure on terrorist groups. The United States made itself a far harder target, in other words, while also making it far harder for terrorists to survive. Three analysts, writing roughly a decade ago, summed up the effect of post-9/11 policies:

> Since 2001, the United States has relentlessly hunted terrorists around the world, shut down training facilities, dried up sources of funding, disrupted active plots, and maintained constant pressure on terrorist networks. Al Qaeda operatives and leaders have reportedly been killed, captured, or reduced to preserving their personal safety. Evidence also suggests that US homeland security has improved since September 11. High value targets have been hardened; coordination between military, intelligence and law enforcement agencies has increased; and authorities at every level of government have heightened the scrutiny of suspicious behavior.[7]

These policies were so successful that Barack Obama, despite having campaigned against the excesses of Bush's war on terror, ended up adopting many of them.[8] There has emerged a bipartisan consensus supporting the quieter aspects of counter-terrorism since 9/11 out of recognition that those measures have consistently proven their worth.

Moreover, the United States has protected itself without destroying its domestic institutions in the process. To be sure, the post-9/11 use of torture left a moral stain, even if overall interrogation efforts may have contributed – in coordination with other tools – to preventing subsequent attacks. The USA Patriot Act and domestic-surveillance programmes have modestly decreased privacy for some Americans. On balance, however, the American way of life has survived largely intact. Prior to the COVID-19 pandemic, Americans continued to enjoy free movement across jurisdictional lines and, for the most part, internationally. Identification checks to prevent terrorism are not a frequent or normal part of American life, except in specific places such as iconic sites and skyscraper entrances. The burden of tighter airport security is modest and sensible. And the US government hardly possesses untrammelled powers to pry into Americans' private lives, as Apple's refusal to unlock the iPhone of a terrorist involved in the San Bernardino shootings of 2015 demonstrates. Not all is well; American Muslims have sometimes been the victims of persecution, vigilantism and (under Trump) political demagoguery. But the United States has attained greater security, with greater regard for civil liberties, than many experts thought possible in 2001.

Denying and dismantling safe havens

One reason for this is that America has also fared well in denying terrorist adversaries the geographic sanctuaries they require to plan and operate effectively. Some scholars contend that the importance of territorial safe havens is overblown, because modern terrorist organisations can thrive even without controlling large swathes of land. Yet since 2001, US officials have believed – correctly – that safe havens are a critical force-multiplier for extremist groups.

Dating back to the 1980s, many terrorist groups – including al-Qaeda – took root when extremists occupied specific pieces of territory where they could assemble and organise. Admittedly, most detailed planning for 9/11 occurred outside of Afghanistan. But terrorist networks were largely built there, and al-Qaeda used its stronghold in that country as a platform from which to recruit, organise and execute progressively more ambitious attacks. The Islamic State made even greater use of the lands it conquered in Iraq and Syria in 2013–14. It exploited its territorial gains to train operatives that struck France, Belgium and other countries; to produce propaganda that radicalised and attracted tens of thousands of foreign fighters; and to control oil and other resources that funded its attacks in the Middle East and beyond. It did all this while avoiding much of the sort of intelligence penetration that is more feasible when security services have geographic access to the areas where terrorist groups plan and organise.

Denying safe havens has thus been the prime operational objective of the GWOT. After 9/11, US special-operations forces and intelligence operatives worked with the Northern Alliance to overthrow the Taliban and deprive al-Qaeda of its principal base. Over the succeeding years, and with considerable difficulty, the United States used its bases in Afghanistan, as well as a quietly lethal drone campaign, to reduce al-Qaeda's freedom to operate in the nearby Federally Administered Tribal Areas of Pakistan. Washington inadvertently created terrorist sanctuaries by invading Iraq in 2003 and again by withdrawing prematurely from that country in 2011. Yet in both cases, American forces and their local partners subsequently destroyed the 'caliphates' that had emerged, killing or capturing large numbers of the terrorists that inhabited them. By the end of 2017, for instance, the Islamic State had lost 95% of the chunks of Iraq and Syria it previously controlled.[9] Similarly, the French, with American help, took back large sections of Mali that had fallen to extremists. Unfortunately, parts of Somalia, northeastern Nigeria, Pakistan, Afghanistan and Syria remain relatively hospitable to terrorist groups. But the United States has repeatedly demonstrated its ability to disrupt those havens if the threat reaches intolerable levels.[10]

Its approach to doing so has, of course, evolved considerably. The initial model for denying safe havens, which involved state-building efforts with 100,000 or more troops deployed in Iraq and Afghanistan, was far too costly in blood as well as treasure to be sustained indefinitely. After US forces found and killed Osama bin Laden in 2011, the Obama administration shifted to a lighter-footprint approach, featuring drones and special-operations forces, that ultimately failed to prevent extremist groups from reconstituting themselves in Iraq, Syria and Yemen. From 2014 onward, Washington thus shifted towards something like a 'medium-footprint' approach in key areas, relying heavily on local forces, enabled by American airpower, logistics, training and assistance, and modest numbers of US ground forces to clear out safe havens and maintain pressure. This approach, when coupled with multilateral diplomatic, demographic and economic isolation of the terrorist movements, is relatively cost-effective.[11] It can generally be conducted with a few thousand US forces, together with deployed air assets capable of delivering up to thousands of strikes a year in certain circumstances. Over the past several years, for example, the US military presence in Iraq has averaged around 5,000 troops, and that in Afghanistan between 5,000 and 10,000 troops, complemented by several thousand NATO troops.

Yet the strategy remains an intuitively unsatisfying 'mowing the grass' approach, focused on suppressing enemies rather than destroying them permanently. By design, it must therefore be continued indefinitely, until local politics or other indigenous factors deprive future terrorists of the ability to train, recruit and organise. As the US intelligence community warned in 2019, the Islamic State 'will exploit any reduction in [counter-terrorism] pressure to strengthen its clandestine presence and accelerate rebuilding key capabilities'. Left undisturbed, the group 'very likely will continue to pursue external attacks from Iraq and Syria against regional and Western adversaries, including the United States'.[12] The good news, then, is that America has gradually developed a sustainable approach to denying or disrupting terrorist safe havens. The bad news is that this approach promises little rest for the weary.

Decapitation of leadership and decimation of the ranks

Then there is the matter of terrorist leadership. To be sure, not all extremist organisations require continuity in top leadership and other key positions: the Taliban in Afghanistan have lost many of their field commanders, not once or twice but multiple times. Organisations that have developed a straightforward method of operation, or adequate depth in their hierarchy, can often survive the loss of key leaders and operatives.

Yet individuals still matter. When new, complex plots are to be attempted, or terrorist groups undertake major campaigns on the battlefield, individuals with strong technical and organisational skills are essential. When an organisation seeks to develop a narrative of long-term survival and inevitable victory, the resilience of its top leadership can itself serve as testament to the credibility of the group's vision.[13] Arrests or killings of leaders, by contrast, can fracture groups, as would-be successors contend for influence. Effective attacks on leaders can force successors to spend most of their energies avoiding targeting – which also means avoiding modern communications – and simply staying alive. Removal of financiers, facilitators and operational commanders disrupts existing routines, destroys institutional memory and keeps terrorist groups in a state of ongoing churn. This is why counter-terrorism is, at a tactical level, often synonymous with manhunting. And the United States has built a manhunting machine unparalleled in human history.[14]

After 9/11, by some estimates, US forces and their international partners killed or captured 80% of al-Qaeda leaders and operatives in Afghanistan.[15]

These included Khalid Sheikh Mohammed and later Osama bin Laden in Pakistan, Abu Musab al-Zarqawi in Iraq, Abu Bakr al-Baghdadi in Syria and, over the years, most second-tier al-Qaeda leaders in the tribal areas of Pakistan. These ruthless yet talented individuals, in addition to countless other mid- and upper-tier members of al-Qaeda, the Islamic State and other groups, have been taken off the battlefield. The late Mullah Omar of the Taliban spent his later years in increasing obscurity, just trying to stay alive. Ayman al-Zawahiri, bin Laden's successor, now appears to be doing largely the same.

This progress has not come cheaply. It is an understatement to say that Washington has taken a resource-intensive approach to capturing or killing relatively small numbers of terrorists. But the combination of ever more refined surveillance tools from reconnaissance drones to signals-intelligence capabilities, the tactical proficiency of American special-operations and paramilitary forces, the expansion of intelligence-liaison and other information-sharing programmes, and continual innovation in military, law-enforcement and intelligence operations honed by 20 years of conflict has afforded the United States an unprecedented ability to find and neutralise its enemies, even in some of the most remote areas of the world.

If offered this deal shortly after 9/11, the outcomes the United States and its partners have achieved to date – no major follow-on attacks on American soil; no transformation of the country into an illiberal 'garrison state'; the consistent disruption or destruction of terrorist sanctuaries, especially in the heart of the Arab world; and the severe attrition of terrorist leaders and other operatives – most policymakers would have unhesitatingly accepted it. Alas, there have been major failures which complicate the net assessment – and which have ensured that America's achievements in the GWOT remain continually fragile.

Metrics of failure

From 9/11 onward, it was clear that any lasting victory in the GWOT would require translating tactical gains into longer-term diminution of Salafist movements and amelioration of the political conditions that allowed them to flourish. On this score, the record is unimpressive, even ugly.

Size, strength and lethality of Salafist movements

If violence from Salafist terrorism has been relatively modest in the West since 9/11, that is far from true in the Islamic world itself. There is no religious determinism here: some of the world's largest countries in terms of their Muslim population – including Indonesia, Bangladesh and India – are largely free of Salafist violence. Others, such as Jordan, Morocco, Oman and Tunisia, have been fairly successful in preventing massive violence. But in many of the countries that have been focal points of American strategy – particularly Iraq, Syria, Yemen, parts of West Africa, parts of the Horn of Africa and parts of Afghanistan and Pakistan – levels of terrorism and religious violence have reached appalling heights.

The annual number of victims of terrorism peaked in 2014–15, the time of the Islamic State's greatest military success. Yet despite declining since then, the annual number of victims is still – depending on the exact measure or database – three to five times higher than it was at the time of the 9/11 attacks, even counting the aberrational year of 2001.[16] Similarly, death tolls from civil wars – most of which have occurred in the broader Islamic world in recent years, often stoked by an Islamist or Salafist element – are greater than global aggregates during the 1990s and 2000s (if still lower than those in the 1960s, 1970s and 1980s).[17] In the late twentieth century, the world's worst civil conflicts were in Africa, Southeast Asia and Central America; they have since been more concentrated in the broader Islamic world. Most of this violence does not claim American lives.[18] But it still poses a strategic danger given American interests in the Middle East, and has produced humanitarian devastation.

It is simplistic to say that the violence is the result of America's war on terror, and it is logical that Washington would be most deeply involved in countries where Salafists run amok. In Iraq and the Levant, security deteriorated most dramatically amid relative American disengagement from counter-terrorism operations in 2011–14. Likewise, violence has increased in Afghanistan as America and NATO's role has ended; it may well spike further as the Taliban and its enemies contend for power undeterred by outside parties.[19] The persistently high level of terrorism in these locales mainly reflects the enduring failures of local governance, the perversion of Islam by groups that weaponise its tenets, and other pathologies that Washington has neither solved nor created.

Yet there have been cases in which US policy has accelerated rather than retarded the momentum of Salafist movements. US intelligence officials conceded in 2006 that 'the Iraq war has made the overall terrorism problem worse' by inflaming anti-Americanism, producing a new cohort of recruits and turning Iraq into a training ground for the next generation of zealots. The US-led humanitarian intervention in Libya in 2011 had a similarly counterproductive, if more modest, effect. In the Syrian civil war, America did just enough to encourage and stoke opponents of the Bashar al-Assad regime, without providing the means for their success; terrorist-friendly anarchy ensued.[20] At minimum, the growth of terrorist activity since 9/11 shows that America is nowhere close to achieving the objective that key policymakers identified early on: pushing terrorism to the margins, cutting off the flow of recruits, and otherwise creating conditions that would allow Washington to declare victory and come home. 'Are we capturing, killing or deterring and dissuading more terrorists every day than the madrassas and the radical clerics are recruiting, training and deploying against us?' Donald Rumsfeld asked in 2003.[21] The question continues to haunt us, because the answer is clearly no.

Promoting political reform and stability in the greater Middle East
Sadly, the same answer must be given to the related question of whether political conditions in the greater Middle East have changed for the better. American officials typically saw the GWOT ending through political and social transformation, leading ultimately to greater regional stability. Bush advanced this thesis with his Freedom Agenda; technocratic analysts pushed for educational reform and expanded economic opportunity as ways of draining the terrorist swamp.[22] Yet for the past decade, after a period of great expectations in Iraq and Afghanistan, and the fleeting opportunity created by the Arab Spring, the regional situation has been mainly terrible.

Violent instability convulses countries from the Arabian Peninsula to North Africa. The International Crisis Group's list of ten conflicts to watch in 2021 includes five in the Sunni Arab world.[23] The Arab Spring ultimately led to jihadist-fuelled chaos, severe repression or both in far more countries than those where it led to pluralistic stability.[24] Iraq is, at best, a semi-functioning democracy. Democratic governance in Afghanistan has been sustained only by foreign aid, military support and political intervention. It may not survive the departure of US and NATO forces, although it is possible that a de facto rump state may emerge in the country's north, even as the Taliban gradually seize large portions of the south. There are a few relatively bright spots – Jordan, Morocco, Oman and Tunisia – and the Saudi government has recently tempered its penchant for brutal repression and state violence with a more promising effort to break the grip of a toxic religious establishment. Without American support, key US partners such as Saudi Arabia and Jordan could have been far more seriously destabilised after 9/11, or during the Islamic State's rampage.[25] But on the whole, no American policymaker can look with satisfaction on what the region has become.

The invasion of Iraq looms large in this regard. That country was supposed to serve as the keystone of a larger project of regional transformation. Instead, the US invasion and mishandled occupation unleashed waves of instability and violence, in all likelihood discouraging democratic reform in the region.[26] The subsequent US surge delivered remarkable results, both in reducing violence and creating hints of a non-sectarian politics. But so much had to go well to make it work, and so many of its benefits proved transient, that it may demonstrate as much about the inherent difficulty of state-building in divided societies with violent pasts as about the possibility of its success.[27] In any event, much of that success was lost as Nuri al-Maliki, the Iraqi prime minister from 2006 to 2014, governed in an increasingly sectarian fashion from 2010 onward – especially after the US departure and the start of the civil war in neighbouring Syria in 2011.[28]

The Iraq experience demonstrates why regional political progress has proved so elusive. In Iraq and Afghanistan, the United States set remarkably high goals for itself, then failed to stick to consistent state-building strategies for more than a few years at a time. Across the broader region, a daunting combination of factors – rapidly growing populations, stagnant wages, a perceived lack of opportunity, corruption, autocracy and long legacies of political violence – skewed developments towards instability and repression. The United States was not the source of most of these problems.

Yet it did – in Iraq, Libya and elsewhere – periodically make them worse, and it certainly never showed sufficient skill in or commitment to solving them. On balance, moreover, American intervention contributed to costs far higher than virtually any leading policymaker anticipated in 2001.

The price

Start with the human and financial toll. The direct costs of campaigns in Iraq and Afghanistan have each been about $1trn; factoring in knowable and inevitable costs of future veterans' benefits, even a conservative calculation pushes the tab to roughly $4trn, equal to some 20% of total US publicly held federal debt.[29] The dollar costs pale next to the human costs. More than 7,000 Americans died. Ten times that number were seriously wounded or maimed, many suffering from post-traumatic stress and other mental challenges, with resulting implications for increased suicide and divorce rates, all borne by an all-volunteer force that constitutes roughly one-half of 1% of the nation's population.[30] These costs must be kept in perspective – the total number of US fatalities from 20 years of the GWOT remains roughly half the number of fatalities American forces suffered in the single worst year of the Vietnam War – but they are tragic nonetheless.

The cost in lives paid by other people has been even greater. In Iraq, for instance, it is estimated that somewhere between 100,000 and 600,000 people were killed in the American invasion and its long aftermath. That fact represents a major humanitarian travesty. It has also taken a strategic toll on America by fuelling cynicism about the moral claims underpinning its foreign policy throughout the broader region.

On top of this, the GWOT – particularly the Iraq War under George W. Bush – inflicted geopolitical costs. It ruptured relations with European allies, stirred up long-standing rivals such as Russia, decreased freedom of action to confront (even diplomatically) rogue-state proliferators in Iran and North Korea, and distracted attention from the emerging yet visible challenge of a rising China. The Bush administration initially saw the GWOT as a way of reinvigorating American leadership and primacy, yet Washington ultimately exited the most intense period of that struggle in a geopolitically worse position than it was in when the conflict had started.[31]

Some would argue that the catalogue of costs also includes serious domestic problems such as militarised policing, xenophobia and political violence.[32] Here, the accounting becomes more tenuous. It is easy to identify ways – the provision of surplus military goods to police departments, for instance – in which the GWOT has 'come home'.[33] But many problems attributed to the GWOT predate, and have roots that run much deeper than, that conflict.

If one contends that the GWOT has had a corrosive, illiberal effect on the nation's policies, it is essential to consider the counterfactual. Had the United States taken a more relaxed attitude towards terrorism and paid no price for it in terms of security, America's domestic politics might well have been more stable and tranquil today. Yet if that attitude had led to additional attacks and heightened insecurity, the result might have been a climate even more conducive to xenophobia and fearmongering of the sort Trump practised at the height of the Islamic State's power in 2015 and 2016. Alternatively, if the United States had chosen a strategy that focused almost exclusively on domestic hardening rather than attacking terrorist organisations militarily, it might have required more restrictions on civil liberties than the country experienced after 9/11. And the Middle East could be in significantly more turmoil as well, perhaps even including war or extreme instability in places like Saudi Arabia.

Crucially, moreover, the GWOT's costs have fallen dramatically over time. The number of American servicemembers killed in combat has been in the low dozens each year since 2015, compared to the high hundreds at the peak of the Iraq and Afghanistan wars. The overall US military presence and strategy for the broader Middle East region costs some $50 billion to $60bn a year now, as measured in terms of 'overseas contingency operations' costs, but these include deterrence of Iran and general vigilance in a region that is still important, if somewhat less so than 20 or 30 years ago, to US and allied security and prosperity. The United States currently stations between 50,000 and 60,000 military personnel in the greater Middle East, compared to well over three times that number roughly a decade ago. The problem of geopolitical distraction has become more pressing as security challenges elsewhere intensify, but even that toll has fallen along with the size of the American military commitment. This reduction of costs is evidence of how much more bearable American strategy has become. But it is also an implicit reproach of how costly American strategy once was.

Assessing US strategy and Biden's Afghanistan decision

So far, the United States has mostly achieved its fundamental strategic objective in the GWOT. The American homeland, citizenry, polity, economy and way of life have been reasonably well protected, in no small part because the United States has inflicted such severe punishment on the extremist groups that threaten the country most. But the United States and its allies appear no closer to safely bringing the GWOT to a conclusion because the problems of Salafist violence and regional instability are significantly worse than they were when the conflict began. In short, American strategy has produced acceptable but hardly desirable outcomes, and the fact that the costs have been so high suggests to some that Washington might have made do with a less resource-intensive approach all along.

There is something to this critique. The need to wage the GWOT in a cost-controlled, politically sustainable manner eventually produced what might be called a medium-footprint approach – neither the heavy interventions employed in Iraq and eventually in Afghanistan, nor the minimalist approach first attempted in Afghanistan. This strategy of focusing on counter-terrorism operations, supporting local partners (even very flawed ones) and eschewing armed state-building never delivered a measure of stability to Afghanistan in the early 2000s, which is why the United States gradually – and, ultimately, enormously – expanded its presence there in the latter Bush and early Obama years. (The scar tissue from that difficult experience, in turn, may have influenced the psychological and strategic outlook underlying Biden's decision to end the US and NATO military mission in 2021.) Consistently pursuing a more disciplined, counter-terrorism-focused strategy also would have required Americans to accept, from the outset, a bitter reality: that the GWOT was destined to be unsatisfying and indefinite because its underlying causes would remain unaddressed. Yet, on balance, this probably would have been the wiser course.

It is certainly the wiser course today. For all the handwringing about 'forever wars' over the past several years, the United States has arrived at a reasonably effective, reasonably sustainable strategy for managing a terrorism problem that will not be solved anytime soon. By maintaining numerous regional footholds with military and intelligence capabilities, using trainers and enablers to empower committed local forces, and suppressing the most serious threats while playing a long game with respect to political reform, the United States can likely achieve an acceptable degree of security at an acceptable cost.

This is what makes the course that the Biden administration is following in Afghanistan so fraught. Biden's decision to withdraw from Afghanistan is, in some ways, a viscerally understandable response to the high cumulative costs and frustrating results of US intervention there. But his announcement of the withdrawal was more a critique of the unsustainably expensive GWOT that America was fighting in 2009, when he was vice president, than the more efficient, slimmed-down conflict it had recently been prosecuting.[34] The US presence in Afghanistan, as of 2020, had already been scaled back roughly 95% from peak troop levels – and even more than that in terms of the number of American casualties suffered each year. By withdrawing from Afghanistan, Biden is ending, for now, hands-on American involvement in a conflict that was not likely to be resolved in a satisfactory fashion soon. Unfortunately, the administration is also accepting a significantly higher chance that Afghanistan will once again become a terrorist sanctuary, either through a takeover by the Taliban – which remains closely linked to al-Qaeda – or a collapse into the violent chaos in which extremist groups thrive.

> *The US has arrived at a sustainable strategy*

There are steps that the United States can take to mitigate that danger from afar. It can fly military aircraft out of air bases in the Persian Gulf, off aircraft carriers or large amphibious ships in the Indian Ocean, or perhaps facilities yet to be acquired in Central Asia to strike the personnel or assets of resurgent terrorist groups. It might mount periodic raids against terrorist targets using special-operations forces or paramilitaries. These intermittent military efforts would be paired with the ongoing provision of funding, equipment and other security assistance to Afghan forces seeking to hold the Taliban and their allies at bay. The threat of economic sanctions and international opprobrium might be wielded to discourage the Taliban from allowing terrorist proxies to operate freely, or running any territories it controls in a future Afghanistan with a brutal, misogynistic hand. As CIA Director William Burns and US Central Command commander General Frank McKenzie have publicly argued, addressing the ongoing terrorism threat in Afghanistan from neighbouring regions will be very difficult, but perhaps not impossible.[35]

Yet this strategy – if pursued proactively – may not be significantly cheaper than the boots-on-the-ground presence of late 2020 and early 2021, which cost US taxpayers some $10–20bn annually. It may not wind up being safer for American personnel, as the country begins to fall apart and over-the-horizon raids have to be conducted in an increasingly hostile, inaccessible environment. And it almost certainly would not be more effective in containing threats, because conducting counter-terrorism from a distance – particularly in landlocked Afghanistan – is extraordinarily hard.

With American forces and at least some diplomatic personnel having departed, the United States will lose some of its influence with the Afghan government, just as the Obama administration lost influence with an increasingly sectarian Iraqi government following the US withdrawal in 2011. Once the United States is operating from over the horizon, it will also lose much of its awareness of what is happening on the ground. Human-intelligence networks are the best means of finding terrorist needles among civilian-population haystacks, but they only work if Americans are present to build rapport and trust with likely sources – and if Afghanistan's own intelligence agencies maintain access to large parts of their own country. Drones can provide some situational awareness, but only when cued to a small region: their soda-straw photographic apertures cannot scan large land masses comprehensively, and they work far better when deployed from nearby bases than from distant bases in Qatar or the Indian Ocean. Unless the United States negotiates access to a Central Asian country, airstrikes or surveillance flights from the Gulf would also require permission from Pakistan, which looks to be at best an unreliable future partner. In this light, the expansion of extremist sanctuaries, with or without explicit Taliban blessing, seems not merely possible but probable.

*   *   *

The Biden administration is undertaking a risky experiment in Afghanistan and in America's larger campaign against violent extremism. For years, American leaders implicitly accepted the proposition that the falling but non-trivial costs of continued military engagement in Afghanistan and the greater Middle East constituted the price of sustaining progress in the GWOT and avoiding the still-higher costs of renewed insecurity. Biden is now wagering that the US can sustain that progress while reducing the military commitments that enabled it. If that gamble pays off, Americans may rightly wonder why their leaders continued the GWOT as long as they did. If it doesn't, the logic of America's long struggle will, once again, receive rueful vindication. The greater Middle East remains the land of bad options, where, as awful as things may be today, they can always get worse. That is why America still needs persistence and patience in its global counter-terrorism campaign, a full 20 years after it began.

Notes

1   See Thomas E. Ricks, *Fiasco: The American Military Adventure in Iraq, 2003 to 2005* (New York: Penguin Books, 2006). On polling, see J. Baxter Oliphant, 'The Iraq War Continues to Divide the US Public, 15 Years After It Began', Pew Research Center, 19 March 2018, https://www.pewresearch.org/fact-tank/2018/03/19/iraq-war-continues-to-divide-u-s-public-15-years-after-it-began.

2   See, for example, George Tenet, *At the Center of the Storm: My Years at the CIA* (New York: HarperCollins Books, 2007), pp. 232–72.

3   See Peter Bergen, 'Terrorism in America After 9/11', New America, January 2021, https://www.newamerica.org/

in-depth/terrorism-in-america/what-threat-united-states-today.

4   See Ron Suskind, *The One Percent Doctrine: Deep Inside America's Pursuit of Its Enemies Since 9/11* (New York: Simon & Schuster, 2006).

5   The Hart–Rudman Commission reports of the late 1990s warned presciently and repeatedly about the likelihood of terrorist attacks against the United States. See 'Alarms Unheeded: Lessons on the 13th Anniversary of the Final Hart–Rudman Report', Aspen Institute, February 2014, https://www.aspeninstitute.org/wp-content/uploads/files/content/upload/Alarms%20Unheeded_0.pdf. See also Daniel Benjamin and Steven Simon,

The Age of Sacred Terror (New York: Random House, 2003); and Richard A. Clarke, *Against All Enemies: Inside America's War on Terror* (New York: Free Press, 2004), pp. 160–5.

6   See Raymond Odierno and Michael O'Hanlon, 'Securing Global Cities: Best Practices, Innovation, and the Path Ahead', Brookings Institution, March 2017, https://www.brookings.edu/research/securing-global-cities-2.

7   Dallas Boyd, Lewis A. Dunn and James Scouras, 'Why Has the United States Not Been Attacked Again?', *Washington Quarterly*, vol. 32, no. 3, Summer 2009, pp. 4–5.

8   See Jack Goldsmith, *Power and Constraint: The Accountable Presidency After 9/11* (New York: W. W. Norton & Co., 2012).

9   See Cameron Glenn et al., 'Timeline: The Rise, Spread, and Fall of the Islamic State', Wilson Center, October 2019, https://www.wilsoncenter.org/article/timeline-the-rise-spread-and-fall-the-islamic-state.

10   See, for example, 'Islamic State and the Crisis in Iraq and Syria in Maps', BBC, 28 March 2018, https://www.bbc.com/news/world-middle-east-27838034.

11   For one thoughtful analysis – though also an argument that the Islamic State, at least when running a caliph-ate, should not be seen as a classic terrorist organisation – see Audrey Kurth Cronin, 'ISIS Is Not a Terrorist Group: Why Counterterrorism Won't Stop the Latest Jihadist Threat', *Foreign Affairs*, vol. 94, no. 2, March/April 2015, pp. 87–98.

12   Daniel R. Coats, Director of National Intelligence, 'Statement for the Record: Worldwide Threat Assessment of the U.S. Intelligence Community', Office of the Director of National Intelligence, 29 January 2019, https://www.dni.gov/files/ODNI/documents/2019-ATA-SFR---SSCI.pdf.

13   For a thorough, balanced, judicious discussion of the likely benefits – and limitations thereof – from taking terrorist leaders off the battlefield through killing or arrest, see Paul Pillar, *Terrorism and US Foreign Policy* (Washington DC: Brookings Institution Press, 2001), pp. 121–3, 136–7. See also Audrey Kurth Cronin, *How Terrorism Ends: Understanding the Decline and Demise of Terrorist Campaigns* (Princeton, NJ: Princeton University Press, 2009).

14   See Hal Brands and Timothy Nichols, 'Special Operations Forces and Great-power Competition in the Twenty-first Century', American Enterprise Institute, 4 August 2020, https://www.aei.org/research-products/report/special-operations-forces-and-great-power-competition-in-the-21st-century/; and Aki Peritz and Eric Rosenbach, *Find, Fix, Finish: Inside the Counterterrorism Campaigns that Killed bin Laden and Devastated Al Qaeda* (New York: PublicAffairs, 2013).

15   See Lawrence Wright, 'The Rebellion Within: An Al Qaeda Mastermind Questions Terrorism', *New Yorker*, 2 June 2008. See also Daniel Byman, 'Are We Winning the War on Terrorism?', Middle East Memo, Brookings Institution, 23 May 2003, https://www.brookings.edu/research/are-we-winning-the-war-on-terrorism/.

16   Institute for Economics & Peace, 'Global Terrorism Index 2020: Measuring the Impact of Terrorism',

November 2020, p. 15, https://visionofhumanity.org/wp-content/uploads/2020/11/GTI-2020-web-1.pdf. This report draws on data from the National Consortium for the Study of Terrorism and Responses to Terrorism, led by the University of Maryland.

17 Julia Palik, Siri Aas Rustad and Fredrik Methi, 'Conflict Trends: A Global Overview, 1946–2019', PRIO Paper, Peace Research Institute of Oslo, pp. 8–11, https://www.prio.org/Publications/Publication/?x=12442.

18 The countries most severely afflicted in 2019 were Afghanistan (the worst-affected country), Iraq, Nigeria, Syria, Somalia, Yemen, Pakistan, India, Democratic Republic of the Congo and the Philippines. See Institute for Economics & Peace, 'Global Terrorism Index 2020', p. 18.

19 See Carter Malkasian, 'The Taliban Are Ready to Exploit America's Exit', Foreign Affairs, 14 April 2021, https://www.foreignaffairs.com/articles/afghanistan/2021-04-14/taliban-are-ready-exploit-americas-exit.

20 See Richard Hanania, 'Worse than Nothing: Why US Intervention Made Government Atrocities More Likely in Syria', Survival, vol. 62, no. 5, October–November 2020, pp. 173–92.

21 Memo from Donald Rumsfeld re: Global War on Terrorism, 16 October 2003, available at https://fas.org/irp/news/2003/10/rumsfeld101603.pdf.

22 See White House, 'Fact Sheet: President Bush's Freedom Agenda Helped Protect the American People', January 2009, https://georgewbush-whitehouse.archives.gov/infocus/freedomagenda; Kenneth M. Pollack, A Path Out of the Desert: A Grand Strategy for America in the Middle East (New York: Random House, 2008); and Tamara Cofman Wittes, Freedom's Unsteady March: America's Role in Building Arab Democracy (Washington DC: Brookings Institution Press, 2008).

23 Robert Malley, '10 Conflicts to Watch in 2021', International Crisis Group, 30 December 2020, https://www.crisisgroup.org/global/10-conflicts-watch-2021.

24 For a riveting, concise and honest treatment, see William J. Burns, The Back Channel: A Memoir of American Diplomacy and the Case for Its Renewal (New York: Random House, 2019), pp. 300–36.

25 See Tenet, At the Center of the Storm, pp. 229–56.

26 See Richard K. Betts, American Force: Dangers, Delusions, and Dilemmas in National Security (New York: Columbia University Press, 2012), pp. 145–70; and George Packer, The Assassins' Gate: America in Iraq (New York: Farrar, Straus and Giroux, 2005).

27 See Peter R. Mansoor, Surge: My Journey with General David Petraeus and the Remaking of the Iraq War (New Haven, CT: Yale University Press, 2013).

28 See Joel Rayburn, Iraq After America: Strongmen, Sectarians, Resistance (Stanford, CA: Hoover Institution Press, 2014); and Emma Sky, The Unraveling: High Hopes and Missed Opportunities in Iraq (New York: PublicAffairs, 2015).

29 The leading advocate of this 'indirect costs' approach is the Watson Institute for International and Public Affairs at Brown University. One need not endorse every part of its analysis or its larger cost estimate to agree that the overall costs of these wars are

significantly more than the direct US government expenditures to date. See Michael E. O'Hanlon, *Defense 101: Understanding the Military of Today and Tomorrow* (Ithaca, NY: Cornell University Press, 2021), pp. 58–61.

30 See David A. Blum and Nese F. Debruyne, 'American War and Military Operations Casualties: Lists and Statistics', Congressional Research Service, 29 July 2020, https://fas.org/sgp/crs/natsec/RL32492.pdf; and iCasualties.org, January 2021, http://icasualties.org.

31 The costs are summarised in Hal Brands, *What Good Is Grand Strategy? Power and Purpose in American Statecraft from Harry S. Truman to George W. Bush* (Ithaca, NY: Cornell University Press, 2014), chapter 4.

32 See, for example, Van Jackson, 'The Liberal Internationalist Origins of Right-wing Insurrection', *Inkstick*, 11 January 2011, https://inkstickmedia.com/the-liberal-internationalist-origins-of-right-wing-insurrection/.

33 See Mitt Regan, 'Citizens, Suspects, and Enemies: Examining Police Militarization', *Texas National Security Review*, Winter 2020/2021, https://tnsr.org/2020/12/citizens-suspects-and-enemies-examining-police-militarization/.

34 See White House, 'Remarks by President Biden on the War Forward in Afghanistan', 14 April 2001, https://www.whitehouse.gov/briefing-room/speeches-remarks/2021/04/14/remarks-by-president-biden-on-the-way-forward-in-afghanistan/.

35 See Missy Ryan and Karoun Demirjian, '"Extremely Difficult, But Not Impossible": General Provides Assessment of Afghan Counterterrorism Effort after US Troops Depart', *Washington Post*, 20 April 2021, https://www.washingtonpost.com/national-security/afghan-war-us-withdrawal/2021/04/20/d9b05468-a201-11eb-8a6d-f1b55f463112_story.html.

Trump's Russia Legacy and Biden's Response

Angela Stent

After all the controversy, accusations, angry tweets, impeachment hearings and conspiracy theories, how is the Trump administration's Russia policy to be assessed? Countless publications have explored questionable links between former president Donald Trump, his family and close allies, and a motley group of Russians and Russian-connected Ukrainians. Russia consumed an unprecedented amount of domestic energy in the United States during Trump's presidency, casting a shadow over the White House during the four years Trump lived there. And yet there has been scant systematic analysis of US–Russian relations under Trump, or of the troubled relationship he bequeathed to the Biden administration as it works to remove Russia as a domestic problem and to focus on managing it as a foreign-policy issue.

The Trump administration's dealings with Russia represent the most controversial part of its foreign-policy legacy. Russia was from day one a polarising issue because of questions about Moscow's role during the 2016 election campaign and accusations that the Trump campaign had colluded with Russia to get Trump into the White House. The president's consistent and extravagant public praise for Russian President Vladimir Putin baffled many. For four years, every White House contact with Russia was carefully scrutinised for signs of nefarious intent. Yet a careful examination of the outcomes of US–Russian engagement on a range of multilateral problems

Angela Stent is a Senior Non-Resident Fellow at the Brookings Institution, a Professor Emerita at Georgetown University and the author of *Putin's World: Russia Against the West and with the Rest* (Twelve, 2020). She is a contributing editor to *Survival*.

Survival | vol. 63 no. 4 | August–September 2021 | pp. 55–80   https://doi.org/10.1080/00396338.2021.1956191

reveals a mixed legacy, one that informed policy in the lead-up to the first summit between Putin and new President Joe Biden.

There has been considerable continuity in US policy toward Russia since the collapse of the Soviet Union because the character of the difficulties between the countries has not changed that much in the past 30 years.[1] Republican and Democratic administrations since 1992 have each tried to reset ties with Russia and to find a better way of dealing with Moscow, only to end their respective terms in disappointment because US and Russian definitions of a productive relationship are so different. In that sense, Trump's refrain, both during the 2016 campaign and after he was elected, that 'it would be great if we could get along with Russia' may have lacked subtlety, but resonated with his predecessors' attitudes.[2] The Biden administration's advocacy of a 'stable, predictable relationship' with Moscow echoes that view, even though the administration has explicitly said it is not seeking a reset.[3] The administration is dealing with a legacy that has laid the groundwork both for bilateral engagement and for the growing number of regional challenges which both countries confront.

Russiagate

Russia became a domestic issue in the United States during the 2016 campaign. Not since the era of Joseph McCarthy had Russia (or the Soviet Union as it was then) played such an outsize role in US politics. Trump was dogged by accusations that his campaign was working with the Russians to bring him to power. These suspicions were amplified by Trump's unprecedented praise for Putin and his reluctance to support Ukraine in its war with Russia. When Buzzfeed published the contents of the so-called 'Steele dossier' purporting to document Russian collusion with the Trump campaign, Russia became a key focus of America's highly polarised political discourse.[4] The Obama administration was slow to react to evidence of Russian meddling in the 2016 election but, on its way out, imposed sanctions on Moscow for its hacking and leaking of Democratic Party emails and its use of social media to inflame the public debate against Hillary Clinton. Days before Trump came to office, the American intelligence community published a declassified version of its report on Russian interference. It concluded:

> We assess Russian President Vladimir Putin ordered an influence campaign in 2016 aimed at the US presidential election. Russia's goals were to undermine public faith in the US democratic process, denigrate Secretary Clinton, and harm her electability and potential presidency. We further assess Putin and the Russian Government developed a clear preference for President-elect Trump.[5]

For many Democrats and others opposed to Trump, this was proof that he had not been legitimately elected. Trump himself would never admit that there had been Russian interference, because he understood that this would cast doubt on his right to occupy the White House. A wiser course might have been to acknowledge possible interference, appoint a commission and move on. He cast even more doubt on his dealings with Russia during a controversial press conference following a summit with Putin in Helsinki in 2018. In answer to a question about whether he agreed with his own intelligence experts about Russian interference, he responded: 'President Putin says it's not Russia. I don't see any reason why it would be.'[6] As Dana Allin has written: 'No president or major presidential candidate in living memory had ever publicly expressed indifference to a foreign power subverting the American political process.'[7]

Throughout the Trump presidency, there were a series of inquiries into the relationship between Russia and members of the Trump administration, the most extensive of these carried out by former FBI director Robert Mueller. While his report detailed illegal acts by a number of people close to Trump, it did not establish that there had been collusion between the president himself and the Russians.[8] Further investigation would later cast doubt on the validity of the Steele dossier.[9] Nevertheless, Trump's consistent praise for Putin continued to raise questions about the nature of their relationship.

Senior officials who worked with Trump attribute his views to his fascination with Russia going back to his days as a young real-estate developer who viewed the Russian market as an exciting business opportunity. One official said Trump had a nostalgic view of Russia, formed when he first visited the country in the late 1980s, during the era of major summits between US leaders and Mikhail Gorbachev.[10] Others attribute his refusal to criticise Russia to his general admiration for strongman rulers who are able to get their own way.[11] Trump believed that he understood Putin well, and that together they could get things done. Former national security advisor John Bolton recalled in his memoir that Trump 'never offered an opinion' on Putin, 'at least in front of me. I never asked what Trump's view was, perhaps afraid of what I might hear. His personal take on the Russian leader remained a mystery.'[12]

Trump's lavish praise for Putin stands in sharp contrast to his harsh criticism of some US allies, particularly German Chancellor Angela Merkel, whom he paradoxically accused of allowing Germany to fall 'captive' to Russia.[13] Trump's own rhetoric and refusal to criticise Moscow ensured that Russia became such a toxic subject domestically that it was impossible for the president to implement his version of a reset with Russia that he had advocated on the campaign trail.

The making of Trump's Russia policy

Inconsistency was the hallmark of Trump's Russia policy. He often seemed to personally favour a forward-looking policy, seeking to have Russia readmitted to the G8 (from which it had been excluded after its annexation of Crimea) and inviting Putin to a summit in Washington. According to Fiona Hill, senior director at the National Security Council (NSC) for Russia and Eurasia from 2017–19, Trump had for some time been focused on issues of nuclear weapons and arms control, believing that he could conclude a 'huge' arms-control deal with Putin – as Ronald Reagan and Gorbachev had done.[14] Trump also believed that improving ties with Russia would persuade Moscow to rethink its increasingly close ties with China, which the White House perceived as the real threat.

So confident was Trump in his ability to understand Russia that he declined preparatory 'deep dives' on the subject ahead of phone calls and meetings with Putin throughout his presidency. Trump took his regular intelligence briefings, but was not interested in discussions of policy.[15] Yet he was unable to achieve his goals, partly because of bureaucratic infighting, partly because of the high turnover of White House staff working on these issues, and partly because of his erratic moves and complete disregard of official expertise. Hill has recounted that she rarely attended Oval Office meetings on Russia, and recalled only one dedicated meeting ahead of the 2018 Helsinki summit when Jon Huntsman, the US ambassador, was visiting.[16] The president may have had his own informal advisers on Russia who did not brief NSC officials on their conversations. Hill's testimony to the congressional impeachment hearings in January 2020, for example, showed that Ukraine policy on key issues was made by a group of Trump's close allies without any communication with the NSC.[17]

While some in the White House tried to improve ties with Russia, national security advisors H.R. McMaster and Bolton, along with their staffs, pursued a tougher line, working with the rest of the executive branch, which saw things differently. When Rex Tillerson was chosen as secretary of state, many assumed, because he had been CEO of ExxonMobil and had worked with Russian oil giant Rosneft and its CEO Igor Sechin (one of Russia's most powerful men), that he would be favourably inclined toward Russia. Indeed, prominent Russian lawmaker Alexei Pushkov welcomed his appointment as a 'sensation'.[18] By the time of Tillerson's dismissal by presidential tweet, however, Putin opined that he had 'fallen in with bad company'.[19] Just before he stepped down, Tillerson backed the British claim that the Russians were responsible for the poisoning with the chemical agent Novichok of former GRU double agent Sergei Skripal and his daughter in Salisbury. 'Russia', he said, 'continues to be an irresponsible source of instability in the world, acting with open disregard for the sovereignty of other states and the life of their citizens.'[20]

Tillerson's successor, former CIA director Mike Pompeo, led a State Department that continued to support sanctions against Russia for its election interference, the Skripal poisonings and its determination to complete the Nord Stream 2 gas pipeline. Pompeo criticised Russia for election interference, its treatment of dissident anti-corruption activist Alexei Navalny and its hacking of the US SolarWinds platform. But while the State Department's public statements and actions were often highly critical of Russia, Trump himself remained silent.

The US Congress was deeply divided over most issues during Trump's presidency, but on Russia it seemed to speak with one voice. There was a bipartisan consensus on the need to impose sanctions on Russia for its actions and to ensure that the president could not remove them. Barack Obama had sanctioned Russia in December 2016 by executive order, sanctions which Congress soon acted to preserve. Throughout the Trump administration, the same Republican senators who usually supported Trump voted for punitive measures against Russia.

Arms control

US–Russia ties are largely defined by the countries' status as the world's two nuclear superpowers. Arms-control treaties and negotiations have been a feature of this relationship since Richard Nixon first visited Moscow in 1972 and signed the SALT I treaty limiting strategic nuclear weapons with Leonid Brezhnev. Despite Trump's initial wish to conclude a major arms-control treaty, he ultimately did more to dismantle the 50-year-old arms-control regime. Indeed, during Bolton's tenure, doing so was a key focus. Long a sceptic about arms control, Bolton ensured that the US withdrew from the 1987 Intermediate-Range Nuclear Forces (INF) Treaty after both sides accused each other of cheating. This opened the possibility of the US once again deploying intermediate-range weapons in Europe or Asia. At the end of the Trump administration, the US pulled out of the multilateral 2002 Treaty on Open Skies, which permits each state party to conduct short-notice, unarmed reconnaissance flights over the others' entire territories to collect data on military forces and activities. Russia withdrew six months later.

The one remaining treaty was New START limiting strategic nuclear weapons, which was set to expire on 5 February 2021. The treaty might have been extended for five years without a Senate vote, but the administration was determined to negotiate a new deal that would include China's nuclear weapons. The Chinese repeatedly refused to join the negotiations, pointing out that their own nuclear arsenal was much smaller than those of the US and Russia.[21] Rather belatedly, arms-control negotiator Marshall Billingslea began to negotiate with his Russian counterpart Sergei Ryabkov to replace New START, but insisted that 'the next arms control agreement must cover all nuclear weapons, not just so-called strategic nuclear weapons'.[22] In the end, both sides were unable to reach an agreement, and by the time Trump left office it was unclear whether New START would survive.

The Trump administration did participate intermittently in talks begun during the Obama years on strategic stability, but Bolton once told German Foreign Minister Heiko Maas that 'strategy stability' referred to 'what Russia didn't like about America's national missile defense program, which we had no intention of negotiating, let alone modifying or abandoning'.[23]

Sanctions and economic relations

During Trump's presidency a raft of sanctions were imposed on Russian entities and individuals that had been implicated in the 2016 election interference, the poisoning of the Skripals, cyber attacks and a range of other activities deemed to be malign. In July 2017, the US Senate passed the Countering America's Adversaries Through Sanctions Act (CAATSA) by a vote of 98–2. Among other provisions, the law requires the White House to submit to Congress lists of oligarchs and political figures linked to Putin who might be personally sanctioned.[24] The legislation allows for 'blocking sanctions', which block all transactions with listed persons and their property in the jurisdiction of a sanctioning country, and 'sectoral sanctions', which prohibit entities from participating in select energy projects in Russia, and in new debt and equity transactions with listed entities. The US has targeted 336 individuals and 536 entities with blocking and sectoral sanctions since 2014, the majority since 2017. Congressional sanctions, unlike those imposed by presidential executive order, are virtually impossible to remove. Since they are largely punitive, they contain few incentives for Russia to modify its behaviour. Indeed, the Kremlin has no expectation that these sanctions will be lifted, and even anticipates more. Despite hundreds of designations, Russia has not changed its behaviour to conform with the Minsk agreements to end the conflict in Ukraine, and has not withdrawn support for separatist forces in the Donbas. Sanctions have, however, adversely affected the Russian economy. They have also adversely affected US companies in terms of lost business opportunities and negative impacts on global competitiveness.[25]

Trump himself mostly opposed the sanctions, saying when he signed CAATSA into law that he believed the act was 'seriously flawed –

particularly because it encroaches on the executive branch's authority to negotiate … I built a truly great company worth many billions of dollars', he added, claiming that 'as president, I can make better deals with foreign countries than Congress'.[26] Trump did, however, support sanctions on the Nord Stream 2 gas pipeline, which targeted not only Russian entities, but German and European companies as well. Trump told Merkel that Germany was 'controlled' by Russia and inaccurately accused Germany of becoming 'totally dependent on Russian energy'.[27]

The Kremlin retaliated against the sanctions by seizing two diplomatic properties and ordering the United States to reduce its Moscow Embassy staff by 755 people. The US then ordered the closure of the Russian consulates in San Francisco and Seattle. Eventually, the US consulate in St Petersburg was itself forced to close. The consequence of all these closures was a severe hollowing out of both countries' diplomatic presence even down to the most basic activities.

While Congress and the executive branch were busy imposing sanctions, the White House tried to promote a high-level business dialogue with Russia. Trump, who had for decades unsuccessfully tried to secure Russian business deals, favoured this, as did Huntsman, his first ambassador to Russia. Preparations had begun for this dialogue prior to the 2018 Helsinki summit, and both presidents announced it during their joint press conference.[28] Unfortunately for the business community, however, Trump's denial of Russian election interference during the same press briefing immediately undermined the establishment of the working group, which was intended to create space for both business and political dialogue. American CEOs faced the political fallout from the press conference and the limitations imposed by the sanctions, which placed restrictions on US businesses and listed a number of key Russian CEOs. Russia did not help matters by arresting Michael Calvey, a prominent US businessman and advocate for closer economic ties with Russia, over a dispute with a Russian partner. Instead of being adjudicated in a civil proceeding, the dispute became a criminal case. Daniel Russell, president of the US–Russia Business Council, has concluded that the high-level business dialogue was the 'right initiative at the wrong time'.[29]

NATO

One of the reasons for the Kremlin's interest in Trump's bid for the White House was his denigration of the NATO Alliance, which for Putin is 'the main opponent'.[30] Trump consistently criticised NATO, calling it 'obsolete' and accusing most of its members of acting as free-riders on the US taxpayer by not living up to their 2014 commitment to spend 2% of GDP on defence by 2024. Trump became increasingly irritated with the allies and convinced that the United States should leave the Alliance, a move that would have demolished the post-war transatlantic security architecture. In his memoir, Bolton recalled tense moments during the July 2018 NATO summit, when even he was unsure whether Trump would announce that the US was pulling out. In the end, Trump told the allies that he was with NATO 'a thousand million percent' while admonishing them to double their contributions.[31] As one senior official put it: 'We saved NATO.'[32]

While Trump was clearly unconvinced of the value of NATO, much of his administration understood the need to shore up the Alliance against an increasingly assertive Russia. In his speech to the 2017 Munich Security Conference, vice president Mike Pence pledged US support to NATO and acknowledged the need to contain Russia.[33] All of Trump's defense secretaries reiterated this stance. Moreover, the administration strengthened its military presence in the Baltic states and Poland, signing the US–Poland Enhanced Defense Cooperation Agreement in 2020 to increase the number of US troops and military installations in Poland. At the same time, Trump announced that the US would pull 12,000 troops out of Germany because Berlin was not fulfilling its NATO obligations.

Even though NATO was 'saved', the experience of dealing with an unpredictable US administration can be expected to have a long-term impact on NATO. Its other members have realised that, given the volatility of American politics, the US commitment to the Alliance cannot be counted on.

Ukraine

Ukraine, and Ukrainians with ties to Russian intelligence, occupied an outsize role in the events leading to Trump's first impeachment trial in January 2020, and in the 2020 presidential campaign. Trump had always been ambivalent about Ukraine, possibly because his first campaign manager, Paul Manafort, had worked for ousted Ukrainian president Victor Yanukovych and a number of prominent Russian oligarchs, and viewed the post-2014 Ukrainian government as hostile to his interests. Trump had implied on the campaign trail that Crimea was Russian and that Russia had not invaded Ukraine.[34] Once in office, his scepticism about Ukraine grew, as he became convinced that the Ukrainians had interfered on Clinton's behalf in the 2016 election.

Throughout Trump's time in the White House, a group of close aides and advisers led by Rudy Giuliani pursued an agenda in Ukraine that was at odds with the priorities of the rest of the executive branch. Gordon Sondland, the US ambassador to the European Union, was one of their recruits. As Hill put it, Sondland's role was to carry out a 'domestic political errand' that undermined US national security and foreign policy, as well as the diplomatic apparatus that was in place to serve those ends.[35] This 'errand' was securing Trump's re-election by collecting negative information on Ukraine's role in 2016 and on the activities of Joe Biden's son Hunter, who sat on the board of Ukrainian gas company Burisma. It also involved engineering the firing of the well-respected US ambassador in Kyiv, Marie Yovanovitch, whose firm anti-corruption message to the Ukrainians was weakened by requests from Trump's inner circle for compromising material on the Bidens. Ultimately, Trump told Ukrainian President Volodymyr Zelensky that the US would withhold security assistance to Ukraine unless the Ukrainians provided damaging information on the Bidens. This information was leaked to the media, and Ukraine blew up in the White House's face. After riveting testimony about his dealings with Ukraine, Trump was impeached by the House of Representatives for abuse of power, only to be acquitted by the Senate.

While the White House pursued its own Ukraine policy, the rest of the executive branch increased its support for Kyiv by supplying it with defensive lethal weapons, something the Obama administration had refused to do. Tillerson appointed Kurt Volker, the former US ambassador to NATO, as special representative for Ukraine negotiations, in which role he met with his Russian counterpart, Vladislav Surkov, in Kyiv, the Donbas and

Moscow to try to resolve the frozen conflict in the Donbas. Volker's negotiations paralleled the French and German efforts to implement the Minsk II agreements, but were unable to advance the peace process.

In April 2021, the Treasury Department sanctioned Konstantin Kilimnik and 15 others for interfering in the 2020 US election. Kilimnik is a Russian-Ukrainian intelligence operative who worked with Manafort to spread disinformation about the Bidens during the 2020 campaign. Investigators are also looking into whether Andriy Derkach, a member of the Ukrainian parliament, was also working with Giuliani and others to provide damaging information during the campaign.[36]

Syria and the Middle East

The Trump administration's dealings with Russia in the Middle East were complex, cooperative in some instances and confrontational in others. Both Russia and the US were committed to defeating the Islamic State (ISIS), but Russia focused more on other anti-Assad groups. When Trump proposed to pull all US troops out of Syria, Putin agreed, arguing that the US had no right to a military presence there, unlike Russia, which had been invited in by President Bashar al-Assad in September 2015.

In the event, most US troops did leave Syria, but a contingent remained in the northeast. It was there that they came into direct conflict with troops from Wagner, a mercenary group owned by Yevgeny Prigozhin, a close Putin associate. The Russian troops had entered an area controlled by US and allied forces next to the Tabiya natural-gas plant formerly owned by Conoco in Deir ez-Zor. In the ensuing battle, 200–300 Russians were killed, but Russia refused to even acknowledge that the firefight had taken place.[37] Senior US officials say that Russia admitted that the Wagner troops had violated an agreement signed with the US, and accepted the casualties without pushing back.[38] When the Trump administration bombed Syrian chemical-weapons facilities after Assad used chemical weapons on his own people, the Russians were given advance warning.

The focus of Trump's Middle East policy was to counter Iran and, if possible, change the regime in Tehran. The administration pulled out of the Joint Comprehensive Plan of Action (JCPOA) that the Obama administration, along with the other permanent members of the United Nations Security Council (the P5) and Germany, had negotiated with Iran. Moscow criticised the withdrawal and Washington's decision to subsequently impose sanctions on Iran, but was clearly ambivalent about Iran's role in Syria and its support of Hizbullah, a group with which Russia was working, at least in theory, to keep Assad in power. On several occasions, Putin told Bolton that Russia did not want the Iranians in Syria.[39] According to James Jeffrey, Trump's special envoy for Syria, the Russians realised that the Iranians were trying to create a state within a state in Syria and to bypass existing institutions.[40] At an unusual meeting with the Israeli and Russian national security advisers in Israel, Bolton and his counterparts agreed that Iran should eventually leave Syria, although Nikolai Patrushev, secretary of Russia's Security Council, continued to praise Russia's ties with Tehran.[41]

Trump's major achievement in the Middle East was the Abraham Accords, which normalised relations between Israel and Bahrain, Morocco, Sudan and the United Arab Emirates (UAE). Some of the work to facilitate the accords was carried out through a private channel between Trump's son-in-law Jared Kushner and Kirill Dmitriev, head of the Russian Direct Investment Fund, whom Putin had used as an envoy to the Trump administration when it first came into office and who had business interests in the UAE.[42]

North Korea

Trump began his presidency convinced that he could resolve the North Korean crisis and persuade Kim Jong-un to give up his nuclear weapons in exchange for generous US economic assistance. Indeed, the NSC produced a bizarre four-minute 'movie trailer' for an audience of one, showcasing a future North Korea as a desirable tourist destination with elegant hotels and attractive beaches, and promoting the theme 'two men, two leaders, one destiny'.[43] Trump met with Kim three times, but the North Korean dictator was not persuaded to give up his nuclear programme. Not wanting to be left out, Putin met with Kim for the first time in Vladivostok in April 2019. According to a senior Trump administration official, Russia wanted to be seen as a player on the Korean Peninsula, even though it accepted that it would follow China's lead there.[44] Like the United States, Russia preferred that North Korea halt its nuclear-weapons programme, and took some helpful steps toward this outcome. In December 2019, for instance, when North Korea grew impatient with the lack of sanctions relief, Russia joined China in pressuring Kim not to proceed with any provocations. The Russians understood that the key to persuading Kim to renounce his nuclear weapons lay in Washington, even though the US attempt to denuclearise North Korea failed.

Venezuela

The Trump administration and Russia were firmly at odds over Venezuela. After the authoritarian Nicolás Maduro took power in a disputed election in 2018, Russia was instrumental in thwarting the Trump administration's attempts to support his rival, Juan Guaidó (president of the National Assembly of Venezuela), who was recognised by 60 countries, including the United States, as the legitimate president, in line with the constitution. Venezuela was in debt to Russia to the tune of $6 billion, and Rosneft was active in Venezuela's oil sector. Russia sent around 200 government troops to back Maduro, as well as officials to train the security services, although Cuba remains the backbone of Maduro's security structure. According to Elliott Abrams, Trump's special representative for Venezuela, Moscow wanted to 'ensure that the US did not create a colour revolution in Venezuela'.[45] In April 2019, an attempted uprising by forces loyal to Guaidó failed to install him as president. There is some evidence that in May, Russia dissuaded Maduro from leaving the country to go into exile.[46] Trump officials viewed Russia as the main spoiler as Venezuela descended into poverty and violence.

The Trump administration's balance sheet

By the end of Trump's presidency, US–Russian relations were worse than they had been when he entered the White House because of continuing questions about election interference in 2016 and 2020, the ongoing war between Russia and Ukraine, cyber attacks, and the poisoning and imprisonment of the Kremlin's opponents. The COVID-19 pandemic complicated the administration's outreach to Russia because it prevented the in-person meetings that both leaders sought, including Trump's attendance at the Victory Day parade in Moscow in June 2020 to commemorate the 75th anniversary of the end of the Second World War, and Putin's hosting of a P5 summit at the UN to discuss the future of world order. By November 2020, the Russians had come to believe that Trump was too unpredictable and unable to deliver the improved relationship he had initially promised, and that Moscow desired. Yet Putin waited until 14 December 2020, after the vote of the electoral college, to congratulate Biden on his victory in the presidential election in November, and some Russian media outlets continued to propagate the Trumpian 'stolen election' myth both before and after the 6 January 2021 assault on the US Capitol.

The Biden administration's approach to Russia

The major difference between Biden's approach to Russia and Trump's is that, under Biden, Russia has ceased to be a domestic political issue. No one has suggested that there are questionable ties between Biden and Russian actors. Indeed, Biden has on several occasions reminded Americans that he told Putin in 2011 that he 'had no soul'.[47] Shortly after taking office, Biden felt it necessary to differentiate himself from Trump by acknowledging in an interview that he believed Putin was a 'killer'.[48] (During his own presidency, Trump's response to interviewer Bill O'Reilly's statement that 'Putin is a killer' was to declare: 'There are a lot of killers. We have a lot of killers. Well, you think our country is so innocent?'[49]) Biden has also gone out of his way to reject the idea that his administration is seeking a 'reset' with Russia. The toxic legacy of the past five years means that the White House's ties with Russia will face extra scrutiny for some time to come. Moreover, Biden's main priorities are domestic, and his top foreign-policy priority is China, not Russia.

A key difference between the Biden administration and its predecessor is the former's emphasis on mending alliance relationships, both in Europe and in Asia. Moreover, Biden has stressed the need to coordinate on Russia policy with the United States' European allies, particularly Germany, Russia's most important European partner. At the Munich Security Conference in 2021, Biden reaffirmed America's commitment to honouring Article V of the Washington Treaty, something that Trump had refused to do.[50] The White House has also announced that it will freeze the Trump administration's decision to withdraw 12,000 troops from Germany pending a broader review of troop deployments around the world.[51] The US has rejoined the Paris climate accords and the World Health Organization, in both of which Russia seeks to play a greater role.

Another way in which Biden's White House contrasts with Trump's is in its explicit commitment to democracy promotion and human-rights advocacy. On the eve of his departure for his first major European trip, which included a summit with Putin, Biden wrote:

> When I meet with Vladimir Putin in Geneva, it will be after high-level discussions with friends, partners and allies who see the world through the same lens as the United States, and with whom we have renewed our connections and shared purpose. We are standing united to address Russia's challenges to European security, starting with its aggression in Ukraine, and there will be no doubt about the resolve of the United States to defend our democratic values, which we cannot separate from our interests.[52]

The administration's criticisms of Russia for its repression of the country's political opposition have elicited strong Russian responses: Putin upbraided the US for violating the human rights of the 6 January insurrectionists in the US Capitol, for instance.[53]

So far, the Biden administration's policy toward Russia has been well coordinated. The administration is disciplined and speaks with one voice on Russia, unlike the Trump administration. And despite the pervasive and often dysfunctional partisanship in the US Congress, Russia remains an issue on which both the House and the Senate appear to be united, occasionally chiding the Biden administration for not being tougher about sanctions.

Arms control
One of the Biden administration's first acts was to renew New START for five years, without which there would be nothing to regulate the strategic

nuclear arsenals of the world's two nuclear superpowers. As it is, the current treaty does not cover new classes of strategic and non-strategic weapons, nor does it cover cyber weapons or space weapons. Both Russia and the United States accept that it would be best to agree on a new treaty to replace New START by 2026, though such a treaty would need to be ratified by the US Senate, which would not be easy to achieve.

The Biden administration is working with Russia to re-establish a dialogue on strategic stability, which would begin to tackle the complex issues involved in negotiating the next arms-control treaty. 'Strategic stability' is a broad and protean concept that can encompass a range of issues beyond nuclear weapons. For instance, the Russians have favoured including the US missile-defence system in any discussion, while both countries might want to include the new class of hypersonic weapons that both have been developing.[54] The history of such talks is not encouraging, but the Biden administration understands that in a time of heightened political and military tensions, it is necessary to re-engage on these issues.

Iran has also become an issue on which the Biden administration and Russia have been working together. Biden would like the US to rejoin the JCPOA, and has been negotiating with Russia and the other signatories in Vienna to complete a new agreement to limit Iran's nuclear-weapons programme.

Ukraine

President Biden was the point man for Ukraine during the Obama administration, and visited Kyiv six times during his vice presidency. He focused on working with the Poroshenko administration to tackle Ukraine's endemic corruption while it was fighting Russia in the Donbas. He knows the country and its major players well, and has supported it during difficult times.

Weeks after Biden took office, Russia began to amass troops and military hardware on the border with Ukraine, ostensibly to counter a planned NATO exercise called *Steadfast Defender*. There was great concern about Russian intentions and the possibility that Russia was planning to invade. Both Biden and Secretary of State Antony Blinken warned Russia against taking more aggressive steps. Russia subsequently said that it was withdrawing some of its troops, although up to 80,000 remained near the border. Blinken visited Ukraine and sought to reassure President Zelensky – previously snubbed by Trump – that the US would support him in the face of Russian pressure. It was unclear why Russia made this provocative move, but it may have been to intimidate Zelensky as he sought to restrict pro-Russian media and politicians in Ukraine, and to test the Biden administration's resolve. It remains to be seen how deeply involved in Ukraine the administration will choose to become, and whether it will take on a more active role in pushing the Minsk agreements. President Zelensky finally received his invitation to the White House in June 2021, two years after Trump declined to invite him.

Sanctions

Biden has ordered the Treasury Department to review the US sanction regime to see how effective it has been. Although not opposed to sanctions in principle, the White House appears to accept that they have often failed to change the behaviour of the targeted countries. As the review has pro-ceeded, however, the administration has had to respond to the evidence that in 2020, hackers based in Russia penetrated SolarWinds, a major US information-technology firm, in a cyber attack that spread to its clients and went undetected for months, affecting both private and public platforms.[55] Evidence has also emerged indicating that Russia spread misinformation about Biden and his son during the 2020 election.[56]

On 15 April 2021, the United States imposed new sanctions related to Russia's interference in the 2020 US election, its disinformation campaigns, the SolarWinds hack and its occupation of Crimea. These included a ban on the participation by US financial institutions in the primary market for rouble-denominated bonds issued after 14 June 2021 by Russia's central bank, National Wealth Fund or Ministry of Finance, and on lending rouble-denominated funds to these entities. These bans do not apply to the secondary market for Russian sovereign debt. They do include designations of multiple Russian individuals and entities, including six technology companies, for supporting Russia's malicious cyber activities, attempts to influence the 2020 US elections, disinformation activities and the occupation of Crimea. Ten diplomats from the Russian

Embassy in Washington DC, including those the White House described as 'representatives of Russian intelligence services', were expelled from the United States.[57]

On the same day that these sanctions were announced, Biden offered an olive branch to Putin, saying: 'The United States is not looking to kick off a cycle of escalation and conflict with Russia. We want a stable, predictable relationship.'[58] He went on to announce that he would be meeting Putin for a summit, and that there were areas in which the two countries could work together.

The Biden administration parted ways with its predecessor by choosing not to prevent the completion of the Nord Stream 2 gas pipeline from Russia to Germany. Even though both Biden and Blinken had said they opposed it, they decided in the end that it was more important to avoid a further rupture with Germany given that the pipeline was almost fully laid. When the time came for the State Department to report to Congress on the progress of the sanctions pursuant to the Protecting Europe's Energy Security Act (PEESA), Blinken said he had determined that it was in the US national interest to waive the application of sanctions on the company Nord Stream AG, its corporate officers and CEO Matthias Warnig, a former East German Stasi officer and close associate of Putin. 'It's almost completely finished', Biden told reporters as he walked across the White House lawn. 'To go ahead and impose sanctions now, I think is counter-productive in terms of our European relations.'[59]

Regional issues

There are a number of regional issues on which Russia and the US may continue to work together, as they did episodically during the Trump administration. Russia is concerned about what will follow the US troop withdrawal from Afghanistan, and about the potential consequences of any return to power by the Taliban and continued fighting for the stability both of the region and of Russia itself. In March, Moscow hosted a peace conference with representatives from several Afghan factions that was attended by Zalmay Khalilzad, US special representative for Afghanistan reconciliation, who played the same role in the Trump administration.[60] Moscow and Washington may well continue to work together as they both seek to minimise the possibility of renewed conflict in the region.

The Middle East could also present opportunities for cooperation, although US–Russian competition there will also continue. Putin is adamant that the United States should leave Syria, but is also wary of Iran's presence in that country, and concerned about Russia's own future influence there. After the US launched a strike on Iranian-backed militias in eastern Syria in February 2021, Russian Defence Minister Sergei Shoigu said: 'I will not hide the fact that in Syria, at the operational and tactical level, we have very close contacts with our American colleagues … We have contacts at the level of our … airspace managers and in the conduct of work in the air to combat terrorism several times a day.'[61]

Although it seeks to diminish the US presence in the region, the Biden administration was drawn back to the Middle East after war broke out between Israel and Hamas in May. Unlike its predecessor, the Biden administration has re-engaged with the Palestinians, announced its intention to reopen the US consulate in Jerusalem that serves Palestinians, and may revive an Israel–Palestinian negotiating track that the Trump administration abandoned. Russia has close ties with Israel, the Palestine Liberation Organization and Hamas (which the US designates as a terrorist organisation), and could play a role in a revived multilateral peace process via the Quartet on the Middle East (comprising the EU, Russia, the UN and the US) should the Biden administration choose this route.

The Arctic is another arena in which the US and Russia both cooperate and compete. As climate change makes the Arctic more accessible, global interest in the region's natural resources, navigation routes and strategic position has grown among members of the Arctic Council, as well as China. Russia assumed the rotating chairmanship of the Arctic Council in May 2021 and has ambitious plans for its two-year term. Its official priorities include the social and economic development of the region, preservation of biodiversity, extraction and processing of natural resources, intensification of cargo transportation along the Northern Sea Route, and growing tourism and trade.[62] These are areas where the US and Russia could work together. However, Russia is also building up its military forces and conducting exercises in the Arctic, and has criticised the NATO presence in the Bering Sea. When Blinken met with Russian Foreign Minister Sergei Lavrov in Reykjavik for an Arctic Council session in May, they agreed to cooperate on Arctic-related issues. But Blinken also sought to persuade other Arctic Council members to oppose Moscow's plans to establish maritime rules in the Northern Sea Route, which runs from the Kara Sea to the Bering Strait, and to frustrate its desire to resume high-level military talks within the eight-nation bloc. Those talks were suspended in 2014 after Russia's annexation of Crimea.

Stability and predictability?

Biden and his colleagues have been clear-eyed about the challenges that Russia poses both to US domestic politics and to American interests abroad. The administration has imposed new sanctions and criticised Moscow's repressive actions against critics of President Putin. Nevertheless, the White House accepts that there are urgent issues on which it must seek to work with Russia. Chief among these are arms control and strategic stability at a time when Russian rhetoric about the possibility of a nuclear confrontation is becoming shriller, and both countries are modernising their nuclear and conventional arsenals. The administration's focus on climate change offers new channels for cooperation, as does the pandemic and the challenge of global health. In theory, counter-terrorism is another potential area for cooperation, although it is hampered by the fact that the US and Russia define 'terrorism' differently.

The Biden administration has singled out China as its major foreign-policy challenge, and is also monitoring the development of the increasingly robust Russian–Chinese strategic partnership. Some in the administration believe, like their predecessors, that the US should seek to prise Russia away from China, suggesting a more forward-leaning policy toward Moscow. Encouraging Moscow to rethink what Bobo Lo has called its 'wary embrace' of China promises to be a difficult task.[63] At the very least, the Biden team must ensure that the US does not take actions that push Russia and China closer together, as the Trump administration's trade war with China and sanctions on Russia did.[64]

Two days before he shook Putin's hand outside the eighteenth-century villa in Geneva where the two leaders held their first summit, Biden called his Russian counterpart 'a worthy adversary'.[65] That was a far cry from Trump's hope that Putin would be his friend, but also from Obama's likening of Putin to a 'bored kid in the back of the classroom'.[66] Expectations for the summit were limited, and the focus was on restoring some diplomatic ties after waves of expulsions and agreeing to launch strategic-stability talks. Both of these goals were accomplished. The administration had emphasised the need to establish 'guard rails' on the relationship, to obviate the need to respond to future unexpected Russian provocations. To that end, Biden gave Putin a list of 16 critical-infrastructure entities which, if they were the subject of a cyber attack from Russia, would evoke swift retaliatory action.[67] Since the summit, however, there have been renewed ransomware attacks in the US attributed to criminals operating from Russian territory, highlighting how challenging the cyber dimension is. Biden has said that the US will know whether the summit was a success by the end of 2021. 'The proof of the pudding', he said, 'is in the eating.'[68]

If Russia undertook escalatory actions in Ukraine or in cyberspace, the US would be obliged to respond. That being the case, can a stable and predictable relationship ever be achieved? Putin's modus operandi is to use Russia's unpredictability to keep the West off-kilter. He likes to surprise. The massing of Russian troops on Ukraine's border with no explanation, and the threat that they could invade or return at any time, was surely designed to test the Biden administration, as are repeated cyber intrusions and ransomware demands, some attributed to criminal groups operating in Russia. Russian foreign policy toward the West is evidently designed not to be predictable.

Russia claims that it seeks stability, but that presupposes some basic agreement between Moscow and Washington as to where each side's red lines lie. Expectations must be carefully managed in what will surely remain a brittle and volatile relationship for the foreseeable future. The erratic policy of the Trump administration is gone, but the challenge of dealing with Putin's Russia remains.

Notes

1 See Angela Stent, *The Limits of Partnership: US–Russian Relations in the Twenty-first Century* (Princeton, NJ: Princeton University Press, 2015).

2 See Dan Mangan, 'President Donald Trump Says Getting Along with Russia Is "Not Terrible, It's Good"', CNBC, 16 February 2021, https://www.cnbc.com/2017/02/16/president-donald-trump-says-getting-along-with-russia-is-a-good-thing.html.

3 White House, 'Readout of President Joseph R. Biden, Jr. Call with President Vladimir Putin of Russia', 13 April 2021, https://www.whitehouse.gov/briefing-room/statements-releases/2021/04/13/readout-of-president-joseph-r-biden-jr-call-with-president-vladimir-putin-of-russia-4-13/.

4 Ken Bensinger, Miriam Elder and Mark Schoofs, 'These Reports Allege Trump Has Deep Ties to Russia', BuzzFeed News, 10 January 2017, https://www.buzzfeednews.com/article/kenbensinger/these-reports-allege-trump-has-deep-ties-to-russia.

5 US Office of the Director of National Intelligence, 'Assessing Russian Activities and Intentions in Recent US Elections', 6 January 2017, p. ii, https://www.dni.gov/files/documents/ICA_2017_01.pdf.

6 'Trump Sides with Russia Against FBI at Helsinki Summit', BBC News, 16 July 2018, https://www.bbc.com/news/world-europe-44852812.

7 Dana H. Allin, 'Donald Trump's Legacy', *Survival*, vol. 62, no. 6, December 2020–January 2021, p. 263.

8 See Robert S. Mueller, 'Report on the Investigation into Russian Interference in the 2016 Presidential Election', March 2019, https://www.justice.gov/archives/sco/file/1373816/download.

9 See Holman W. Jenkins, 'Two Grifters and a Dossier', *Wall Street Journal*, 25 May 2021, https://www.wsj.com/articles/two-grifters-and-a-dossier-11621982038?mod=trending_now_opn_5.

10 Author's interview with senior Trump administration official, May 2021.

11 See, for example, Thomas Wright, 'Trump's 19th Century Foreign Policy', *Politico*, 20 January 2016, https://www.politico.com/magazine/story/2016/01/donald-trump-foreign-policy-213546/.

12 John Bolton, *The Room Where It Happened: A White House Memoir* (New York: Simon & Schuster, 2020), p. 63.

13 See Ewan MacAskill, 'Angela Merkel Hits Back at Donald Trump at Nato Summit', *Guardian*, 11 July 2018, https://www.theguardian.com/us-news/2018/jul/11/nato-summit-donald-trump-says-germany-is-captive-of-russians.

14 Author's interview with Fiona Hill, May 2021.

15 *Ibid.*

16 See Adam Entous, 'What Fiona Hill Learned in the White House', *New Yorker*, 22 June 2020, https://www.newyorker.com/magazine/2020/06/29/what-fiona-hill-learned-in-the-white-house.

17 See Nicholas Fandos and Michael D. Shear, 'Fiona Hill Testifies "Fictions" on Ukraine Pushed by Trump Help Russia', *New York Times*,

21 November 2019, https://www.
nytimes.com/2019/11/21/us/politics/
fiona-hill-impeachment-ukraine.html.

18 Denis Pinchuk and Olesya Astakhova,
'Russia Sees Exxon Boss, Tipped
To Be Secretary of State, as an Old
Friend', Reuters, 12 December
2016, https://cn.reuters.com/article/
us-usa-trump-russia-tillerson/
russia-sees-exxon-boss-tipped-to-be-
secretary-of-state-as-an-old-friend-
idUSKBN14114E.

19 'Putin: Tillerson Fell into "Bad
Company"', UAWire, 8 September
2017, http://www.uawire.org/
putin-tillerson-fell-into-bad-company.

20 John Cassidy, 'Rex Tillerson Gets
Fired the Day After He Criticized
Russia', *New Yorker*, 13 March 2018,
https://www.newyorker.com/news/
our-columnists/rex-tillerson-gets-
fired-the-day-after-he-criticized-russia.

21 See Leanne Quinn, 'China's Stance
on Nuclear Arms Control and New
START', Arms Control Association, 23
August 2019, https://www.armscontrol.
org/blog/2019-08-23/chinas-stance-
nuclear-arms-control-new-start.

22 'U.S. Pushes for Broadening of New
START Treaty, Pushes for China to
Join Accord', Radio Free Europe/Radio
Liberty, 23 June 2020, https://www.
rferl.org/a/u-s-pushes-for-broadening-
of-new-start-treaty-pushes-for-china-
to-join-accord/30686509.html.

23 Bolton, *The Room Where It Happened*,
p. 162.

24 US Department of the Treasury,
'Counter America's Adversaries
Through Sanctions Act', https://
home.treasury.gov/policy-issues/
financial-sanctions/sanctions-
programs-and-country-information/

countering-americas-adversaries-
through-sanctions-act.

25 See US–Russian Business Council,
'USRBC Compendium of Worldwide
Sanctions Against Russia', 24 May 2021.

26 White House, 'Statement by President
Donald J. Trump on Signing the
"Countering America's Adversaries
Through Sanctions Act"', 2 August
2017, https://ru.usembassy.gov/
statement-president-donald-j-
trump-signing-countering-americas-
adversaries-sanctions-act/.

27 Rick Noack, 'Trump Accused
Germany of Becoming "Totally
Dependent" on Russian Energy at
the U.N. The Germans Just Smirked',
Washington Post, 25 September
2018, https://www.washingtonpost.
com/world/2018/09/25/
trump-accused-germany-becoming-
totally-dependent-russian-energy-un-
germans-just-smirked/.

28 Jennie Neufeld, 'Read the Full
Transcript of the Helsinki Press
Conference', Vox, 17 July 2018, https://
www.vox.com/2018/7/16/17576956/
transcript-putin-trump-russia-
helsinki-press-conference.

29 Author's interview with Daniel
Russell, May 2021.

30 Vladimir Putin, *First Person* (New
York: PublicAffairs, 2000), p. 6.

31 Bolton, *The Room Where It Happened*,
p. 145.

32 Author's interview with senior Trump
administration official, May 2021.

33 Mike Pence, address at the 53rd
Munich Security Conference, 18
February 2017, available at https://
www.americanrhetoric.com/speeches/
mikepencemunichsecurityconference
2017.htm.

34 See Brian Naylor, 'How the Trump Campaign Weakened the Republican Platform on Aid to Ukraine', NPR, 6 August 2016, https://www.npr.org/2016/08/06/488876597/how-the-trump-campaign-weakened-the-republican-platform-on-aid-to-ukraine.

35 Zack Beauchamp, 'The Key Moment from Fiona Hill's Testimony', Vox, 21 November 2019, https://www.vox.com/policy-and-politics/2019/11/21/20976364/impeachment-hearing-dr-fiona-hill-trump-errand.

36 See William K. Rashbaum et al., 'Prosecutors Investigating Whether Ukrainians Meddled in 2020 Election', New York Times, 27 May 2021, https://www.nytimes.com/2021/05/27/nyregion/trump-ukraine-rudy-giuliani-2020-presidential-election.html.

37 See Thomas Gibbons-Neff, 'How a 4-hour Battle Between Russian Mercenaries and U.S. Commandos Unfolded in Syria', New York Times, 24 May 2018, https://www.nytimes.com/2018/05/24/world/middleeast/american-commandos-russian-mercenaries-syria.html.

38 Author's conversation with senior Trump administration official.

39 Bolton, The Room Where It Happened, p. 130.

40 Author's interview with James Jeffrey, May 2021.

41 See Tovah Lazaroff, 'US, Russian, Israeli Understanding Iranian Forces Will Leave Syria', Jerusalem Post, 25 June 2019, https://www.jpost.com/middle-east/us-russia-and-israel-meet-in-unprecedented-trilateral-summit-watch-live-593609.

42 See Erin Banco, 'Revealed: Jared Kushner's Private Channel with Putin's Money Man', Daily Beast, 24 August 2020, https://www.thedailybeast.com/jared-kushners-private-channel-with-putins-money-man-kirill-dmitriev.

43 See Emily Stewart, 'Watch the "Movie Trailer" Trump Showed Kim Jong Un About North Korea's Possible Future', Vox, 12 June 2018, https://www.vox.com/world/2018/6/12/17452876/trump-kim-jong-un-meeting-north-korea-video.

44 Author's interview with senior Trump administration official, May 2021.

45 Author's interview with Elliott Abrams, May 2021.

46 See Nicole Gaouette and Jennifer Hansler, 'Pompeo Claims Russia Stopped Maduro Leaving Venezuela for Cuba', CNN, 1 May 2019, https://www.cnn.com/2019/04/30/politics/pompeo-maduro-russia/index.html.

47 See 'U.S. Vice President Biden Says Putin Has No Soul: New Yorker', Reuters, 21 July 2014, https://www.reuters.com/article/us-usa-russia-biden/u-s-vice-president-biden-says-putin-has-no-soul-new-yorker-idUSKBN0FQ1CU20140721.

48 See Dan Mangan, 'Biden Believes Putin Is a Killer, Vows Russian Leader "Will Pay a Price" for Trying to Help Trump Win the Election', CNBC, 17 March 2021, https://www.cnbc.com/2021/03/17/biden-says-putin-is-a-killer-will-pay-for-trying-to-help-trump-win-election.html.

49 See Abby Phillip, 'O'Reilly Told Trump that Putin Is a Killer: Trump's Reply: "You Think Our Country Is So Innocent?"', Washington Post, 5 February 2017,

https://www.washingtonpost.com/
news/post-politics/wp/2017/02/04/
oreilly-told-trump-that-putin-is-a-
killer-trumps-reply-you-think-our-
countrys-so-innocent/.

50 White House, 'Remarks by
President Biden at the 2021 Virtual
Munich Security Conference',
19 February 2021, https://www.
whitehouse.gov/briefing-room/
speeches-remarks/2021/02/19/remarks-
by-president-biden-at-the-2021-
virtual-munich-security-conference/.

51 See Helene Cooper, 'Biden Freezes
Trump's Withdrawal of 12,000 Troops
from Germany', *New York Times*, 4
February 2021, https://www.nytimes.
com/2021/02/04/us/politics/biden-
germany-troops-trump.html.

52 Joe Biden, 'Joe Biden: My Trip
to Europe Is About America
Rallying the World's Democracies',
Washington Post, 5 June 2021,
https://www.washingtonpost.
com/opinions/2021/06/05/
joe-biden-europe-trip-agenda/.

53 See 'Putin Sees "Double Standard" in
US Capitol Riot Prosecutions', BBC
News, 5 June 2021, https://www.bbc.
com/news/world-us-canada-57366668.

54 See 'Putin Boasts About New
Russian Weapons, Calls Them
Defensive', *Military Times*, 2 March
2020, https://www.militarytimes.
com/news/your-military/2020/03/03/
putin-boasts-about-new-russian-
weapons-calls-them-defensive/.

55 See Isabella Jibilian and Katie Canales,
'The US Is Readying Sanctions Against
Russia Over the SolarWinds Cyber
Attack', *Business Insider*, 15 April
2021, https://www.businessinsider.
com/solarwinds-hack-explained-

government-agencies-cyber-
security-2020-12.

56 See US National Intelligence
Council, 'Foreign Threats to the
2020 US Federal Elections', 10
March 2021, available at https://int.
nyt.com/data/documenttools/2021-
intelligence-community-
election-interference-assessment/
abd0346ebdd93e1e/full.pdf.

57 White House, 'Fact Sheet: Imposing
Costs for Harmful Foreign Activities
by the Russian Government',
15 April 2021, https://www.
whitehouse.gov/briefing-room/
statements-releases/2021/04/15/
fact-sheet-imposing-costs-for-
harmful-foreign-activities-by-the-
russian-government/.

58 White House, 'Remarks by President
Biden on Russia', 15 April 2021, https://
www.whitehouse.gov/briefing-
room/speeches-remarks/2021/04/15/
remarks-by-president-biden-on-russia/.

59 Jennifer Jacobs and Jennifer
Epstein, 'Biden Says He Waived
Nord Stream Sanctions Because
It's Finished', Bloomberg, 25 May
2021, https://www.bloomberg.
com/news/articles/2021-05-25/
biden-says-he-waived-nord-stream-
sanctions-because-it-s-finished.

60 See Vladimir Isachenkov, 'Russia
Hosts Afghan Peace Conference,
Hoping to Boost Talks', AP, 18 March
2021, https://apnews.com/article/
peace-process-afghanistan-moscow-
kabul-taliban-b842bfee387bbf3f08d-
404d285c39c81.

61 'My Budem Zhit' Vmeste i v Mire'
[General of the Army Sergei Shoigu:
'We Will Live Together in Peace'], *Red
Star*, 19 March 2021, http://redstar.

ru/general-armii-sergej-shojgu-my-budem-zhit-vmeste-i-v-mire/.

62   Arctic Council, 'Russian Chairmanship 2021–2023: Responsible Governance for a Sustainable Arctic', https://arctic-council.org/en/about/russian-chairmanship-2/.

63   Bobo Lo, 'A Wary Embrace', Lowy Institute Papers, 3 April 2017, https://www.lowyinstitute.org/publications/wary-embrace.

64   See Angela Stent, 'Russia and China: Axis of Revisionists?', Brookings Institution, February 2020, https://www.brookings.edu/research/russia-and-china-axis-of-revisionists/.

65   Anita Kumar and Myah Ward, 'Biden Calls Putin a "Worthy Adversary" Ahead of Meeting', *Politico*, 14 June 2021, https://www.politico.com/news/2021/06/14/biden-putin-meeting-494376.

66   See 'Trump: I Hope One Day Putin Will Be My Friend', *Daily Beast*, 12 July 2018, https://www.thedailybeast.com/trump-i-hope-one-day-putin-will-be-my-friend; and Steve Holland and Margaret Chadbourn, 'Obama Describes Putin as "Like a Bored Kid"', Reuters, 9 August 2013, https://www.reuters.com/article/us-usa-russia-obama/obama-describes-putin-as-like-a-bored-kid-idUSBRE9780XS20130809.

67   White House, 'Remarks by President Biden in Press Conference', 16 June 2021, https://www.whitehouse.gov/briefing-room/speeches-remarks/2021/06/16/remarks-by-president-biden-in-press-conference-4/.

68   Miranda Bryant, 'First Thing: Proof of Putin Pudding Is in the Eating, Says Biden After Summit', *Guardian*, 17 June 2021, https://www.theguardian.com/us-news/2021/jun/17/first-thing-proof-of-putin-pudding-is-in-the-eating-says-biden-after-summit.

Competing with the BRI: The West's Uphill Task

James Crabtree

Speaking at the close of June's G7 summit, US President Joe Biden talked up a new high-profile push to build infrastructure in developing economies. Dubbed the 'Build Back Better World Partnership' – B3W for short – it envisions bringing the G7's members together to funnel private capital into a new wave of global projects. But behind it, Biden admitted, lay a larger challenge: mounting an effective Western response to China's rising geo-economic power. 'China has its Belt and Road Initiative', he said, referring to President Xi Jinping's giant infrastructure programme. 'We think that there's a much more equitable way to provide for the needs of countries around the world.'[1] Making that effort competitive with China's, however, appears to be a far harder task.

China's formidable initiative

Since its 2013 launch, China's Belt and Road Initiative (BRI) programme has produced hundreds of billions of dollars' worth of rail lines, ports, roads, metro systems and power plants across the developing world. Originally conceived as a way of forging new land and maritime connections across Eurasia, it has since expanded to encompass Africa, Latin America, the Arctic and even a spin-off in space.[2] At its best, the programme mixes China's deep capital reserves, experienced infrastructure companies and powerful state-backed banks to construct new projects quickly and at reasonable cost.

James Crabtree is Executive Director of IISS–Asia.

Survival | vol. 63 no. 4 | August–September 2021 | pp. 81–88   https://doi.org/10.1080/00396338.2021.1956189

The BRI's expansion has caused problems, however. Western critics says its infrastructure is low-quality and marred by corruption, opaque governance and weak environmental standards. Its financing terms can be generous, but it often yields white-elephant projects that are hard to justify on a cost–benefit basis. Other BRI projects come with more expensive commercial loans that leave recipient nations struggling to repay debts. In some instances, China has been accused of 'debt-trap diplomacy', in which investment projects are structured so they cannot easily be repaid, allowing China eventually to assume outright ownership in debt-for-equity rescue deals.[3] In other cases, critics suggest, Chinese-backed projects with strategic implications – such as ports around the Indian Ocean – could in time develop civil–military dual uses.[4]

Yet while Western leaders decry the BRI's failings in public, in private they are more likely to worry about its ongoing successes. The project has undeniably helped Beijing to deepen economic and political ties with emerging nations across Asia and Africa. If the West continues to fall short in providing alternatives, those same governments are likely to keep turning to Beijing as a partner. Western actors have tried to compete with the BRI in recent years, but mostly with little impact. Biden and other Western leaders, such as British Prime Minister Boris Johnson, hope B3W can do better. But their plan faces two awkward questions, one practical and the other geopolitical. Firstly, and most obviously, can B3W actually do much to build new infrastructure? Secondly, if it can, will the effort help to increase Western geo-economic influence?

A sketchy debut

B3W arrived with few firm details. A post-G7 statement described it as a 'values-driven, high-standard, and transparent infrastructure partnership led by major democracies to help narrow the $40+ trillion infrastructure need in the developing world'.[5] That need is real enough: estimates suggest that Asian emerging economies alone will need $1.7trn in infrastructure investment each year until 2030 to support development.[6] A new G7 task force is now set to move these plans forward. Although the United States said it would 'work with Congress to augment' its 'development finance toolkit', there were no commitments for new money to fund the programme beyond those already made by the G7's members.

B3W's projects will focus on four specific areas: climate, health, digital technology and gender. These priorities look a little curious. They imply that B3W plans to ignore critical areas like rail, road and energy, all of which have been mainstays of the BRI's influence and tend to be among the most important infrastructure requirements of emerging nations. There may be some logic in focusing on areas in which China is not already dominant. Green financing is one obvious opportunity. An earlier version of B3W, developed by the United Kingdom, was even slated to be called the 'clean green initiative' until Biden and his team intervened.[7] Digital infrastructure also makes some intuitive sense, given that the US and its partners have strengths in areas such as data centres and submarine cables. But without dedicated new financing, B3W planners will be left merely hoping to find ways to bring in money from others to develop new projects.

Propitious moment, vexing challenge

B3W does appear to have arrived at an opportune time. BRI lending has declined over recent years. At a summit marking its five-year anniversary in 2019, China's leadership responded to Western critics by promising to improve project transparency and environmental sustainability.[8] Research from Boston University showed global lending by two of China's development banks, the anchors of BRI finance, falling from $75bn in 2016 to $4bn three years later, as Beijing pulled back from some of the more lavish projects it supported in the BRI's earlier years.[9] While these trends pre-dated COVID-19, they are likely to have been extended by the pandemic. COVID-19 made foreign infrastructure harder to build and delayed projects, and prompted China's leadership to concentrate financial resources on a new wave of domestic-stimulus investment rather than spending freely abroad.

This funding decline creates a gap that a well-funded, determined, Western-led infrastructure programme could exploit. But to do so, B3W must overcome a range of substantial barriers, the most obvious being the limitations of its own proposed model. To finesse its lack of funding, the G7's plan aims to attract hundreds of billions of dollars of infrastructure investment for low- and middle-income countries by channelling capital from institutional investors such as insurance companies and pension funds. This idea is not new; indeed, it is arguably the technocratic holy grail of infrastructure development. Back in 2015, the World Bank pushed the slogan 'billions to trillions' to argue that limited state support might unlock far larger private flows to support global development goals.[10] Multilateral banks like the World Bank and Asian Infrastructure Investment Bank (AIIB) have put substantial effort into encouraging private capital investment.

Yet such attempts to coax private capital into new infrastructure have had only limited success. The challenge is not one of liquidity: there is plenty of private finance sloshing around the global economy seeking projects. The problem is rather that private investors balk at the risks that most emerging-market infrastructure deals entail, including project delays, political interference, corruption and mismanagement. Investors prefer stable, pre-existing assets, like toll roads and business parks, to completely new ones. They are also wary of risky greenfield projects. Recent decades have revealed flaws in public–private partnership approaches to infrastructure, in which private companies build projects before handing them back to the state. More enticing models tend to involve governments building infrastructure before selling it to private enterprises to manage later.

These points explain not just why B3W faces an uphill task, but also why earlier Western BRI rivals made little progress. In 2019, US president Donald Trump launched the so-called Blue Dot Network to encourage private investment by providing information about potential projects. The network rapidly receded from view, only to be revived by Biden and given a new home at the Organisation for Economic Co-operation and Development. Back in 2014, the G20 launched a new Global Infrastructure Hub designed to improve flows of information about infrastructure projects. A host of other efforts – from Japan and India's grand-sounding Asia–Africa Growth Corridor plan to build infrastructure around the Indian Ocean in 2017 to the European Union's EU–Asia Connectivity Strategy the following year – have failed to make major impacts.

*   *   *

How might B3W do better? Providing superior information about potential infrastructure projects could help to attract financing in some circumstances, but it will do little to overcome the real risks that deter many investors. A more promising approach could focus on more discriminating project selection and improvement – that is, finding ways to help emerging economies refine nascent project plans, making them more appealing to private investors. Recent International Monetary Fund research suggests that governments could help to 'crowd in' private finance by, among other things, mitigating risks at the start of a project and offering compensation if things go wrong at the end.[11] Yet most multilateral development banks already offer these kinds of sweeteners, alongside financing of their own.

B3W faces a second hindrance involving the type of projects it seeks to build. On the one hand, the G7's new programme aims to increase infrastructure-investment levels. On the other, however, it also hopes to raise infrastructure quality. This second objective is partly a familiar dig at China, which the US and others, like Japan, often accuse of churning out substandard work. At the 2019 Osaka Summit, Japan pushed the G20 to launch a set of voluntary guidelines called the 'principles for quality infrastructure investment'. (For instance, Japan favours a 'life-cycle' approach to infrastructure development to avoid situations in which projects that look cheap turn out to be more expensive in the long run, as when crumbling roads or inefficient power stations need to be replaced.) Tokyo hoped such rules would drive up global infrastructure standards, in the process helping its own companies compete more effectively with China in developing projects around Asia.

The idea of building high-quality infrastructure is admirable. But truly sound projects also tend to be more expensive up front, making them less attractive to governments in developing countries. Japan remains Southeast Asia's largest infrastructure investor, backing $367bn worth of projects compared to China's $255bn.[12] But Japan has managed to compete with China only because it has provided loans to fund its higher-quality projects. Without access to similar funding, B3W is likely to face a trade-off between infrastructure quality and geo-economic influence. Indeed, a similar tension is found within China's own institutions. Launched in

2016, the Beijing-based AIIB has grown into an exemplary development bank, with high governance standards and cautious lending practices. This year it will bankroll $10bn worth of projects – an impressive record for a new body, but still tiny in the context of global annual infrastructure spending. The BRI, by contrast, won influence because it moved quickly to deliver hundreds of billions' worth of high-risk projects. Had China relied only on the kind of approach taken by the AIIB, its geo-economic gains would have been far smaller.

Overall, B3W's road looks daunting. Infrastructure is expensive. As currently configured, the G7's plan will struggle not merely to develop infrastructure but also to catalyse private investment. Its focus on infrastructure quality, laudable though it is, may be less attractive to many poorer nations. Western governments could mitigate some of these difficulties by better coordinating the money each of them spends. But so far they have generated little apparent cohesion. Leaders of the Quadrilateral Security Dialogue – a partnership comprising Australia, India, Japan and the US – say they plan to launch a new infrastructure-funding scheme later this year.[13] Meanwhile, the EU is preparing to initiate another BRI rival of its own to replace its existing EU–Asia connectivity plan. Without much closer cooperation, these disparate initiatives risk becoming far less than the sum of their parts. And regardless of B3W's noble aspirations, without dedicated funding and political leadership, the programme looks unlikely to cause much consternation in Beijing.

Notes

[1] White House, 'Remarks by President Biden in Press Conference', 13 June 2021, https://www.whitehouse.gov/briefing-room/speeches-remarks/2021/06/13/remarks-by-president-biden-in-press-conference-2/.

[2] See Michael S. Chase. 'The Space and Cyberspace Components of the Belt and Road Initiative', in Nadège Rolland (ed.), 'Securing the Belt and Road Initiative: China's Evolving Military Engagement Along the Silk Roads', NBR Report #80, National Bureau of Asian Research, September 2019, pp. 19–32, https://www.nbr.org/wp-content/uploads/pdfs/publications/sr80_securing_the_belt_and_road_sep2019.pdf.

[3] See, for example, 'Chinese Firm

Pays $584 Million in Sri Lanka Port Debt-to-equity Deal', Reuters, 20 June 2018, https://www.reuters.com/article/us-sri-lanka-china-ports-idUSKBN1JG2Z6. See also Jordan Calinoff and David Gordon, 'Port Investments in the Belt and Road Initiative: Is Beijing Grabbing Strategic Assets?', *Survival*, vol. 62, no. 4, August–September 2020, pp. 59–80.

4   See, for instance, Daniel R. Russel and Blake H. Berger, 'Report: Weaponizing the Belt and Road Initiative', Asia Society Policy Institute, 8 September 2020, https://asiasociety.org/sites/default/files/2020-09/Weaponizing%20the%20Belt%20and%20Road%20Initiative_0.pdf.

5   White House, 'Fact Sheet: President Biden and G7 Leaders Launch Build Back Better World (B3W) Partnership', 12 June 2021, https://www.whitehouse.gov/briefing-room/statements-releases/2021/06/12/fact-sheet-president-biden-and-g7-leaders-launch-build-back-better-world-b3w-partnership/.

6   Asian Development Bank, 'Asia Infrastructure Needs Exceed $1.7 Trillion Per Year, Double Previous Estimates', 28 February 2017, https://www.adb.org/news/asia-infrastructure-needs-exceed-17-trillion-year-double-previous-estimates.

7   See Alberto Nardelli, 'G-7 Set to Back Green Rival to China's Belt and Road Program', Bloomberg Green, 1 June 2021, https://www.bloomberg.com/news/articles/2021-06-01/g-7-set-to-back-green-rival-to-china-s-belt-and-road-program.

8   See 'List of Deliverables of the Second Belt and Road Forum for International Cooperation', Second Belt and Road Forum for International Cooperation, 27 April 2019, http://www.beltandroadforum.org/english/n100/2019/0427/c36-1312.html.

9   See Rebecca Ray and Blake Alexander Simmons, 'Tracking China's Overseas Development Finance', Boston University, Global Development Policy Center, 7 December 2020, https://www.bu.edu/gdp/2020/12/07/tracking-chinas-overseas-development-finance/.

10 See Gavin E.R. Wilson, 'Billions to Trillions: Financing the Global Goals', World Bank Blogs, 24 September 2015, https://blogs.worldbank.org/voices/billions-to-trillions-financing-the-global-goals.

11 See Luc Eyraud et al., 'Private Finance for Development: Wishful Thinking or Thinking Out of the Box?', Departmental Paper No. 2021/011, International Monetary Fund, African Department, 14 May 2021, https://www.imf.org/en/Publications/Departmental-Papers-Policy-Papers/Issues/2021/05/14/Private-Finance-for-Development-50157.

12 See Eduard Fernandez, 'Japan Still Reigns in South-east Asia Infra', *Infrastructure Investor*, 16 July 2019, https://www.infrastructureinvestor.com/japan-infra-player-in-south-east-asia-china-belt-and-road-initiative/.

13 White House, 'Quad Leaders' Joint Statement: "The Spirit of the Quad"', 12 March 2021, https://www.whitehouse.gov/briefing-room/statements-releases/2021/03/12/quad-leaders-joint-statement-the-spirit-of-the-quad/.

Enabling US Security Cooperation

Bilal Y. Saab

One of US President Joe Biden's top foreign-policy priorities is to rebuild America's alliances and partnerships, which are vital to US strategic interests and international security. Yet to 'pick up the pieces of Donald Trump's broken foreign policy', as Biden tweeted in January 2020, will require a great deal of effort given the harm that his predecessor inflicted on the country's reputation as a partner of choice.[1]

Biden's foreign-policy team has moved quickly to reinvigorate global agreements and institutions. It immediately re-established the United States' participation in the 2016 Paris agreement on climate change, and is trying to negotiate terms for rejoining the Iran nuclear deal from which Trump withdrew. It is building an international coalition to contain China and holding a global 'Summit for Democracy'. But truly burying Trump's transactional approach to foreign relations will entail not only a return to diplomacy but also a renewed emphasis on security cooperation with the allies and regional partners that play vital roles in the United States' strategic calculations. Aligning smaller and less capable powers, and enlisting them in the implementation of US strategy, is indispensable to Washington's effective performance in the great-power competition that is now under way.

To strengthen the United States' defence ties with its regional friends and enable them to share some of the burdens of collective security, Washington

Bilal Y. Saab is a senior fellow and director of the Defense and Security Program at the Middle East Institute. He served as Senior Advisor for Security Cooperation in the US Department of Defense's Office of the Under Secretary of Defense for Policy, with oversight responsibility for US Central Command.

Survival | vol. 63 no. 4 | August–September 2021 | pp. 89–99   https://doi.org/10.1080/00396338.2021.1956188

needs to overhaul how it conducts security cooperation. For too long, this enterprise, run mainly by the US Department of Defense since 9/11, has lacked vision, leadership and organisation. It is too narrowly focused on US military sales and tactical and operational support to partners, and insufficiently attentive to the defence governance and institutional enabling mechanisms that allow for the proper employment and sustainment of US military assistance.[2] More particularly, the Defense Department and the State Department – the latter having primary statutory authority over security assistance[3] – have not effectively conducted joint planning on institutional capacity-building, despite the congressional laws and executive directives calling for it, and they have not been able to pool their resources and nourish each other's activities.

A long-term project

The 9/11 attacks catapulted security cooperation to prominence in US national-security policy. Today, it is a central pillar of the National Defense Strategy and arguably one of Washington's most precious and singular strategic tools.[4] US decision-makers increasingly recognise that security cooperation is an invaluable tool for fighting terrorists, countering rogue regimes and competing with great powers: exploiting an unparalleled network of alliances and partnerships serves as a force multiplier. Substantially through security cooperation, the United States has been able to achieve major foreign-policy objectives over the past 50 years. These have included protecting Europe from the Soviet threat, liberating Kuwait, checking North Korea, policing the energy-rich Persian Gulf, sustaining Arab–Israeli peace agreements, neutralising terrorists and, recently, destroying the self-proclaimed caliphate of the Islamic State (ISIS). Massive US foreign military sales to international partners have also benefited the US economy, generating billions of dollars in revenue, creating hundreds of thousands of jobs in the American defence industry and boosting efficiency in US military budgets by reducing unit costs.

Because America faces borderless and ever more complex security challenges that require collective action, security cooperation has only become more important, and is likely to have priority under the Biden administration. Yet US security cooperation has failed at its most critical task: to significantly bolster the military abilities of less capable regional partners so they can safeguard security interests they share with the United States. Despite US complaints about regional partners free-riding on US security and talk about achieving security integration or higher levels of defence inter-operability with those partners, that goal has only been partially met. Building the required institutions in other countries cannot be done quickly or incidentally. Even if the drive and determination are strong, the money is available and the politics is right, it is a generational endeavour.

The United States' own experience in defence reform arguably started in 1903 with the Militia Act, under which Congress asserted federal control over state military forces and strengthened the national guard, thus allowing it to function as a strategic reserve. The United States did not undertake wholesale defence reform until after it fought two world wars, with the National Security Act of 1947, which fundamentally reorganised and modernised the nation's armed forces, in addition to its foreign-policy and intelligence architecture. The next major overhaul occurred during the last few years of the Cold War, when Congress passed the 1986 Goldwater–Nichols defence-reform act. This sweeping law established strategic and operational jointness on the US military for the first time in its history, enabling it to maintain its status as the most capable fighting force in the world. Even so, there is still much room for reform for the US military.

America's regional partners have neither huge militaries that require enormous bureaucracies nor global interests and responsibilities comparable to those of the United States. Their defence reforms – which will vary from one country to another depending on their initial institutional baseline, economic development and internal politics – need not require as much time or effort as the evolution of the US defence establishment has required. But no credible attempt at reorganising defence establishments and building more effective militaries is likely to succeed in the short term. It is at least a decade-long process.

Accordingly, Washington should approach security cooperation the same way it does great-power competition: by taking the long view, which means investing in the key drivers of positive change and resisting the temptation to settle for more immediate tactical and operational gains. Key to this is a determination by US officials not just to train and equip the armed forces and security services of its regional friends, but also to assist them to the extent possible in developing the strategic, institutional, organisational and programmatic fabric of their defence and security sectors. Institutional capacity-building is integral to the success of US security cooperation and assistance programmes because it helps partners improve their abilities to oversee, manage and employ human, materiel and financial resources. It also enables them to formulate appropriate policies, strategies, operational concepts and doctrine, without which a military is unlikely to perform effectively on the battlefield.

Washington has underachieved in helping its regional partners build their defence institutions for three main reasons. Firstly, it is extremely difficult to push autocratic governments to engage in structural reform. They are simply not interested in opening up their security sectors and possibly their political systems for fear of loss of control and economic privileges. Secondly, US officials worry about getting on a slippery slope towards nation-building, for which they currently have no appetite or resources. Thirdly, and perhaps most crucially, American civilian and military decision-makers have been unable to push for the creation of a functioning organisational framework for security cooperation in the US inter-agency structure that can effectively implement this priority. As a result, the US government could not meet the new legal requirement of institutional capacity-building – mandated by the US Congress in the 2017 security-cooperation reforms – with those partners who are most in need even if it wanted to. Fortunately, the United States has some of the world's best soldiers, military trainers and professional educators. What it needs is a system that can set the security-cooperation activities of its deployed uniformed personnel on a more strategic and sustainable course.

A global command

US officials could match rhetoric about the growing significance of security cooperation in American statecraft with actual deeds by forming a global security-cooperation command. Such a command could integrate the US security-cooperation community on a global level, centrally manage and coordinate its activities, and emphasise institutional capacity-building with foreign partners.

The example of Special Operations Command (SOCOM) offers guidance as to why a global command for security cooperation is not just desirable but probably necessary. On 24 April 1980, US special-operations forces (SOF) were sent by then-president Jimmy Carter to a desolate staging area in Iran, designated 'Desert One', to rescue 53 Americans held captive by the Iranian regime at the US Embassy in Tehran. *Operation Eagle Claw*, as it was codenamed, failed miserably. The US aviation assets flown to the area faced significant mechanical problems, and only six of the eight arrived at the location. The mission had to be aborted. As the withdrawal of US forces proceeded, a helicopter crashed into a C-130 military transport plane carrying fuel and American servicemen. The collision killed eight of them. The Desert One debacle was followed three years later by another tactical failure of US SOF in Grenada. In *Operation Urgent Fury*, American forces managed to effortlessly invade the tiny island nation, rescue Americans and roll back communist influence in the Caribbean. But the way the mission was executed brought back painful memories of Desert One. The US Marine Corps and the US Army led totally separate operations and could not even communicate with each other because their radios were not technically compatible. Flaws in joint command structures hampered the operation's overall effectiveness.

Despite the strong objections of the Pentagon and the tepid endorsement of the Reagan administration, SOCOM was established in 1987 by way of the bipartisan Nunn–Cohen amendment. In line with the recommendations of several retired and active-duty generals and admirals, Congress made SOCOM a four-star command to afford it the gravitas required to secure adequate funding, appropriations and authorities, and to interact on an equal footing with other military commands. By combining the skill sets of special operators from distinct elements in the US military and developing a joint culture that stressed cooperation, SOCOM turned its most stubborn doubters into its most ardent believers.

A global security-cooperation command would essentially seek to solve problems similar to those that afflicted the special-operations community in the past: competition and lack of effective communication and integration among the geographic combatant commands on security cooperation. Such a command would have budget authority and organise, employ, train, equip and sustain a joint security-cooperation force. It would provide a coherent global framework for action and synthesise the perspectives and inputs of the geographic commands into a single comprehensive assessment of the Pentagon's security-cooperation efforts worldwide. It would help adjudicate security-cooperation prioritisation and resourcing, which every fiscal year turns into an unproductive food fight among the geographical commands that ends up getting resolved in rather haphazard and less than strategic ways by the Office of the Under Secretary of Defense for Policy. It would introduce the same kind of discipline into the security-cooperation system that SOCOM did into special operations. And like SOCOM, it would be a functional command and thus a force provider.

Like special operators, security-cooperation officers are not general-purpose forces. They are low-density, high-demand personnel, and they ought to be treated as such. Given that these officers would still come from the individual US armed services, ensuring their proper training in the integration of institutional capacity-building into security-cooperation planning would be paramount.

Likely sources of opposition and support

There are various psychological, political and budgetary obstacles that would have to be overcome to create a security-cooperation command. It took a tragedy – Desert One – for Washington to rethink how it did special operations. Major reforms in the US intelligence community were instituted only after terrorists struck New York City and the Pentagon. It's hard to foresee misfortune as visible and catastrophic as Desert One or 9/11 occurring in the realm of security cooperation that could prompt an overhaul of the enterprise. While deeply troubling, the possibility that American weapons could occasionally end up in the hands of terrorists or be misused by regional partners is not likely to be a major catalyst. In fact, US-supplied weapons have found their way to the Islamic State and other anti-American jihadist groups, and Saudi Arabia has devastated the civilian population of

Yemen substantially using American weapons and intelligence assistance, to little effect on thinking in Washington.

Bureaucratic inertia is a significant impediment. Active resistance to standing up a security-cooperation command is likely to arise from various stakeholders largely because the new command would require dedicated money, authorities and access to US political and military leadership that have traditionally been the prerogatives of the individual services. The same, of course, was true of SOCOM.

One source of opposition is likely to be the Defense Security Cooperation Agency (DSCA), which not only executes and administers all security-cooperation programmes and activities for the Defense Department but also helps conduct planning and set priorities. DSCA would be forced to surrender those security-cooperation authorities. Next in line is the Office of the Under Secretary of Defense for Policy because it seems to be happy with the current state of play, having failed to provide effective policy oversight and guidance for resource allocation for security cooperation.

If history is any guide, the service chiefs and the joint staff would vehemently oppose a new security-cooperation command as a dilution of their resources and supervisory power. In turn, the secretary of defense is not likely to be very sympathetic to the idea either, precisely because of the headache it would cause him or her vis-à-vis the service chiefs and the joint staff. But the secretary of state might be agnostic or even supportive, since a security-cooperation command would theoretically yield better global strategic planning, which would provide a stronger basis for foreign military sales, over which the State Department has statutory authority.

The geographic combatant commands probably would not contest the formation of a security-cooperation command as long as it did not take away from them what they care about the most: funds to secure and maintain access and influence in partner nations – that is, so-called 'phase zero' activities that seek to shape the regional environment during peacetime. The executive body that would have the most credibility, clout and positioning to push effectively for the establishment of a security-cooperation command is the National Security Council Principals Committee, which is the pre-eminent inter-agency forum for consideration of policy issues affecting US national security. Whether the current array of senior officials would be able to reach consensus on such a major defence reform – or even be willing to try – is an open question.

In any case, Congress would ultimately play the most important and decisive role in the potential creation of a security-cooperation command. The history of SOCOM shows that were it not for far-sighted leaders on Capitol Hill – in particular, senators Sam Nunn and William Cohen – the executive branch would have never agreed to establish SOCOM. Like Nunn and Cohen, senator John McCain was a visionary, and he was the main author of security cooperation's most significant reforms. New congressional leaders in the current, highly polarised US political environment are not likely to push for reforms that might be unpopular and politically costly. But the establishment of a new security-cooperation command, supported by a rigorous argument for its national-security benefits and advantages, might be sufficiently non-partisan and technocratic to gain legislative traction.

Effective civilian oversight

If a security-cooperation command were established, it would be headed by a four-star general or admiral, subject to oversight by senior civilian leaders in the Pentagon. A new position of an under secretary of defense for security cooperation could be formed to ensure effective civilian oversight. Some might view this as unnecessary given that the current chain of command provides the under secretary of defense for policy – the Pentagon's top policy official – with the authority to steer security cooperation and make sure its output is in line with the priorities of the National Defense Strategy. But because he or she has several other priorities and a saturated agenda, that responsibility tends to fall by the wayside. The under secretary of defense for policy does have two deputies, one at the assistant-secretary level and one at the deputy-assistant-secretary level, helping him or her fulfil oversight duty, but neither official has the bureaucratic heft to instruct four-stars to pursue courses of action that they might otherwise perceive as contradictory to their commands' missions and priorities.

Just as a four-star commander for security cooperation would immediately send a strong signal to the military community of the increased strategic significance of the enterprise, an under secretary would swiftly elevate it within the civilian community in ways a deputy assistant secretary or assistant secretary could not. Again, the case of SOCOM is instructive. Per the Nunn–Cohen amendment, an assistant secretary of defense for special operations and low-intensity conflict is responsible for providing oversight over all special-operations forces. However, the officials filling that slot have often been unable to effectively perform their statutory duties for two reasons. Firstly, their interlocutors in SOCOM have been four-star generals, who clearly outrank them, complicating the chain of command. Secondly, the special-operations community has become so large and active since 9/11 that an assistant secretary of defense is incapable of managing it on their own. Just as there is an under secretary of defense for intelligence and security, there should be one for special operations and low-intensity conflict.

The same goes for security cooperation, which costs the United States billions of taxpayer dollars every year, directly shapes events on the ground and affects US security interests on a daily basis as very few tools of US foreign policy do. An under secretary of defense for security cooperation – dedicated full-time to managing the enterprise, implementing statutory missions and reforms, evaluating trade-offs and making decisions – would emphasise to all civilian and military stakeholders that pursuing defence institution-building in conjunction with train-and-equip programmes is neither a charity nor a luxury, but rather a strategic necessity.

In line with this reform, it would also make sense, as recently proposed by Max Bergmann and Alexandra Schmitt, to create a senior position on the National Security Council staff to facilitate inter-agency coordination of security cooperation.[5] Defence institution-building requires a whole-of-government approach due to its multi-sectoral nature. Capacity-building involves planning, management, human resources, budgeting, human-rights training and knowledge of the rule of law. Therefore, it is part and parcel of the development universe, in which the State Department and the United States Agency for International Development (USAID) are better versed than the Defense Department and the US military. It is one thing to help a partner train and equip its coastguard or police force – a Department of Defense function. It is quite another to help its government create legal systems and authorities that are necessary for that security service's role and jurisdictions – a Department of State responsibility. The two functions are, of course, complementary, but the Defense Department and the State Department have not worked well together since the end of the Cold War for various reasons, including the absence of top-level stimuli and the persistence of turf battles and competition for authority, influence and resources. With NSC-level guidance, coordination and support, a global security-cooperation command could ameliorate this problem.

*　　*　　*

The United States is trying to reduce its involvement in the greater Middle East in part to engage more effectively in other priority regions such as the Indo-Pacific. Yet the United States could have difficulty devoting due attention to China and Russia, and find itself deploying American troops to the Middle East again, if US regional military partners are unable or unwilling to step up.[6] Stronger and more sustainable security ties with regional militaries that are focused less on trucks and guns and more on defence institution-building and comprehensive defence reform would mitigate these risks, and better position the United States to achieve some of its more important strategic objectives. A security-cooperation command would enable it to consolidate and enhance those ties.

Notes

[1] See Joe Biden (@JoeBiden), tweet, 2 January 2020, https://twitter.com/joebiden/status/1213217722508570624?lang=en.

[2] See generally Bilal Y. Saab, 'Broken Partnerships: Can Washington Get Security Cooperation Right?', *Washington Quarterly*, vol. 32, no. 3, Fall 2019, pp. 77–89.

[3] Under the Foreign Assistance Act of 1961, 'the Secretary of State is responsible for the continuous supervision and general direction of economic assistance, military assistance, and military education and training, including determining whether there shall be a security assistance program and the value thereof, to the end that such programs are effectively integrated both at home and abroad, and

that the foreign policy of the United States is best served thereby'.

4   See US Department of Defense, 'Summary of the 2018 National Defense Strategy of the United States of America', pp. 8–10, https://dod. defense.gov/Portals/1/Documents/ pubs/2018-National-Defense-Strategy-Summary.pdf.

5   Max Bergmann and Alexandra Schmitt, 'A Plan to Reform U.S. Security Assistance', Center for American Progress, 9 March 2021, https://www. americanprogress.org/issues/ security/reports/2021/03/09/496788/ plan-reform-u-s-security-assistance/.

6   See David B. Roberts, 'Lifting the Protection Curse: The Rise of New Military Powers in the Middle East', *Survival*, vol. 63, no. 2, April–May 2021, pp. 139–54.

Noteworthy

Israel: end of an era?

'The settlers are thieves supported by the government. We will not leave our homes.'

Muhammad al-Sabbagh, a plumber who has lived in the Sheikh Jarrah neighbourhood of Jerusalem for 56 years, comments on a pending court case about the ownership of homes in the neighbourhood, a case that contributed to an outbreak of violence between Jews and Arabs across Israel and Gaza in May 2021.[1]

'We emphatically reject the pressures not to build in Jerusalem. Unfortunately, these pressures have been increasing of late. Just as every people builds its capital and in its capital, so too do we reserve the right to build Jerusalem and in Jerusalem.'

Benjamin Netanyahu, then prime minister of Israel, defends plans to evict Palestinian families from their homes in Sheikh Jarrah to make way for Israeli settlers.[2]

'Tampering with Jerusalem will burn the heads of the occupiers.'

Saleh al-Arouri, a senior Hamas official.[3]

'Israel will respond with great force. We will not tolerate attacks on our territory, on our capital, on our citizens and on our soldiers. Whoever attacks us will pay a heavy price.'

Netanyahu launches a military campaign against Hamas in Gaza after rockets were fired by the group at targets in Israel on 10 May.[4]

'We were not careful in Jerusalem. At a very delicate time toward the end of Ramadan, they gave [Hamas military commander Muhammad] Deif and the militants in Gaza the motivation to do what they did.'

Giora Eiland, a retired Israeli general and former national security adviser, describes what he sees as Israel's contribution to the outbreak of violence.[5]

'Why have they been attacking the Aqsa Mosque during Ramadan? The Aqsa Mosque is a sacred place for Muslims. Israel is starting a religious war.'

Khaled Zabarqa, a lawyer who said he had been praying at the Aqsa Mosque in Jerusalem before it was raided by Israeli forces on 10 May, blames Israel for provoking the violence.[6]

'I think it's important to note, as I think you'd agree, that these rockets are coming and these attacks are coming from Hamas. And many Palestinian people are being put in danger because of the violence that is happening back and forth.'

Jen Psaki, the White House press secretary, defends Israel's right to respond to rocket attacks from Gaza in remarks on 13 May.[7]

'Every couple of years there is a conflict of magnitude in Gaza that leaves it even more desperate and destitute than before because of the ongoing blockade. Now the health infrastructure which is already weak has to also grapple with Covid-19.'

Tamara al-Rifai, a spokesperson for the United Nations Relief and Works Agency for Palestine Refugees in the Near East (UNRWA).[8]

Survival | vol. 63 no. 4 | August–September 2021 | pp. 100–102   https://doi.org/10.1080/00396338.2021.1956190

'This fire has been simmering this entire time – it's like a bubble that the Palestinian citizens of Israel have been told to live in, but we can't do it any more.'

Documentary filmmaker Tony Copti.[9]

'There is talk about international pressure. There is always pressure but all in all we are receiving very serious backing, first of all from the US.'

Netanyahu comments on the military campaign in Gaza after a meeting of Israel's security cabinet on 16 May.[10]

'Our approach is through quiet, intensive diplomacy, and that's where we feel we can be most effective.'

Psaki takes questions on the White House's efforts to help end the violence during a press briefing on 17 May.[11]

'The Security Cabinet, this evening, unanimously accepted the recommendation of all of the security officials, the IDF Chief-of-Staff, the head of the ISA, the head of the Mossad and the head of the National Security Council to accept the Egyptian initiative for a mutual ceasefire without pre-conditions, to take effect at a time to be determined.'

Israel announces a ceasefire on 20 May.[12]

'The Palestinian resistance will abide by this agreement as long as the occupation abides by it.'

Hamas spokesperson Taher al-Nono announces the group's acceptance of the ceasefire.[13]

'I am proud of the ability to sit together with people with very different views from my own. To continue on in this way – more elections, more hatred, more vitriol on Facebook – is just not an option.'

Naftali Bennett delivers his inaugural speech as prime minister of Israel on 13 June after the Israeli parliament voted in an eight-party coalition to form the government.[14]

Belarusian pirates

'Don't do this, they will kill me, I am a refugee.'

Words attributed to Belarusian dissident Roman Protasevich as the Ryanair flight he had boarded in Greece bound for Lithuania was forced to land in Minsk on 23 May 2021.[15]

'When we landed people were standing around the plane doing nothing, looking pleased with themselves. They didn't let us out for half an hour. If there was a bomb on the plane, why would they not let us out?'

Saulius Danauskas, a passenger on the diverted flight, questions claims by Belarusian authorities that the diversion was necessary because of a bomb threat.[16]

'We strongly condemn the Lukashenko regime's brazen and shocking act to divert a commercial flight and arrest a journalist.'

US Secretary of State Antony Blinken.[17]

'This is an attack on democracy. This is an attack on freedom of expression. And this is an attack on European sovereignty … This outrageous behaviour needs a strong answer.'

European Commission President Ursula von der Leyen calls for sanctions on Belarus.[18]

'We consider this issue to be a domestic affair of Belarus. The actions of the Belarusian aviation authorities were in line with international standards.'

Maria Zakharova, spokesperson for the Russian Foreign Ministry, defends Belarus's actions.[19]

'They've moved on from preparing revolts to suffocating us. They are looking for new weaknesses.'

Belarusian President Alexander Lukashenko accuses Western countries of launching a 'hybrid modern war' against Belarus.[20]

'With regards to Belarus, we will no longer only sanction individuals but also areas of the economy which are important to the regime. We want to make Lukashenko's regime run dry financially.'

German Foreign Minister Heiko Maas comments on the imposition of a new round of sanctions on Belarus by the European Union on 21 June.[21]

Sources

1 Emma Graham-Harrison, Harriet Sherwood and Sufian Taha, 'A Raid, a March, a Court Case: How Israel Spiralled into a Deadly Conflict', *Guardian*, 16 May 2021, https://www.theguardian.com/world/2021/may/16/a-raid-a-march-a-court-case-how-israel-spiralled-into-a-deadly-conflict.

2 Mehul Srivastava, 'Israel Delays East Jerusalem Evictions over Warnings of Growing Violence', *Financial Times*, 9 May 2021, https://www.ft.com/content/fefe28b4-91ef-41ad-9087-adcab31e0b55?emailId=6098bb1ef070f60004123398&segmentId=22011ee7-896a-8c4c-22a0-7603348b7f22.

3 Patrick Kingsley and Isabel Kershner, 'After Raid on Aqsa Mosque, Rockets from Gaza and Israeli Airstrikes', *New York Times*, 10 May 2021, https://www.nytimes.com/2021/05/10/world/middleeast/jerusalem-protests-aqsa-palestinians.html.

4 *Ibid.*

5 *Ibid.*

6 *Ibid.*

7 White House, 'Press Briefing by Press Secretary Jen Psaki', 13 May 2021, https://www.whitehouse.gov/briefing-room/press-briefings/2021/05/13/press-briefing-by-press-secretary-jen-psaki-may-13-2021/.

8 Heba Saleh and Mehul Srivastava, 'Gazans Describe Terror of Israeli Bombing: "Together We Count Out the Loud Explosions"', *Financial Times*, 16 May 2021, https://www.ft.com/content/bcae7fc5-165c-4d9b-93c0-0e478bb2dd9e.

9 Mehul Srivastava, 'Arab–Israeli Uprising: "This Time It's Different"', *Financial Times*, 14 May 2021, https://www.ft.com/content/6d733289-fa86-4087-abee-036d8b1e07c8?emailId=609e637f74dd9400047546cd&segmentId=c393f5a6-b640-bff3-cc14-234d058790ed.

10 Mehul Srivastava and Kiran Stacey, 'Netanyahu Warns Israel's Offensive Against Hamas "Will Take Time"', *Financial Times*, 16 May 2021, https://www.ft.com/content/d13105d9-468d-4b1d-8f4d-4ea1fa5b8b45?emailId=60a1f23950485e0004084e6c&segmentId=22011ee7-896a-8c4c-22a0-7603348b7f22.

11 White House, 'Press Briefing by Press Secretary Jen Psaki', 17 May 2021, https://www.whitehouse.gov/briefing-room/press-briefings/2021/05/17/press-briefing-by-press-secretary-jen-psaki-may-17-2021/.

12 Prime Minister's Office, 'Prime Minister's Office Statement', press release, 20 May 2021, https://www.gov.il/en/departments/news/spoke_cabinet200521.

13 Patrick Kingsley, 'Israel and Hamas Agree to End a Brief War that Reverberated Worldwide', *New York Times*, 20 May 2021, https://www.nytimes.com/2021/05/20/world/middleeast/israel-gaza-ceasefire.html?name=styln-jerusalem-palestinian&region=TOP_BANNER&block=storyline_menu_recirc&action=click&pgtype=Article&variant=show&is_new=false.

14 Mehul Srivastava, 'End of Era in Israel as Netanyahu Is Ousted', *Financial Times*, 13 June 2021, https://www.ft.com/content/f0824e22-2e42-4d80-b0fa-574c6b12b9dd?emailId=60c6df285593a30004df42cb&segmentId=22011ee7-896a-8c4c-22a0-7603348b7f22.

15 Andrew Roth and Helena Smith, '"They Will Kill Me": Belarusian Blogger's Descent into Horror', *Guardian*, 24 May 2021, https://www.theguardian.com/world/2021/may/24/belarus-blogger-roman-protasevich-minsk-ryanair.

16 Ivan Nechepurenko, 'Passengers Recall the Fear that Gripped the Dissident Journalist as Their Flight Was Diverted', *New York Times*, 24 May 2021, https://www.nytimes.com/2021/05/24/world/europe/passengers-recall-the-fear-that-gripped-the-dissident-journalist-as-their-flight-was-diverted.html?action=click&module=Spotlight&pgtype=Homepage.

17 Anton Troianovski and Ivan Nechepurenko, 'Belarus Forces Down Plane to Seize Dissident; Europe Sees "State Hijacking"', *New York Times*, 26 May 2021, https://www.nytimes.com/2021/05/23/world/europe/ryanair-belarus.html?action=click&module=RelatedLinks&pgtype=Article.

18 European Commission, 'Opening Remarks by President von der Leyen at the Joint Press Conference with President Michel Following the Special Meeting of the European Council of 24 May 2021', https://ec.europa.eu/commission/presscorner/detail/en/statement_21_2661.

19 Anton Troianovski, 'Belarus Is Isolated as Other Countries Move to Ban Flights', *New York Times*, 24 May 2021, https://www.nytimes.com/2021/05/24/world/europe/belarus-flight-ban.html?action=click&module=Spotlight&pgtype=Homepage.

20 Andrew Roth, 'Belarus President Calls Backlash Against Plane Incident a "Planned Provocation"', *Guardian*, 26 May 2021, https://www.theguardian.com/world/2021/may/26/belarus-president-accuses-west-of-launching-hybrid-modern-war.

21 German Foreign Office (@GermanyDiplo), tweet, 21 June 2021, https://twitter.com/GermanyDiplo/status/1406907849440178176.

Ditch the NPT

Joelien Pretorius and Tom Sauer

The Treaty on the Non-Proliferation of Nuclear Weapons (NPT) has become an impediment to a world free of nuclear weapons, and it is time to move beyond it. We first suggested as much in a September 2019 opinion piece in the *Bulletin of the Atomic Scientists*, in which we asked whether it was time to ditch the treaty.[1] We wrote the article to coincide with preparations for the treaty's 50th anniversary and the critical 2020 NPT Review Conference. The view that the non-proliferation and disarmament regime is in serious trouble is not unique to us, yet our opinion piece caused something of a furore in the arms-control and peace community. Some observers even argued that we were being 'woefully irresponsible' by daring to imagine the NPT's collapse and replacement.[2] For many, our call to abandon a treaty that came as a great relief at the height of the Cold War was blasphemous. But, at 100 seconds to midnight,[3] there can be no sacred cows. The problem must be looked at from all angles.

Why ditch the NPT?

For decades the NPT has been called the 'cornerstone' of the nuclear non-proliferation and disarmament regime, a designation that has become common sense, applied automatically and uncritically. However, experts and decision-makers are increasingly perceiving that the NPT is in trouble.[4] The extent of the trouble, and its potential consequences for both the treaty and the

Joelien Pretorius is Associate Professor in Politics at the University of the Western Cape, South Africa. **Tom Sauer** is Professor in International Politics at the University of Antwerp, Belgium.

Survival | vol. 63 no. 4 | August–September 2021 | pp. 103–124   https://doi.org/10.1080/00396338.2021.1956197

arms-control regime, is still a matter for debate. Most observers seem to believe that the NPT will be around forever, or at least for a very long time.[5] In contrast, we argue that, just like many other arms-control agreements (the Anti-Ballistic Missile Treaty, the Intermediate-Range Nuclear Forces Treaty, the Treaty on Open Skies), the NPT may come to an end, possibly sooner rather than later.[6]

Arguably, the NPT, which was concluded in 1968 and entered into force in 1970, has helped to contain the spread of nuclear weapons, but has not stopped it altogether. Since 1967, four states have acquired nuclear weapons: Israel, India, Pakistan and North Korea.[7] Any state that is willing to devote the necessary money, personnel and time to acquire nuclear weapons may succeed,[8] and can always withdraw from the NPT if needed, as North Korea did. Israel, India and Pakistan never joined the treaty, because they planned to acquire nuclear weapons. Indeed, one-third of all nuclear-armed states do not belong to the NPT. Of these, Pakistan was implicated in the widespread trafficking of nuclear technology to countries such as Iran, Libya and North Korea. Israel had a significant hand in making apartheid South Africa's nuclear programme possible, offering it *Jericho* missiles likely fitted with nuclear warheads;[9] providing it with enough tritium to help build its nuclear bombs;[10] and likely testing a nuclear weapon with South Africa.[11]

The NPT framework is incapable of dealing with nuclear-armed states that tested after 1967, because allowing such states to join the treaty as nuclear-weapon states would reward proliferation and undermine the non-proliferation norm. This dilemma is symptomatic of the basic flaw of the NPT, namely that its implementation is one-sided. Contrary to most arms-control agreements, the NPT is discriminatory, drawing a distinction between the five states that could sign up as nuclear-weapon states because they had exploded a nuclear device before 1967, and all other states, which had to sign up as non-nuclear-weapon states.[12] The latter had to promise never to acquire nuclear weapons. The continuation of this distinction between a small club of 'haves' and a very large group of 'have nots' is not sustainable. The negotiators of the treaty knew this, which is why Article VI of the NPT demands that signatory parties start multilateral negotiations towards a world without nuclear weapons. If Article VI were not there, many states would not have signed up in the first place.

The legitimacy of a treaty depends on its implementation. If all states carry out what they have promised, a treaty can exist for a very long time, as demonstrated by some treaties establishing nuclear-weapon-free zones. If, however, one group of states does not fulfil its obligations under the treaty while another group does, its legitimacy and ultimately its survival may be called into question. That is the case with the NPT. The intention behind the treaty was to build a house in which nuclear weapons would eventually become illegitimate and illegal. But the house that was actually built is not the one that the architects promised. Today, the treaty is the cornerstone of a severely hypocritical nuclear order in which a few states claim the right to wield their nuclear weapons while proscribing this right to other states – a situation that India has dubbed 'nuclear apartheid'.[13]

The NPT is at best a status quo treaty

The unwillingness of the nuclear-weapon states to eliminate their arsenals – there are still in excess of 13,000 nuclear weapons on earth – has yielded significant frustration among many of the non-nuclear-weapon states. This frustration was first canalised by the Non-Aligned Movement (NAM), and then by the New Agenda Coalition (NAC) after the NPT was extended indefinitely in 1995, 25 years after coming into force. This extension may not have been the right thing for the non-nuclear-weapon states, as it deprived them of the leverage that a fixed-period or rolling extension could have given them to hold nuclear-weapon states to account.[14] As the NPT does not contain a deadline for nuclear disarmament, the treaty's indefinite extension freed the nuclear-weapon states of any immediate legal pressure to disarm.[15] From that point onwards, the NPT became at best a status quo treaty. At worst, the treaty's extension may have emboldened nuclear-weapon states to treat Article VI with impunity. Meanwhile, none of the three major demands that were part of the package deal to achieve indefinite extension in 1995 have been implemented: the conclusion and entry into force of a Comprehensive Nuclear-Test-Ban Treaty (CTBT); the conclusion and entry into force of a fissile-materials cut-off treaty; and the creation in the Middle East of a zone free of nuclear, biological and chemical weapons.[16] In our estimation, the indefinite extension of the NPT is an important explanatory factor for the slowdown of nuclear arms control and disarmament since the mid-1990s.

At the five-yearly review conferences, the non-nuclear-weapon states regularly complain about the lack of nuclear disarmament, a grievance that has led to failures to adopt a consensus document at many of the conferences. In fact, more review conferences have failed than have succeeded. Conferences that succeeded generated promises that, like those made in 1995, were not implemented: neither the 13 arms-control and disarmament steps agreed at the 2000 Review Conference, nor the 64 steps agreed upon in 2010, have been implemented in any meaningful way.

Most of the non-nuclear-weapon states have had enough. Fifty years ago, they signed up to a discriminatory treaty that was disadvantageous to their side based on a promise that the situation would be rectified in good faith. It has not been rectified. As Richard Falk and David Krieger put it,

> the NPT was drafted to reflect an acceptance of a denuclearization agenda, but it has been geopolitically interpreted over its more than half century of existence from an arms control perspective that seeks to lower some costs and risks of nuclearism but implicitly rejects the treaty premise of denuclearization.[17]

Moreover, the NPT is commonly interpreted as giving the five nuclear-weapon states the right to keep their nuclear weapons, as long as they pass civilian nuclear technology to states without nuclear weapons.[18]

The nuclear-weapon states – along with many observers[19] – seem insensible to the frustration of non-nuclear-weapon states not allied to nuclear-armed states, which constitute the majority of NPT members. Some nuclear-weapon states – in particular France and the United States – have even questioned the steps that had been promised.[20] Put on the spot, defenders of the nuclear order concede that the house built over the last 50 years is not the one that the NPT promises, but argue that the world must be patient. The house, they claim, is simply not finished.[21] The nuclear-weapon states defend themselves by saying that more time is needed for the implementation of NPT obligations, because the world is not yet safe for the elimination of nuclear weapons.[22] Nuclear-weapon states therefore argue for a step-by-step approach to nuclear disarmament in the form of arms control (that is, limitations on nuclear arsenals) rather than for the one-step abolition of nuclear arsenals. The US initiative Creating an Environment for Nuclear Disarmament (CEND) even discards the step-by-step approach, postulating mythical prerequisites for the implementation of nuclear disarmament. Some states and scholars rightly call out the CEND initiative as just the latest excuse to delay giving up nuclear weapons.[23] As the only country that can claim role-model status for nuclear disarmament, South Africa's refusal to participate in the CEND initiative is an indictment of this approach.

Proof that even a protracted step-by-step approach is not really happening, and that nuclear-weapon states have no intention to give up their nuclear weapons, can be found in the modernisation activities that these states are carrying out. The US is planning to spend $1.2 trillion to modernise its nuclear weapons and their delivery vehicles over the next 30 years.[24] In other words, 20% of the US defence budget is being spent on nuclear-weapons research, development and procurement (or 30% if the costs of missile defence and the cleaning up of nuclear sites are added to the total).[25] In 2018, Russian President Vladimir Putin announced a series of nuclear-modernisation programmes, including a new intercontinental ballistic missile and a nuclear torpedo.[26] China reportedly plans to double its nuclear warheads in the next ten years.[27] The United Kingdom plans to increase the cap on its nuclear warheads by more than 40%, thereby reversing the gradual nuclear disarmament it embarked on following the end of the Cold War.[28] France has set aside a significant portion of its defence budget to design a next-generation ballistic-missile submarine and new sea- and air-launched ballistic missiles to be operational from 2035.[29] These modernisation activities reflect the intent to ensure that nuclear arsenals can be maintained for 50–80 more years. They make a mockery of Article VI and have reignited a nuclear arms race that some observers fear will be worse than that of the Cold War.[30]

Article VI is not the only section of the NPT that causes frustration for the non-nuclear-weapon states. Article IV states that all signatories – including the non-nuclear-weapon states – have the right to develop civilian nuclear programmes, as long as these are declared to the International Atomic Energy Agency (IAEA), and as long as the IAEA can control the relevant facilities (as specified in Article III). The nuclear-weapon states are exempt from these controls in another instance of discrimination, although some of them have unilaterally agreed to IAEA controls on their civilian facilities. Worse, the benefits of Article IV for the non-nuclear-weapon states are decreasing and the restrictions increasing. While the NPT does not specify the kind of civilian facilities that states can build, there is a tendency (especially in the US) to claim that enrichment and reprocessing facilities do not fall under the heading of Article IV.[31] At the same time, an Additional Protocol to the IAEA was negotiated that gives the agency more power to verify declared and undeclared facilities in the non-nuclear-weapon states. Some states, like Brazil, perceive this as an additional burden and therefore did not sign up to the Additional Protocol.[32] Adding insult to injury, the US applies double standards when supplying nuclear technologies that erode the NPT regime.[33] It turns the screws with respect to safeguards for NPT members, but signed a nuclear deal with India that snubbed the NPT and undermined the non-proliferation norm. As Amitai Etzioni has noted, the result of the US–India nuclear deal was more nuclear know-how for India and more materials that benefit its military programme, despite the Nuclear Suppliers Group's efforts to contain diversion from its civilian programme.[34]

Not only are there serious flaws in the respective implementation of each of the 'three pillars' of the NPT – non-proliferation, disarmament and peaceful use – but these flaws also reinforce each other, meaning that the house that has been built on these pillars is structurally unstable. The way the pillars are interpreted and discussed is like a game of rock–paper–scissors that goes as follows: nuclear disarmament cannot occur while there is a risk of proliferation; proliferation is an inherent risk of peaceful use; and peaceful use is an inalienable right. As a result, the peaceful-use pillar and consequent proliferation risk make nuclear disarmament an impossibility, which in turn unravels the grand bargain of the NPT, which links non-proliferation and disarmament. Thus, non-nuclear-weapon states may think of their peaceful programmes as nuclear hedging, which allows nuclear-weapon states to play up proliferation risks to justify their own nuclear weapons, and so the arguments go round and round. This rhetorical game has not only become standard in the NPT review conferences, but is becoming a self-fulfilling prophecy. It is time to get off the discursive merry-go-round and pursue discussion and practices that move beyond the NPT trinity.

Beyond the NPT

The NPT was never intended to be a full stop in the history of the nuclear order, but rather a comma in a story ending with a nuclear-weapons-free world. So how can we get past the NPT to achieve that world?

Non-nuclear-weapon states and civil-society organisations that are serious about a world without nuclear weapons found a way to harness their growing frustrations after the failed 2005 review conference with the launching of the so-called Humanitarian Initiative. Ronald McCoy, the founder of the Malaysian chapter of the International Physicians for the Prevention of Nuclear War (IPPNW), initiated this humanitarian movement, which led to the creation of the International Campaign to Abolish Nuclear Weapons (ICAN). Taking the initiative further, states including Austria, Norway and Switzerland were able to insert a statement of 'deep concern at the continued risk for humanity represented by the possibility that [nuclear] weapons could be used and the catastrophic humanitarian consequences that would result from [their] use' in the final document of the 2010 NPT Review Conference.[35] In 2013–14, Austria, Mexico and Norway each organised a Conference on the Humanitarian Impact of Nuclear Weapons, with a growing number of states (120–150) attending. The last conference in Vienna led to the 'Austrian pledge', later rebranded the 'Humanitarian Pledge'. The latter called for a new legal instrument that would make nuclear weapons illegal.

Nuclear-armed states were absent from most of these conferences even though the main question being discussed was whether societies are prepared for any future use of nuclear weapons. The consequences of a nuclear attack, much like the effects of the coronavirus pandemic, would not be restricted to the target state. Yet the humanitarian conferences concluded that societies were not ready and – worse – would never be ready to deal with the aftermath of nuclear-weapons use.[36] The COVID-19 pandemic exposed the importance of capacities such as intensive-care beds in dealing with a large-scale medical emergency. How many intensive-care beds would be left after a nuclear-weapons attack, let alone a nuclear war?[37] The conferences strengthened the view that the only way to protect humanity from the use of nuclear weapons was to eliminate them.

One useful way to start eliminating a category of weapons is to ban them and declare them illegal, as in the case of landmines and cluster munitions. In October 2016, a United Nations General Assembly resolution was agreed by 123 states demanding that multilateral negotiations for a legally binding instrument to prohibit nuclear weapons begin in 2017 within the UN framework.[38] These negotiations were concluded on 7 July 2017, at which time 122 states voted in favour of the Treaty on the Prohibition of Nuclear Weapons (TPNW), better known as the Ban Treaty. Despite significant pressure from nuclear-weapon states not to support the Ban Treaty, it nevertheless entered into force in January 2021. The treaty outlaws the development, acquisition, possession, transfer, use and threat of use of nuclear weapons for all states, without exception. The treaty could help to achieve a world without nuclear weapons if every state were to ratify and implement it.

The Ban Treaty is both a prohibition and a disarmament treaty. For the first time, a legally binding international treaty stipulates that nuclear weapons are prohibited and regarded as illegal (at least by the signatories). The ban expands the existing nuclear taboo from use to possession.[39] It aims to strengthen the existing norm against nuclear weapons. The hope of Ban Treaty advocates (including the authors) is that the stigmatising effect of the treaty will trigger a renewed societal and political debate among nuclear-armed states and their allies about the role of such weapons in their defence doctrines.[40]

It is crucial to understand the Ban Treaty as another signal by most of the non-nuclear-weapon states that they fundamentally dislike the current state of affairs with respect to nuclear disarmament. It reflects frustration with the NPT to the point that parties are seeking other forums to enact the treaty's objectives. The Humanitarian Initiative can be regarded as the successor of the NAC in the 1990s, which in turn can be regarded as the successor of the NAM. This time, and for the first time, the non-nuclear-weapon states successfully used the power of their numbers to their advantage. The Ban Treaty shows that, instead of the nine nuclear-armed states and their 30 allies, the 120–130 non-nuclear-weapon states that wish to get rid of nuclear weapons are at the steering wheel of the global non-proliferation and disarmament regime.

Alexander Kmentt has identified a 'conceptual gap' between the nuclear-weapon and the non-nuclear-weapon states.[41] The nuclear-weapon states assumed that any discussion of nuclear matters in their absence would be futile and fizzle out. They boycotted the first two humanitarian conferences, arguing that the initiative was a distraction from, and was undermining, the NPT. Instead, as Kmentt puts it, their absence

> proved almost to a greater degree that the humanitarian approach was valid and provided a possibility to have the kind of nuclear disarmament debate that is usually stifled in other fora. Rather than weakening the humanitarian approach, the nuclear weapon States' dismissive attitude actually provided further impetus to this non-nuclear weapon State-driven initiative.[42]

Realising that their boycott had the opposite effect to that intended, India, Pakistan, the UK and the US officially participated in the Vienna conference, which was now considered part of the mainstream nuclear debate.[43]

Nevertheless, the boycott policy and the critique that the process undermines the NPT returned during the negotiations of the Ban Treaty.[44] Moreover, diplomatic pressure not to sign, or even to un-sign, the Ban Treaty was exerted to hamper its entry into force.[45] For the states most invested in the Humanitarian Initiative, the Ban Treaty is not only complementary to the NPT, but also firmly rooted within the NPT, especially Article VI. It is regarded, in Kmentt's words, as 'fully consistent with their own objective of trying to promote a strong and credible NPT'.[46] The Ban Treaty preamble reaffirms that the NPT is the cornerstone of the non-proliferation and disarmament regime, and plays a vital role in international security. As such, these states find the nuclear-weapon states' claim that the Ban Treaty is incompatible with the NPT especially provocative.

Some commentators saw our 2019 article as playing into the hands of the detractors of the Ban Treaty, because the article suggested that it should replace the NPT.[47] Our article was apparently cited with glee by some of these detractors to show that the Ban Treaty undermines the NPT.[48] To be clear, the NPT inevitably must be replaced with another international agreement – be it the Ban Treaty or a newly negotiated instrument – that abolishes nuclear weapons, oversees their elimination and institutes a universal system to ensure nuclear abstinence for all. This progression from the NPT to other instruments of nuclear disarmament is built in to Article VI. The ideal is that the NPT becomes a dynamic and time-bound forum for the orderly transition to a new nuclear order in which nuclear weapons are illegal for all.

Because of their failure to grasp the frustration that non-nuclear-weapon states experience in the NPT forum, the nuclear-armed states and their allies miscalculated the success of the Ban Treaty. However, they could have welcomed the treaty as a constructive step towards fulfilling the NPT's commitment to a world without nuclear weapons, and engaged creatively with the process to set out short-, medium- and long-term steps to implement their end of the NPT bargain. Unfortunately, they categorically rejected the Ban Treaty, and some of them stated that they would never sign it.[49] From their point of view, nuclear weapons are legitimate defensive tools. In our view, the idea of eliminating them has never been taken seriously by nuclear-armed states.[50]

Our article asking whether it was time to ditch the NPT was criticised on both sides of the argument. The criticism of the nuclear-armed states, their allies and those who agree with their views was understandable. It is in their interest to uphold the NPT-as-cornerstone regime because they cannot imagine a world without the privileged position that it affords nuclear-armed states.

The criticism of ICAN and other peace organisations was possibly more surprising, but also understandable. For some critics of our position, the NPT is regarded as one of the few treaties, albeit an imperfect one, that regulates nuclear weapons, and therefore ditching it will mean that non-nuclear-weapon states give up their only legal leverage over nuclear-weapon states.[51] However, in our estimation, that leverage was already given up with the indefinite extension in 1995, and the nuclear-armed states certainly do not act as if the NPT regulates their nuclear weapons. The only leverage that remains within the NPT framework is withdrawal or acting outside the NPT, as the negotiation process of the Ban Treaty illustrated.

Some criticism can be understood in terms of the nuclear-weapon states' insistence that the Ban Treaty would undermine the NPT. For some non-nuclear-weapon states and peace activists, the 'do no harm' principle applies: they would not like any action to be seen to contribute to the proliferation of nuclear weapons, and fear that ditching the NPT could result in proliferation.[52]

For other actors, our article came at the wrong time. They argue that the Ban Treaty first needed to enter into force. For that to happen, the criticism that the Ban Treaty will undermine the non-proliferation regime needs to be neutralised to attract more signatories and ratifications. The references to the NPT in the Ban Treaty and assurances that it does not contradict the NPT serve this purpose. Irrespective of these references, ratification has become more complicated than previously anticipated because of the pressure by the nuclear-weapon states,[53] just as happened when the NPT was extended indefinitely.[54] Even so, the Ban Treaty achieved the necessary 50 ratifications and entered into force on 22 January 2021.

This is a crucial period for the NPT and the future of nuclear weapons. If the nuclear-armed states and their allies, or at least some of them, heed the grievances and frustrations of the non-nuclear-weapon states and proceed with a clear agenda to eliminate nuclear weapons, the NPT can become a framework for an orderly transition to a world without nuclear weapons under a legal instrument that eventually supersedes the NPT. If, in contrast, the nuclear-armed states and their allies remain tone deaf and obstinate, we do not merely predict the end of the NPT, but also prescribe it. The Ban Treaty puts into effect the grand bargain that the NPT negotiators struck. Its stigmatising effects can be fully realised with the NPT out of the way.

Thinking through NPT withdrawal

What if the nuclear-armed states don't listen? If they haven't picked up on the diplomatic signals for nuclear disarmament so far, it may be time to enlist more allies within the nuclear-armed states themselves. There are several ways to capture the attention of domestic actors inside the nuclear-armed states. One approach would be to withdraw from the NPT. Previously, a decision to withdraw from the NPT was regarded as a rogue act that immediately cast suspicion on a state's nuclear intentions, as was the case with North Korea. But if a large group of states in good standing with their IAEA safeguards agreements that are members of the Ban Treaty or a nuclear-weapons-free-zone treaty walk away from the NPT on the grounds that Article VI is being undermined, the target of the stigmatising effect will shift to the nuclear-armed states.

What about the risk of proliferation in a world without the NPT? When it comes to withdrawal from the NPT, it is possible to distinguish between three kinds of states. For many non-nuclear-weapon states that have signed on to the Ban Treaty and are part of other arrangements, we do not see that withdrawal from the NPT will impact on their nuclear status. These states can transfer their safeguards agreements under the NPT to other legal instruments (such as treaties establishing nuclear-weapons-free zones). The IAEA will still function as the watchdog organisation, in addition to regional organisations such as the Brazilian–Argentine Agency for Accounting and Control of Nuclear Materials (ABACC) and the African Commission on Nuclear Energy (AFCONE). For us, this solves the problem of duplicity in the nuclear order: states that forgo the nuclear option will no longer be beholden to nuclear-weapon states in the unfair and therefore unstable set-up of the NPT, but to like-minded states and the international community more generally on the basis that nuclear weapons are illegal for all. Most states will probably belong to this group.

A second group of states may withdraw from the NPT because they feel insecure and would like to build nuclear weapons. As Mohamed ElBaradei once stated:

> Imagine this: a country or group of countries serves notice that they plan to withdraw from the nuclear Non-Proliferation Treaty (NPT) in order to acquire nuclear weapons, citing a dangerous deterioration in the international security situation. 'Don't worry,' they tell a shocked world. 'The fundamental purpose of our nuclear forces is political: to preserve

peace and prevent coercion and any kind of war. Nuclear weapons provide the supreme guarantee of our security. They will play an essential role by ensuring uncertainty in the mind of any aggressor about the nature of our response to military aggression.'... The rationale I have just cited to justify nuclear weapons is taken from NATO's current Strategic Concept.[55]

Iran is the state most likely to follow this path. If it does go nuclear, the odds are that Saudi Arabia will soon follow. Although their motivation would be distinct from the grievances and frustrations vis-à-vis the nuclear-weapon states and their allies discussed above, both countries may make use of the NPT crisis to leave the treaty. The North Korean precedent will certainly not deter them; on the contrary, North Korea has become a nuclear-armed state without being attacked for doing so. It would not be defensible to treat Iran and Saudi Arabia any differently to North Korea.[56] It should be acknowledged, though, that there is a greater possibility that Israel – and perhaps also the United States – would react differently to Iran's acquisition of nuclear weapons than it did to North Korea's, possibly by way of bombing nuclear installations. Israel could expect substantial retaliatory attacks by Iran if it were to do so. And it is unthinkable that Israel or the US would invade and occupy Iran indefinitely to ensure that it does not acquire nuclear weapons.[57]

Members of the third group of states do not necessarily feel insecure, but do feel unfairly treated by the NPT, and may think of changing their status to nuclear. Only weeks after our 2019 article was published, Turkish President Recep Tayyip Erdogan stated to his ruling Justice and Development Party: 'Some countries have missiles with nuclear warheads, not one or two. But (they tell us) we can't have them. This, I cannot accept.'[58] He repeated these views at the UN General Assembly a few weeks later.[59] Rebecca Davis Gibbons predicts that

> this type of rhetoric will likely increase as leaders from non-nuclear-weapon states grow frustrated with the status of the NPT disarmament bargain … One can imagine nationalistic leaders of non-nuclear-weapon states or members of their foreign ministries making the case that the NPT has been an unfair treaty and it is time to get out.[60]

In the past, statements like Erdogan's have been heard in Brazil. José Alencar, then the country's vice-president, said in 2009: 'The nuclear weapon, used as an instrument of deterrence, is of great importance for a country that has 15,000 kilometers of borders to the west and a territorial sea.'[61] Egypt is also known as being critical of the NPT and has already walked out of an NPT Preparatory Committee. South Africa is resisting watering down or giving up the leftover highly enriched uranium from its apartheid-era nuclear-weapons programme despite intense pressure from the US to do so. It cannot be ruled out that keeping this uranium (which is deemed a 'strategic asset') is a form of nuclear hedging.[62] South Africa also resisted making the Additional Protocol a condition of supply of sensitive nuclear technology in the Nuclear Suppliers Group.[63] It did not join the Proliferation Security Initiative or CEND. These inactions on initiatives ostensibly strengthening non-proliferation, nuclear security and disarmament suggest a form of passive resistance against one-sided interpretations of the NPT that favour nuclear-weapon states' interests in the nuclear order.[64] In short, more states may follow the North Korean example by leaving the NPT or following the South African example, which will result in an increasingly dysfunctional NPT. Both steps would likely signify the end of the treaty.

Ditching the NPT is only a responsible approach if there is an alternative. Not by chance, that alternative exists, namely the Ban Treaty. With the Ban Treaty in force, the upcoming NPT Review Conference promises to be a turning point. If there is still no sign that nuclear-armed states and their allies are substantially moving in the direction of fundamentally delegitimising nuclear weapons, and we predict that there won't be, there is no need for the NPT.

States that withdraw from the NPT have nothing to lose. A discriminatory regime would have been replaced with one in which all states are equal with respect to the possession of nuclear weapons. It would be a world without a treaty that legitimises nuclear weapons for a small group of states while condemning their acquisition by most others. It would be a world in which nuclear-armed states are regarded as pariah states for possessing weapons that are not only inhumane, immoral and illegitimate, but also illegal.[65]

Should the NPT's house of cards fall apart, the nuclear-armed states and their allies could no longer rely on their version of the NPT bargain to legitimise continued possession of nuclear weapons. They would face the choice of becoming nuclear rogues on the wrong side of history or accepting that such a scenario does not serve their interests. In all likelihood, hanging on to nuclear weapons would create a schism between the nuclear-armed states and some of their allies, as well as within their own societies. Indeed, the first indications of such a schism are already visible.[66] Under pressure from civil society and its national parliament, the Netherlands was the only NATO member state to attend the Ban Treaty negotiations in 2017. Due to the insistence of Belgium's Greens and Dutch-speaking socialists, the agreement that created the country's governing coalition in September 2020 contains a positive reference to the Ban Treaty. There is a real chance that the Greens will also enter Germany's government in autumn 2021. Some non-nuclear NATO members are also examining whether they will attend the first meeting of states parties of the Ban Treaty in January 2022 as observers. The pressure exerted by states calling for radical change will grow, as the group of non-nuclear-weapon states is joined by more states or interested domestic actors.

Admittedly, ditching the NPT becomes more complicated if states opt for the nuclear option after withdrawal, or in a first stage threaten to build nuclear weapons. Legally, they would not be doing wrong, as they will have withdrawn from the NPT. An increase in nuclear-armed states would mean an increase in the inherent risks of nuclear-weapons possession: nuclear use, nuclear accidents, nuclear terrorism and catastrophic failure of any perceived deterrence.

The international community may choose to accept the nuclear status of states that withdraw and obtain nuclear weapons in the same way it has largely accepted the status of the four nuclear-armed states outside the NPT. In the worst-case scenario, particular nuclear-armed states may use proliferation as an excuse to start wars against some of these states, which will have dire consequences if the ongoing humanitarian costs and geopolitical instability of the 2003 Iraq War are anything to go by. However, these wars cannot be justified by pointing to the NPT if states have used their sovereign right to withdraw from the treaty and are no longer bound by it. Without the NPT it will be difficult to defend what Richard Falk calls

> an American-led geopolitical regime of 'enforcement' [supplemental to the NPT] that denies certain states their Article X right of withdrawal, and as applied is relied upon to justify sanctions against North Korea and Iran, which constitute unlawful threats and uses force in circumstances other than self-defense, violating the core prohibition of the UN Charter set forth in Article 2(4).[67]

* * *

There comes a point when the lack of or skewed implementation of a treaty argues against its continuation. The NPT is at that point. After 50 years of the treaty's being in force and 25 years since its indefinite extension, it seems almost farcical to contend that the nuclear-armed states are serious about giving up their nuclear weapons. The NPT's historical trajectory, compounded by recent reversals of arms-control measures and a new arms race, will not result in a world without nuclear weapons. It is time to move beyond the NPT.

The indefinite extension of the NPT in 1995 has left the non-nuclear-weapon states with no real legal leverage over the nuclear-armed states except in their ability to withdraw from this forum. The arrival of the Ban Treaty embodies the frustration of this group of states. The nuclear-armed states' reaction to the ban reflects their intransigence with respect to achieving the spirit of the NPT. It is in this context that withdrawal appears to be a legitimate and reasonable option for states that are serious about nuclear disarmament. This is by far the largest group of non-nuclear-weapon states. If enough of these states withdraw, the NPT will collapse. Our analysis offers a way to think about a post-NPT world. The majority of non-nuclear-weapon states will not change their nuclear status, as many are already or will become members of the Ban Treaty. However, if some states acquire nuclear weapons, this kind of proliferation must be seen in the context of the failure of nuclear-armed states to abide by their NPT obligations.

Although the NPT has played a key role in establishing the norm against nuclear weapons, the way nuclear-armed states have interpreted the treaty damages this norm. The danger of proliferation after withdrawal must be weighed against this damage and its effect on non-proliferation and disarmament. Withdrawal does not invalidate the NPT, but represents an indictment of the way it has been interpreted, and an attempt to reclaim its original intent – a world without nuclear weapons. As such, the optimal step towards nuclear disarmament is for states to withdraw from the NPT and to join the Ban Treaty.

Notes

[1]   Joelien Pretorius and Tom Sauer, 'Is It Time to Ditch the NPT?', *Bulletin of the Atomic Scientists*, 6 September 2019, https://thebulletin.org/2019/09/is-it-time-to-ditch-the-npt/.

[2]   Heather Williams (@heatherwilly), tweet, 9 September 2019, https://twitter.com/heatherwilly/status/1170990676227579905.

[3]   The *Bulletin of the Atomic Scientists* set its nuclear doomsday clock at 100 seconds to midnight on 23 January 2020. See 'Closer than Ever: It Is 100 Seconds to Midnight', 2020 Doomsday Clock Statement, *Bulletin of the Atomic Scientists*, 23 January 2020, https://thebulletin.org/doomsday-clock/2020-doomsday-clock-statement/.

[4]   See Tom Sauer, 'The Nuclear Nonproliferation Regime in Crisis', *Peace Review*, vol. 18, no. 3, Fall 2006, pp. 333–40; Paul Meyer, 'The Nuclear Nonproliferation Treaty: Fin de Régime?', *Arms Control Today*, April 2017; Jerry Brown and William Potter, 'Open Forum: Time for a Reality Check on Nuclear Diplomacy', *San Francisco Chronicle*, 24 April 2019, https://www.sfchronicle.com/opinion/openforum/article/Open-Forum-Time-for-a-reality-check-on-nuclear-13793344.php; and Tariq Rauf, 'The NPT at Fifty: Perish or Survive?', *Arms Control Today*, March 2020.

[5]   See, for example, Liviu Horovitz, 'Beyond Pessimism: Why the Treaty on the Non-proliferation of Nuclear Weapons Will Not Collapse', *Journal of Strategic Studies*, vol. 38, no. 1–2, 2015, pp. 126–58; and Adam Scheinman, 'No, It Is Not Time to Ditch the NPT', *Bulletin of the Atomic Scientists*, 7 October 2019, https://thebulletin.org/2019/10/no-it-is-not-time-to-ditch-the-npt/.

[6]   Pretorius and Sauer, 'Is It Time to Ditch the NPT?'

[7]   South Africa built nuclear weapons during the 1980s, but dismantled them and joined the NPT in 1991.

[8]   South Africa proved that this is possible even amid sanctions.

9   See Sasha Polakow Suransky, *The Unspoken Alliance: Israel's Secret Relationship with Apartheid South Africa* (New York: Pantheon Books, 2010), pp. 83, 125.

10 *Ibid.*

11 See Avner Cohen and William Burr, 'Revisiting the 1979 VELA Mystery: A Report on a Critical Oral History Conference', Woodrow Wilson Center Sources and Methods blog, 31 August 2020, https://www.wilsoncenter.org/blog-post/revisiting-1979-vela-mystery-report-critical-oral-history-conference.

12 'Nuclear-*armed* states' comprise the five 'nuclear-weapon states' temporarily recognised by the NPT and the four additional ones mentioned in our text.

13 See Pretorius and Sauer, 'Is It Time to Ditch the NPT?'

14 See, for example, Rebecca Johnson's analysis that led her to conclude that the NPT's 'indefinite extension has exposed more problems than it cured', in 'Troubled Treaties: Is the NPT Tottering?', *Bulletin of the Atomic Scientists*, vol. 55, no. 2, March/April 1999, pp. 16–18.

15 One of the authors, Tom Sauer, predicted this in his article 'Het Nucleair Non-Proliferatie Verdrag' [The Nuclear Non-Proliferation Treaty], *Streven*, vol. 62, no. 4, April 1995, pp. 306–15.

16 Johnson details in 'Troubled Treaties' how some in the nuclear-weapon states saw the strengthened review process agreed to as part of the indefinite extension package as merely a gambit to achieve the NPT's permanence.

17 Richard Falk and David Krieger, 'Biden's Foreign Policy and Nuclear Weapons: A Dialogue', Counterpunch, 4 May 2021, https://www.counterpunch.org/2021/05/04/bidens-foreign-policy-and-nuclear-weapons-a-dialogue/.

18 See Stephen McGlinchey, 'Diplomacy', in Stephen McGlinchey (ed.), *International Relations* (Bristol: E-IR Publications, 2017); and Julian Borger and Ian Sample, 'All You Wanted to Know About Nuclear War, but Were Too Afraid to Ask', *Guardian*, 16 July 2018, https://www.theguardian.com/world/2018/jul/16/nuclear-war-north-korea-russia-what-will-happen-how-likely-explained.

19 See, for example, Bruno Tertrais, 'The Illogic of Zero', *Washington Quarterly*, vol. 33, no. 2, pp. 125–38; and Brad Roberts, 'Ban the Bomb or Bomb the Ban?', ELN Policy Brief, 22 March 2018.

20 See Jean du Preez, 'Half Full or Half Empty? Realizing the Promise of the Nuclear Nonproliferation Treaty', *Arms Control Today*, vol. 36, no. 10, December 2006, pp. 6–12.

21 The nuclear-weapon states and their allies were put on the spot when they had to defend their choice not to support the negotiation of the Ban Treaty in UN forums. See, for example, the UN High-Level Meeting on the Total Elimination of Nuclear Weapons on 27 September 2017, https://www.un.org/press/en/2017/ga11954.doc.htm.

22 See Pretorius and Sauer, 'Is It Time to Ditch the NPT?'

23 See, for example, Tariq Rauf, 'CEND Is Creating the Conditions to "Never Disarm": 74 Years Since Hiroshima and Nagasaki', 5 August 2019, https://www.indepthnews.net/index.php/opinion/2876-cend-is-creating-the-conditions-to-never-disarm-74-years-since-hiroshima-nagasaki.

24 This figure does not account for inflation.

25 Lawrence Korb, 'Trump's 2021 Budget: More Nuclear Spending, Less of Almost Everything Else', *Bulletin of the Atomic Scientists*, 12 February 2020, https://thebulletin. org/2020/02/trumps-2021-budget-more-nuclear-spending-less-of-almost-everything-else/.

26 See Hans M. Kristensen and Matt Korda, 'Russian Nuclear Weapons, 2021', *Bulletin of the Atomic Scientists*, vol. 77, no. 2, 2021, pp. 93–4.

27 See Joe Gould, 'China Plans to Double Its Nuclear Arsenal, Pentagon Says', *Defense News*, 1 September 2020, https://www.defensenews. com/congress/2020/09/01/ china-planning-to-double-nuclear-arsenal-pentagon-says/.

28 See Tom Plant and Matthew Harries, 'Going Ballistic: The UK's Proposed Nuclear Build-up', RUSI Commentary, 16 March 2021.

29 UK House of Commons, 'The French Nuclear Deterrent', 7 October 2020.

30 See, for example, Andreas Kluth, 'This Arms Race Is Worse than the Last One', Bloomberg Opinion, 18 June 2020, https://www.bloomberg. com/opinion/articles/2020-06-18/ this-nuclear-arms-race-is-worse-than-the-last-one.

31 See Joelien Pretorius, 'Nuclear Politics of Denial: South Africa and the Additional Protocol', *International Negotiation*, vol. 18, no. 3, 2013, pp. 379–99, https://brill.com/view/ journals/iner/18/3/article-p379_4.xml.

32 *Ibid.*

33 See George Perkovich, 'The Global Implications of the U.S.–India Nuclear Deal', *Daedalus*, Winter 2010, https:// www.amacad.org/publication/ global-implications-us-india-deal.

34 Amitai Etzioni, 'The Darker Side of the US–India Nuclear Deal', *Diplomat*, 13 February 2015, https://thediplomat. com/2015/02/the-darker-side-of-the-u-s-india-nuclear-deal. The US–India deal was not the first time that the US and its allies helped a proliferator outside the NPT. See Renfrew Christie's 1993 analysis on the substantial help that the South African nuclear-weapons programme received from the West, particularly the US. Renfrew Christie, 'South Africa's Nuclear History', Nuclear History Program Fourth International Conference, Nice, 23–27 July 1993.

35 2010 Review Conference of the Parties to the Treaty on the Non-Proliferation of Nuclear Weapons, 'Final Document', NPT/CONF.2010/50 (Vol. I), p. 12, para. 80, https://www. nonproliferation.org/wp-content/ uploads/2015/04/2010_fd_part_i.pdf.

36 Vienna Conference on the Humanitarian Impact of Nuclear Weapons, 'Humanitarian Pledge', 8–9 December 2014, https://www.bmeia. gv.at/fileadmin/user_upload/Zentrale/ Aussenpolitik/Abruestung/HINW14/ HINW14vienna_Pledge_Document.pdf.

37 See Tom Sauer and Ramesh Thakur, 'How Many Intensive Care Beds Will a Nuclear Weapon Explosion Require?', *Bulletin of the Atomic Scientists*, 28 April 2020, https://thebulletin.org/2020/04/ how-many-intensive-care-beds-will-a-nuclear-weapon-explosion-require/.

38 United Nations General Assembly, 'General and Complete Disarmament: Taking Forward Multilateral

Nuclear Disarmament Negotiations', A/C.1/71/L.41, 14 October 2016.

39 For a discussion of the nuclear taboo, see Nina Tannenwald, *The Nuclear Taboo* (Cambridge: Cambridge University Press, 2007).

40 See Tom Sauer and Mathias Reveraert, 'The Potential Stigmatizing Effect of the Treaty on the Prohibition of Nuclear Weapons', *Nonproliferation Review*, vol. 25, nos 5–6, 2018, pp. 437–55.

41 Alexander Kmentt, 'The Development of the International Initiative on the Humanitarian Impact of Nuclear Weapons and Its Effect on the Nuclear Weapons Debate', *International Review of the Red Cross*, vol. 97, no. 899, 2015, pp. 681–709, https://international-review.icrc.org/sites/default/files/irc97_11.pdf. See also his recent book *The Treaty Prohibiting Nuclear Weapons: How It Was Achieved* (Abingdon: Routledge, 2021).

42 Kmentt, 'The Development of the International Initiative on the Humanitarian Impact of Nuclear Weapons and Its Effect on the Nuclear Weapons Debate', p. 691.

43 China's representative to the Vienna Conference registered as an academic and therefore the country's participation cannot be regarded as official.

44 See 'P5 Joint Statement on the Treaty on the Non-Proliferation of Nuclear Weapons', 24 October 2018, https://www.gov.uk/government/news/p5-joint-statement-on-the-treaty-on-the-non-proliferation-of-nuclear-weapons.

45 See 'US Urges Nations to Withdraw Support for UN Nuclear Weapons Ban Treaty', CBS News, 22 October 2020, https://www.cbsnews.com/news/us-urges-nations-to-withdraw-support-for-un-nuclear-weapons-prohibition-treaty-ap/.

46 Kmentt, 'The Development of the International Initiative on the Humanitarian Impact of Nuclear Weapons and Its Effect on the Nuclear Weapons Debate', p. 685.

47 See, for example, Rob Goldston's comment below the online version of our article, 'Is It Time to Ditch the NPT?', at https://thebulletin.org/2019/09/is-it-time-to-ditch-the-npt/.

48 See Heather Williams, 'What the Nuclear Ban Treaty Means for America's Allies', *War on the Rocks*, 5 November 2020, https://warontherocks.com/2020/11/what-the-nuclear-ban-treaty-means-for-americas-allies/.

49 'Joint Press Statement from the Permanent Representatives to the United Nations of the United States, United Kingdom, and France Following the Adoption of a Treaty Banning Nuclear Weapons', 7 July 2017, available at https://2017-2021-translations.state.gov/2017/07/07/joint-press-statement-from-the-permanent-representatives-to-the-united-nations-of-the-united-states-united-kingdom-and-france-following-the-adoption-of-a-treaty-banning-nuclear-weapons/index.html.

50 For a similar view, see Benoit Pelopidas, 'The Birth of Nuclear Eternity', in Sandra Kemp and Jenny Andersson (eds), *Futures* (Oxford: Oxford University Press, 2021).

51 See Scheinman, 'No, It Is Not Time to Ditch the NPT'.

52 See Sergio Duarte, 'Ditch the Bomb, Not the NPT', *Bulletin of the Atomic Scientists*, 18 November 2019.

53 For pressure from the nuclear-weapon states before November 2016, see Xanthe Hall, 'Under Pressure', International Physicians for the Prevention of Nuclear War Peace & Health blog, 3 November 2016, https://peaceandhealthblog.com/2016/11/03/under-pressure/.

54 See Rebecca Davis Gibbons, 'American Hegemony and the Politics of the Nuclear Non-proliferation Regime', PhD dissertation, Georgetown University, 2016, chapter 6.

55 Mohamed ElBaradei, 'Five Steps Towards Abolishing Nuclear Weapons', *Süddeutsch*, 4 February 2009.

56 The US Senate's recent passing of the so-called Iran War Powers resolution certainly suggests that there is limited appetite outside the White House for war.

57 See John J. Mearsheimer, 'Iran Is Rushing to Build a Nuclear Weapon – And Trump Can't Stop It', *New York Times*, 1 July 2019, https://www.nytimes.com/2019/07/01/opinion/iran-is-rushing-to-build-a-nuclear-weapon-and-trump-cant-stop-it.html.

58 'Erdogan Says It's Unacceptable that Turkey Can't Have Nuclear Weapons', Reuters, 4 September 2019.

59 'Turkey President Recep Tayyip Erdoğan's Full Speech to the UN General Assembly', PBS NewsHour, 24 September 2019, https://www.youtube.com/watch?v=40jXJhEa7jw.

60 Rebecca Davis Gibbons, 'The Outlook for the Nuclear Nonproliferation Treaty', in Sharon Squassoni (ed.), 'The Next Fifty Years of Nuclear Proliferation', George Washington University IISTP Occasional Paper, February 2021, pp. 38–9.

61 See J. Boyle, 'Brazilian Nuclear Ambitions?', *Rio Times*, 25 September 2009.

62 See Peter Fabricus, 'The Highly Enriched Uranium Stored Away at Pelindaba Has Much More than Commercial or Tactical Value for South Africa', Institute for Security Studies, 19 March 2015, https://issafrica.org/iss-today/why-is-pretoria-so-jealously-guarding-it-fissile-material.

63 See Pretorius, 'Nuclear Politics of Denial'.

64 Such measures may be seen as pseudo forms of withdrawal and means of voicing frustration for states in the NPT forum.

65 See Pretorius and Sauer, 'Is It Time to Ditch the NPT?'

66 See Tom Sauer and Claire Nardon, 'The Softening Rhetoric by Nuclear-armed States and NATO Allies on the Treaty on the Prohibition of Nuclear Weapons', *War on the Rocks*, 7 December 2020, https://warontherocks.com/2020/12/the-softening-rhetoric-by-nuclear-armed-states-and-nato-allies-on-the-treaty-on-the-prohibition-of-nuclear-weapons/.

67 Falk and Krieger, 'Biden's Foreign Policy and Nuclear Weapons'.

Response: Keep the NPT

Matthew Harries

Joelien Pretorius and Tom Sauer have presented a boldly argued case for abandoning the Treaty on the Non-Proliferation of Nuclear Weapons (NPT). As they note, they have done so before, having discussed the idea in the *Bulletin of the Atomic Scientists* in September 2019. Contrary to their claim here, however, they were not challenged just because they 'dared to imagine' the collapse of the NPT, but because they actively wished it into being.[1] As they make the same case here, I feel forced to renew the challenge.

The authors' return to the anti-NPT cause rests on a fair assessment of the injustice codified in the treaty and its relative impotence as a driver of nuclear disarmament. Yet proponents of the Treaty on the Prohibition of Nuclear Weapons (TPNW, also known as the Ban Treaty), the authors' preferred alternative, have mostly taken great care to present that treaty as a complement, rather than a rival, to the NPT, and have disavowed the call for NPT parties to withdraw. In taking a more adversarial approach, the authors understate both the value of what would be lost if the NPT fell and the dangers of what could follow. The collapse of nearly all existing arms-control agreements in the past decade has left the global nuclear order wobbly enough. Taking a sledgehammer to one of the few remaining foundations would be reckless.

Matthew Harries is a Senior Research Fellow in the Proliferation and Nuclear Policy Programme at the Royal United Services Institute (RUSI).

Survival | vol. 63 no. 4 | August–September 2021 | pp. 125–130   https://doi.org/10.1080/00396338.2021.1956198

Who wins?

The authors fail to consider what seems to me to be an obvious question: if the NPT is such a rotten deal, why have non-nuclear-weapon states stuck with it? The authors do not properly consider the possibility that the NPT provides benefits for many non-nuclear states in and of itself, regardless of whether the nuclear powers ever disarm. And their argument relies on an unfounded gamble that a mass exodus from the NPT would lead to consternation among the nuclear-armed states which then triggers disarmament. The more likely consequence, in my view, is a world in which disarmament remains just as difficult to achieve but proliferation is now more likely.

The authors overestimate how important the non-proliferation norm is to the nuclear-armed states, and underestimate how important it is to the non-nuclear-armed states. Who is best equipped to live in a proliferating world, if not the nuclear-armed states? Who benefits most from continued non-proliferation, if not the non-nuclear-weapon states? Would Russia, for example, observe states leaving the NPT and become convinced that it had better get serious about disarmament? The opposite is more likely: with arms control already in tatters, the Russian government would become further entrenched in its defensive and distrustful world view, and would feel vindicated in its decision to modernise and diversify its nuclear arsenal.

Similarly, the authors assert that 'if a large group of states in good standing with their IAEA safeguards agreements that are members of the Ban Treaty or a nuclear-weapons-free-zone treaty walk away from the NPT on the grounds that Article VI is being undermined, the target of the stigmatising effect will shift to the nuclear-armed states'. It is hard to see where this logic might work as the authors intend. If a large number of states in China's region left the NPT, for example, would China become more earnest about disarmament out of a sense of guilt? This seems unlikely. China already perceives itself to be encircled by US allies and partners, and the dynamics of US–Chinese military competition are making nuclear weapons more relevant to both countries' regional strategies. Mass NPT withdrawal would not change China's diplomatic rhetoric – it already emphasises its own no-first-use doctrine and modest arsenal – and would simply reaffirm the conviction of defence planners on both sides that they need to prepare for nuclearised strategic competition in Asia.

Review conferences aren't everything

In derisively (and entertainingly) sketching out an NPT 'discursive merry-go-round', in which the risk of proliferation is cited as grounds for avoiding disarmament, the authors allow irritating rhetoric to cloud their judgement of broader reality. Nuclear-armed states have kept their weapons not primarily because of the risk of proliferation, although that is one factor, but because of other, more profound strategic drivers. These include the existence of nuclear-armed rivals with whom they have serious disagreements and whom they do not trust to disarm except as part of a strict and enforceable negotiated process (and even then barely so), and – for all except the United States – the fear of an existential threat from a conventionally superior enemy.

This is characteristic of the authors' tendency to focus on the foibles of NPT diplomacy at the expense of the world outside review-conference sessions. Their comment that universal ratification and implementation of the TPNW, for example, could help to achieve a world without nuclear weapons drastically understates the fraught and complicated process that would be required to negotiate and verify disarmament, even in the event of legal prohibition.[2]

The authors' characterisation of the original NPT bargain also favours states' absolutist rhetoric over their pragmatic interests. The authors state that Article VI of the NPT 'demands that signatory parties start multilateral negotiations towards a world without nuclear weapons'. The provision actually reads:

> Each of the Parties to the Treaty undertakes to pursue negotiations in good faith on effective measures relating to cessation of the nuclear arms race at an early date and to nuclear disarmament, and on a treaty on general and complete disarmament under strict and effective international control.

The hortatory, rather than mandatory, phrasing of Article VI reflected a judgement at the time that the NPT was worth having even if the nuclear-weapon states could not be legally forced to disarm as a binding condition for non-proliferation.[3] This was, and remains, a very difficult political inequality to swallow, and it was, and remains, very important for nuclear-weapon states to acknowledge that difficulty and continue to make good-faith efforts to pursue disarmament. The injustice of the NPT bargain has become more glaringly obvious as the decades have passed, and the authors are right in this respect to pay attention to the implications of the NPT's indefinite extension in 1995, which attempted to turn a time-limited compromise into a lasting normative architecture. It may yet prove an impossible task, and the NPT is certainly losing its effectiveness as an arena for negotiating new bargains, as opposed to reaffirming existing ones. But for the majority of non-nuclear-weapon states, abstract nuclear injustice is probably still worth tolerating as long as it helps ward off real nuclear insecurity.

The authors claim that 'the intention behind the treaty was to build a house in which nuclear weapons would eventually become illegitimate and illegal'. To support this claim, and therefore to support their argument that the house should now be torn down, they would need to have provided evidence that this was the consensus, or at the least majority view, at the time the treaty was negotiated and ratified. This they do not do, and indeed, one of the authors wrote elsewhere only a few years ago that the 'NPT was not … an instrument meant to stigmatize nuclear-armed states'.[4]

Focusing exclusively on the NPT's role in advancing disarmament, meanwhile, leads the authors to neglect the importance of the treaty in underpinning broader global nuclear governance. It may be a cliché to call the NPT the 'cornerstone' of the non-proliferation and disarmament regime, but it is also true. The NPT provides normative and legal support to a range of global instruments regulating proliferation, including cooperation on export controls, the Iran nuclear deal and international responses both to North Korea's nuclear-weapons programme and to the three nuclear arsenals outside the NPT. The NPT, with 190 states parties, has also reached near-universal adherence.

The TPNW, the authors' preferred alternative, does not yet have nearly the same normative breadth and depth as the NPT, and it is unlikely to reach a comparable level of signatures until the day that global nuclear abolition is effectively a fait accompli (because no nuclear-armed state can sign the treaty until it is ready to lay out at least a tentative timetable for unilateral disarmament). Even if my interpretation of the historical purpose of the NPT is wrong, any plan to scrap the treaty needs to consider seriously how the gaps left in the international nuclear architecture would be filled – and, in the short to medium term, they surely cannot. Negotiating, implementing and expanding upon the NPT's provisions was hard enough the first time around. Transferring 50 years of progress in nuclear governance onto a contested treaty which lacks the participation of any of the nuclear-armed states – which is to say, any of the permanent members of the United Nations Security Council – sounds like a recipe for disaster.

*   *   *

There is no doubt that the NPT, as an instrument for disarmament, has failed to escape the unsatisfactory circumstances of its birth. But the diplomatic inadequacies of the NPT have to be measured against the utter catastrophe of nuclear war, which places a high burden of proof on anyone arguing that yet another treaty should be torn up. And in the section on the consequences of NPT withdrawal, the authors show why their critics consider their argument irresponsible. They concede the basic point that abandoning the NPT might help give cover to proliferators, while offering, as supposedly reassuring precedent, the fact that war has not yet broken out with North Korea. They sketch a scenario in which NPT withdrawal forces the existing nuclear powers to decide whether to stick to their weapons or conclude that they are tired of being 'nuclear rogues' and therefore disarm. Given the strong likelihood of the former outcome, it is difficult to understand why the authors would wish to help precipitate such a crisis.

The NPT's fatal crisis might come anyway, because much of the authors' diagnosis of the treaty's ill health is sound. But there is a difference between diagnosis and prescription, and actively advocating the collapse of the treaty goes beyond merely recognising the possibility that it might happen. In this context, the authors' casual admission that ditching the NPT becomes 'more complicated' if states go nuclear as a result is rather breathtaking. This is no abstract thought experiment: attempted proliferation could lead to wars; successful proliferation could lead to nuclear wars. And with arms control in tatters, we need to cling to every instrument of nuclear restraint we have. The NPT must stay.

Acknowledgements

The author would like to thank Gaukhar Mukhatzhanova and Tom Plant for their comments on a draft of this response.

Notes

1   See Joelien Pretorius and Tom Sauer, 'Is It Time to Ditch the NPT?', *Bulletin of the Atomic Scientists*, 6 September 2019, https://thebulletin.org/2019/09/is-it-time-to-ditch-the-npt/; and Joelien Pretorius and Tom Sauer, 'Ditch the NPT', *Survival*, vol. 63, no. 4, August–September 2021, pp. 103–24.

2   See Edward Ifft, 'The Joint Enterprise: Towards a World Without Nuclear Weapons', *Survival*, vol. 61, no. 1, February–March 2019, pp. 115–40.

3   For an expanded version of this assertion with reference to the negotiating record, see Matthew Harries, 'Disarmament as Politics: Lessons from the Negotiation of NPT Article VI', Chatham House, May 2015, https://www.chathamhouse.org/sites/default/files/field/field_document/20150512DisarmamentPoliticsNPTHarries.pdf.

4   Tom Sauer and Mathias Reveraert, 'The Potential Stigmatizing Effect of the Treaty on the Prohibition of Nuclear Weapons', *Nonproliferation Review*, vol. 25, nos 5–6, 2018, p. 4.

Manoeuvre Versus Attrition in US Military Operations

Franz-Stefan Gady

Attrition – defined as the depletion or destruction of an adversary's equipment, personnel and resources through a 'methodical use of battle or shaping operations' at a rate faster than the adversary can replace its losses[1] – has historically constituted American forces' primary modus operandi. But a consensus is rapidly emerging within the United States military that Chinese and Russian war-fighting methods, based on long-range sensors and precision munitions and enabled by emerging technological capabilities, are best countered by so-called multi-domain or all-domain operations.[2] These require the seamless integration of information and military capabilities across the air, sea, land, space and cyber domains. Central to such operations is the synchronisation of multi-domain manoeuvres to impose multiple cognitive dilemmas on an adversary, paralysing its leadership and breaking its cohesion.[3] The theoretical foundations of this way of war were laid by theorists such as J.F.C. Fuller, B.H. Liddell Hart and John Boyd.[4] This thinking, if fully embraced, would inform a new joint war-fighting concept or doctrine, and help determine the types of weapons systems and other equipment that are procured, the types and numbers of soldiers that are needed, and the kind of training that is required.[5]

The US approach has been to seek technical means of expediting Boyd's observation–orientation–decision–action (OODA) cycle through new artificial-intelligence-enabled command-and-control capabilities and Battle

Franz-Stefan Gady is IISS Research Fellow for Cyber, Space and Future Conflict.

Survival | vol. 63 no. 4 | August–September 2021 | pp. 131–148 https://doi.org/10.1080/00396338.2021.1956195

Management Systems that aim to accelerate decision-making and increase operational pace.[6]

Boyd believed that conflict should be conceived as a duel during which the adversaries observe (O) the actions of their enemies, orient (O) themselves and their forces to the evolving scenario, decide (D) on the most appropriate course of action or response, and finally act (A) to execute their plans. For them, the combatant who cycles through the OODA loop fastest is almost certain to gain the advantage by disrupting the adversary's ability to effectively respond.[7] The ultimate objective, however, would be to get inside the adversary's OODA loop. As Boyd put it: 'Such activity will make us appear ambiguous (unpredictable) [and] thereby generate confusion and disorder among our adversaries – since our adversaries will be unable to generate mental images or pictures that agree with the menacing as well as faster transient rhythm or patterns they are competing against.'[8] In the US armed forces, in particular the army and Marine Corps, rapid ground manoeuvres have been seen as one of the most effective means to achieve this goal. Boyd also considered the blitzkrieg campaign of the German Wehrmacht against Allied forces in France in May–June 1940 a prime example of manoeuvre warfare that caused widespread cognitive, psychological and physical paralysis and a swift collapse of the defence.[9]

Boyd downplayed the operational complexities and subtleties of that campaign.[10] More broadly, the practical feasibility of imposing multiple cognitive dilemmas and paralysis through manoeuvre on a capable enemy during high-intensity warfare – which rests on a questionable assumption that offensive elements will inherently dominate future battlespaces – has received insufficient attention. This aspect of multi-domain operations as a basis for American military doctrine should be rethought for three inter-related reasons. Firstly, the proliferation of emerging technologies – in particular, new intelligence, surveillance, target-acquisition and reconnaissance (ISTAR) capabilities – will make offensive military operations easier to detect and hence easier to counter. Secondly, the advantage of the defence will be amplified by an increase of attritable systems and platforms (such as uninhabited aerial and ground vehicles) in the battlespace. This will make detecting and exploiting 'windows of superiority' following paralysis – a core task of multi-domain operations – more difficult. Thirdly, except possibly in the opening phase of a great-power war, defence will likely enjoy the upper hand in cyberspace and thus impede successful manoeuvre in that domain. The same may hold true for the space domain. This is not to say that the concept of manoeuvre itself is outdated or that it has no place in future military doctrine or operations. But relying on imposing cognitive dilemmas through multi-domain manoeuvre is risky.

Origin and tenets of multi-domain operations

The US defence establishment regards the Chinese People's Liberation Army's 'Informationised Warfare' and the Russian 'New Generation Warfare' concepts as direct challenges to existing US military doctrine.[11] In 2015, the US Army was tasked to develop 'AirLand Battle 2.0', which led to the concept of multi-domain operations.[12] For US military planners, a key objective in any future high-intensity great-power warfare scenarios was the defeat of Russian and Chinese anti-access/area-denial (A2/AD) systems following faits accomplis in the Baltics and Taiwan, respectively.[13] These systems were seen as the main impediments to an effective US-led counter-offensive campaign.

According to a provisional definition from the US Army Training and Doctrine Command, multi-domain operations are

> conducted across multiple domains and contested spaces to overcome an adversary's (or enemy's) strengths by presenting them with several operational and/or tactical dilemmas through the combined application of calibrated force posture; employment of multi-domain formations; and convergence of capabilities across domains, environments, and functions in time and spaces to achieve operational and tactical objectives.[14]

This multi-domain operational concept is expected to constitute the foundational element of the new 'Joint Warfighting Concept for All-domain Operations' under development by the Joint Chiefs of Staff.[15]

Key to multi-domain operations is offensive manoeuvre warfare supported by long-range kinetic and non-kinetic precision-strike capabilities for defeating an enemy without necessarily wreaking physical destruction. While attrition-oriented firepower has an important role to play, it is cast primarily as an enabling capability meant to support and facilitate 'freedom of maneuver to achieve operational and strategic objectives by defeating enemy forces in all domains'.[16] In 2020, US Army Futures Command published its own 'Concept for Maneuver in Multi-domain Operations 2028', which details the central idea of manoeuvre under the new operational concept:

> Simultaneous multi-echelon convergence of capabilities from all domains and environments to contest decisive spaces enables Army forces to maneuver to penetrate and dis-integrate the enemy's layered standoff. This maneuver generates temporary windows of superiority, and exploits those opportunities to seize the initiative, gain positions of relative advantage, and generate overmatch.[17]

The publication reiterates that the main objective of the operational concept remains paralysis, leading to the breakdown of the enemy's cognitive cohesion.[18]

How would such paralysis and loss of cohesion look in practice? Imagine an attack launched by a US Army armoured brigade against a hardened Russian defensive position in the Baltics protected by an integrated and layered missile-defence system, often referred to as an A2/AD system. The attack would be preceded by synchronised offensive cyber- and electronic-warfare operations as part of a campaign to suppress enemy air defences so as to disrupt Russian command-and-control nodes, radar stations and missile batteries. It would be further supported by long-range precision strikes on Russian rear-echelon forces to prevent reinforcements from counter-attacking. These operations would incapacitate Russian division- and corps-level leadership. At the same time, air-superiority fighters and ground-based air-defence systems would aim to keep the airspace free of Russian aircraft and defend against incoming missiles. The actual armoured thrust of the brigade would be supported by mechanised artillery and infantry, and directed against an enemy to a large extent already leaderless.

The attack would be coordinated in the mobile headquarters of the US corps commander, who, thanks to an Advanced Battle Management System, would have access to a cross-domain common operational picture providing wide situational awareness and accelerating decision-making.[19] In an ideal scenario, American armour would rapidly encircle enemy forces, cut supply lines and compel the Russian defenders to capitulate.

Perhaps the most comprehensive criticism of multi-domain operations to date has come from Huba Wass de Czege, a retired army officer who led the team that produced the US Army Field Manual for operations – its keystone war-fighting doctrine – and the original AirLand Battle concept in 1982. De Czege notes the absence of precise language, a well-developed theory of the problem and a logical theory of victory. In a direct challenge to its manoeuvre-centric approach, he also criticises the concept's lack of focus on defence and emphasis on symmetrically matching enemy aggression: 'The United States and our allies would conduct a counteroffensive campaign of reconquest in the form of a strategic movement to contact, which plays right into the strong conventional and nuclear defensive posture of our adversaries.'[20] De Czege does not, however, discuss the question of imposing multiple dilemmas on the enemy leading to paralysis. Heather Venable does question the tenet of paralysis, noting that the 'seeming logic of paralysis affects various aspects of past and recent US military doctrine without adequately assessing its embedded assumptions about how well it works in practice'.[21] But she confines her assessment largely to conceptual and historical analysis.

An official US Joint Chiefs of Staff publication sketching out the operating environment in 2035 confronts the paralysis issue more directly. It appears to throw cold water on any assumption of an enemy collapse based on paralysis, and instead suggests that attrition will be the dominant characteristic of future great-power wars. It notes that adversary forces will have the ability to deploy cutting-edge technological innovations, including sophisticated assets such as 'advanced C3/ISR and information technologies', and 'lethal precision strike and area effect weapons'.[22] To counter such capabilities, the study recommends that US forces first reduce adversary defences at range, then deploy 'speedy, targeted offensive actions' against the adversary's 'global and regional strike assets', including nuclear capabilities, and finally utilise combined offensive operations to secure key territories that would permanently eliminate any remnant resistance from the adversary. Most crucially, the study cautions that such future conflict is 'unlikely to be won quickly or cheaply' and may extend into multiple years given the 'global presence and influence of powerful adversaries'.[23]

Constraints on manoeuvre

The principal reason for the advantage of defence over offence in high-intensity great-power war fighting is the spread of ISTAR capabilities in the modern battlespace, which will make the undetected manoeuvre of large formations prohibitively challenging. Early detection of an attacking force would significantly reduce the psychological impact of attack, since the element of surprise – key to inducing shock and paralysis – would likely be lost.

Offensive operations in the modern battlespace have become particularly challenging because moving, shooting, communicating or employing active sensors (for example, radar) can be detected directly or indirectly by radar or electronic, electro-optical and other advanced sensors, placing military assets at early risk of being identified and targeted. Defensive operations, aside from limited local counter-attacks, rely less on manoeuvre and more on concealment and concentrated firepower. Shorter interior communication lines and less need for ad hoc communication and movement significantly reduce a trained defender's exposure in the electromagnetic spectrum.

Armenia's recent experience in the war in Nagorno-Karabakh is an instructive counter-example in this regard. Reconnaissance via uninhabited aerial vehicles (UAVs) afforded Azerbaijani forces advance warning of Armenian concentrations of forces and counter-offensive movements, and the Azerbaijani UAVs were quickly able to identify and target static Armenian positions. But electronic countermeasures (for example, jamming) could have provided significant protection to Armenian forces if they had been embedded in an integrated air-defence system. Furthermore, emerging technological capabilities could allow the quick identification of an attacking force. These include passive radar receivers, which can rely on existing radio and communications networks, and three-dimensional mobile long-range very-high-frequency radar systems that can detect stealth aircraft.[24] These and other low-observable tools would reduce the chances that an attacking force could achieve surprise and, consequently, paralysis. This does not doom offensive operations against well-equipped adversaries to failure. But it does suggest that rapid and decisive results based on disrupting an enemy's OODA loop should not be expected.[25]

Thus, the defence enjoys a structural advantage. Existing and emerging ISTAR capabilities now compel both attacker and defender to build operations around complex multiple defensive layers, and these favour the relatively stationary defender. For an offensive force, there is a greater chance that a crucial defensive layer will be lost or rendered ineffective during rapid manoeuvres. Ground formations may find themselves operating outside their air and electronic-warfare defensive umbrellas, leaving them exposed to kinetic and electromagnetic attacks. The operational history of deep manoeuvres is filled with examples of analogous eventualities.[26] And even assuming offensive forces do stay inside their umbrellas, the very compulsion to do so reduces the speed and operational flexibility of the offensive force. If an attack can only take place under air and electromagnetic protection, it would be difficult for the attacker to achieve an operational tempo high enough to trigger major cognitive dilemmas for the enemy.

More broadly, the multi-domain operational concept poses problems for manoeuvre because it violates a core principle of US military doctrine: simplicity.[27] And lack of simplicity tends to invite Clausewitzian friction. Coordinating and synchronising attacks across multiple domains offer numerous opportunities for mistakes, with the consequences substantially greater for the attacker than for the defender.

The US military is attempting to mitigate the complexity problem by way of the Joint All-Domain Command and Control (JADC2), which connects sensors from the different US service branches into a single network, thereby providing military commanders with a common operating picture.[28] But doubts have arisen about the ability of a centralised architecture to operate in a degraded operating environment.[29] Basing an operating concept substantially on an emerging technological capability also risks a single point of failure. The US Army's failed Future Combat Systems (cancelled in 2009 by Robert Gates, then secretary of defense) had over 60 million lines of code that would have exposed it to cyber vulnerabilities and software-upgrade challenges.[30] It is also unclear how accelerated operational speed and convergence (that is, the synchronised use of kinetic and non-kinetic capabilities from different domains to strike an enemy) based on JADC2 could trigger cognitive dilemmas in an enemy if the latter were already expecting a multi-domain attack.

The return of mass

The spread of ISTAR capabilities and precision-guided munitions has caused US military thinkers to push for a more geographically dispersed force structure, particularly in East Asia. The US Marine Corps' new 'Force Design 2030' advocates the establishment of dispersed units capable of operating within the 'weapons engagement zones' of great-power adversaries.[31] Likewise, the US Navy's 'Distributed Maritime Operations' are based on a dispersed force structure.[32] The US Army's multi-domain operational concept also emphasises dispersal.[33] Combat effectiveness in ground operations, however, is impossible to achieve without some degree of massing, which dispersal renders more difficult. Evolving American doctrine tries to finesse the increased vulnerability that massing implies by prescribing prompt re-dispersal. Following concentrated cross-domain fires from disaggregated locations, formations would 'mass from dispersed locations on multiple axes to defeat opposing adversary forces in swift close maneuver, then quickly disperse, and maneuver to subsequent objectives'.[34] There is no viable alternative to massing, as it is doubtful that offensive cyber operations could achieve cognitive dilemmas comparable to the chaos that massed manoeuvre forces could generate with kinetic firepower. More likely, cyber operations would systematically destroy or disable enemy defences, achieving an effect more akin to attrition than manoeuvre.

The fact remains that it will take time to concentrate dispersed formations, thus jeopardising the element of surprise, which remains crucial to successful manoeuvre warfare. Moreover, the shift from dispersed to massed forces would expose the attacking force to counter-attack. An offensive force could deploy relatively inexpensive drones en masse to overwhelm an adversary, supporting the effort with long-range precision strikes.[35] But it would still find itself at a disadvantage since it would first have to disrupt enemy defensive layers, affording the defender tactical warning. Thus, on balance, the defence is favoured even in a UAV massing scenario, and an attacker's ability to exploit vulnerabilities in defences sinks as total force levels increase.[36] Mass tends to favour the defence. It appears doubtful that synchronised mass attacks from multiple domains would achieve the desired effect of paralysis in a reasonably capable defender.[37]

While dispersal makes considerable tactical sense, 'the proliferation of cheap means of surveillance suggests that forces will have to accept much higher levels of attrition, especially against firepower-heavy militaries like Russia's'.[38] If multilayered defences could reduce these vulnerabilities, it would be at the expense of operational speed and surprise. Ironically, for many future attackers, concentrating rather than dispersing forces under a layered defensive umbrella may turn out to be the most economical and low-casualty move.

US military thinkers are hoping to solve this operational dilemma by accelerating and improving decision-making while degrading the quality and speed of enemy decision-making.[39] Under the Defense Advanced Research Projects Agency's mosaic-warfare concept, for example, the battlefield is viewed as an 'emergent, complex system' in which swarming formations of low-cost UAVs can be augmented by electronic and cyber attacks assisted by artificial intelligence (AI) to overwhelm adversaries, and then be quickly disaggregated to minimise system vulnerability.[40] As with JADC2, however, such a technology-driven solution may produce multiple points of technical failure. It also presupposes the offensive advantage of uninhabited swarms, which appears doubtful. And it is unclear whether an AI-enabled process could compose an effective mosaic of capabilities without understanding an adversary network or system of systems at a level of detail that is unattainable.[41]

Cyber and space

Cyberspace is traditionally thought to favour the offence over defence during peacetime, since the former need only exploit a single vulnerability while the latter has to plug many of them.[42] In 2018, US Cyber Command shifted from a relatively static to a more proactive strategy by which it seeks to seize the initiative.[43] This requires manoeuvre. Manoeuvre in cyberspace involves 'gaining access to adversary, enemy, or intermediary links and nodes and shaping this cyberspace to support future actions'.[44] Peacetime efforts, including forward defence and intelligence operations, can furnish opportunities for offensive cyber manoeuvre at the outset of hostilities. For military commanders to ensure success during high-intensity war fighting, they would have to take several factors into account.[45]

Firstly, actual combat will likely reduce or even negate the utility of prepared cyber-attack packages, and additional cyber-attack options may take too much time to develop to be useful. Given the significant advantages US forces continue to enjoy in cyberspace, peer and near-peer adversaries such as China and Russia are probably already in the process of hardening targets, thus increasing the chances of blunting offensive manoeuvres in cyberspace.[46] Secondly, even if an attack is successful, redundant capacities would most likely mitigate its effect.[47] Thirdly, integrating cyber operations with kinetic operations in other domains may prove difficult because an effective network defender is likely to change and update security protocols more often in wartime. Fourthly, internal and external obstacles that impede information-sharing can diminish the impact of the offence.[48] Fifthly, fears about the collateral damage caused by offensive cyber capabilities and uncertainty about adversaries' resiliency may inhibit offensive operations.[49] Finally, the trend towards multilayered defensive systems may eventually render defence more capable than offence in the cyber realm.[50] These factors suggest that offensive cyber capabilities deployed in high-intensity war-fighting scenarios may not be capable of rapidly and totally paralysing an adversary's critical information, triggering psychological collapse. As a result, achieving cognitive dilemmas by way of manoeuvring in cyberspace may prove difficult for the US military.

Furthermore, a key tenet of multi-domain operations is the denial of the use of the cyber and space domains to the enemy, thereby causing multiple dilemmas and paralysis, while friendly forces continue to exercise freedom of manoeuvre. According to the US Space Force, 'space warfare targets the mind of an adversary and seeks to neutralize their capability and will to resist … Military space forces must prepare to outwit, outmanoeuvre, and dominate thinking, competent, and lethal aggressors who are attempting to thwart US actions.'[51] Doctrine also calls for exploiting 'fleeting battlespace opportunities' while preventing 'decision paralysis' via space-domain awareness.[52] Consequently, the US goal of space warfare is neither attrition nor annihilation, but to break the enemy's will to resist by superior battlespace awareness, accelerated decision-making and manoeuvre, all of which are also core premises of multi-domain operations.

Supporting the emphasis on manoeuvre is the widely held perception that the space domain also favours the offence over the defence. The late Colin Gray, for instance, posited that 'offense may appear to be the stronger form of war in space, given the absence of terrain obstacles, the relative paucity of capital assets (and targets), and the global consequences of military success or failure'.[53] Andrew Krepinevich argued in congressional testimony that space is an 'offense-dominant' domain'.[54] 'Always the predator, never the prey', then-US Air Force secretary Heather Wilson stated in 2019, highlighting the offence-minded disposition of senior American leaders.[55]

A key technical basis for such statements is that satellites appear to be highly vulnerable to attack. They travel in predictable orbits, lack robust defences against kinetic attacks, and can be targeted and disabled by means of offensive cyber operations or electronic attacks. Fears about the vulnerability of satellites and the dependency of the US Armed Forces on space for conducting operations have led to alarm over the prospect of a 'Space Pearl Harbor' inflicted by Russian or Chinese first strikes.[56] However, beyond individual satellite and data-link vulnerabilities, defence may still have the advantage over offence in the space domain on account of the resilience of US space-systems architecture.[57] Redundancy in space assets paired with effective cyber and electronic defences can also protect celestial lines of communication – data links – from degradation, further diminishing the impact of the offence. Most importantly, in a high-intensity war-fighting scenario, mutual great-power dependency on space for military operations is likely to reciprocally deter massive first strikes.[58] Absent a decisive all-out first strike in the space domain, space capabilities that support military operations on earth would likely remain intact, which would decrease the chances that one side could outmanoeuvre or cognitively flummox the other in conventional warfare and potentially give rise to attrition.

*   *   *

The introduction of more sophisticated and readily available ISTAR capabilities, the return of mass to the battlespace, the need for force dispersion, and likely defence advantages in the cyber and space domains will reduce the impact of manoeuvre. Accordingly, the US armed forces should critically re-examine their ability to achieve cognitive dilemmas and paralysis through manoeuvre to inform future US force structures, procurement, war-fighting concepts and military strategy.

For the US military to continue insisting that manoeuvre is central to breaking enemy cohesion under the multi-domain operational concept by imposing multiple cognitive dilemmas risks misreading the future operating environment. For one thing, it is unclear whether the confined geography of the battlespace in some contingencies would permit extensive physical manoeuvres. Furthermore, continuing to pursue a manoeuvre-centric approach may also increase the chances of excessive US casualties in future wars because of the inability of mobility and speed to compensate for layered defences. Doctrinal debates within the French army between 1871 and 1914 might be instructive in this regard. French military leaders incrementally shifted from an approach that emphasised the importance of firepower, dispersion and defence to one focused on offensive manoeuvres and their cognitive dimension – *élan* – as the key to operational success.[59] The most obvious consequence was a reduction in French artillery capabilities in both number and calibre, which, in the defence-dominant operating environment of the First World War, proved disastrous.

The essential question for US doctrine is to what degree a preoccupation with manoeuvre and paralysis would impede the creation of a force structure that can at once yield greater kinetic and non-kinetic firepower and endure in an operating environment dominated by the defence. US strategists should pay more attention to attrition and to positional warfare – that is, the use of force to move the adversary to a desired position or prohibit it from accessing an area in order to exploit one. An attrition- or position-centric approach may place greater emphasis on concentrated firepower, and yield a clearer and more systematic programme for degrading enemy capabilities from a more defensive posture. It would drop the doctrinal ideal of imposing cognitive dilemmas and paralysis through manoeuvre, and instead focus on layered kinetic and non-kinetic strike capabilities for slowly but steadily depleting enemy assets – an updated variant of the French 'Methodical Battle', whereby manoeuvre and precision fires are seen as interchangeable in the future battlespace to neutralise mobile or stationary targets.[60]

The concept of multi-domain operations reflects a concentrated effort to integrate a suite of advanced new technologies and capabilities that have the potential to increase the intensity and speed of otherwise traditional joint and combined-arms operations, and, crucially, to blunt an enemy's efforts to execute them. But the speed and distributed nature of offensive multi-domain operations may ultimately render them even more vulnerable to the traditional weak points of exposed forward elements – namely, supply, repair, lines of communication and force protection. Understanding multi-domain operations as different in degree rather than in kind from traditional military operations should nourish due scepticism about claims that they provide a unique or wholly new ability to achieve strategic or political goals.

Notes

[1] Amos C. Fox, 'A Solution Looking for a Problem: Illuminating Misconceptions in Maneuver-warfare Doctrine', *Armor*, Fall 2017, p. 3, https://www.benning.army.mil/ armor/eARMOR/content/issues/2017/ Fall/4Fox17.pdf.

[2] See the introduction in Thomas G. Mahnken, *Technology and the American Way of War Since 1945* (New York:

Columbia University Press, 2008).

3   'Collectively, convergence of capa-
     bilities and ground-based maneuver
     present a set of dilemmas leading
     to paralysis caused by the over-
     whelming of adversary command
     and control systems.' US Army
     Futures Command, 'Army Futures
     Command Concept for Maneuver in
     Multi-domain Operations 2028', AFC
     Pamphlet 71-20-1, 7 July 2020, p. 27,
     https://api.army.mil/e2/c/downloads/2
     021/01/20/2fbeccee/20200707-afc-71-20-
     1-maneuver-in-mdo-final-v16-dec-20.
     pdf. A provisional definition of
     (multi-domain) manoeuvre is 'the
     employment of forces through
     movement in combination with
     lethal and nonlethal effects across
     multiple domains, the electromag-
     netic spectrum, and the information
     environment to destroy or defeat
     enemy forces, control land areas and
     resources, and protect populations'.
     Ibid., p. 78.

4   See David S. Fadok, *John Boyd and
     John Warden: Air Power's Quest for
     Strategic Paralysis* (Montgomery,
     AL: Air University Press, 1995), p. v,
     https://media.defense.gov/2017/
     Dec/27/2001861508/-1/-1/0/T_0029_
     FADOK_BOYD_AND_WARDEN.PDF.

5   See Andrew Feickert, 'Defense Primer:
     Army Multi-domain Operations
     (MDO)', In Focus Brief, Congressional
     Research Service, updated 22 April
     2021, p. 1, https://fas.org/sgp/crs/
     natsec/IF11409.pdf.

6   See, for example, Robert O. Work,
     'A Joint Warfighting Concept for
     Systems Warfare', Center for a New
     American Security, 17 December 2020,
     https://www.cnas.org/publications/

commentary/a-joint-warfighting-
concept-for-systems-warfare. For a
detailed description of the OODA
cycle, see John R. Boyd, *A Discourse on
Winning and Losing* (Montgomery, AL:
Air University Press, 2018), p. 384.

7   See Stephen Robinson, *The Blind
     Strategist: John Boyd and the American
     Way of War* (Dunedin: Exisle
     Publishing, 2021), p. 11.

8   John Boyd, 'Patterns of Conflict',
     Defense and the National Interest,
     January 2007, http://www.
     projectwhitehorse.com/pdfs/boyd/
     patterns%20of%20conflict.pdf.

9   *Ibid.*, p. 6

10   See generally Robinson, *The Blind
     Strategist.*

11   See Peter L. Jones et al., 'Unclassified
     Summary of the US Army Training
     and Doctrine Command Russian
     New Generation Warfare Study',
     US Army Training and Doctrine
     Command, March 2020, https://www.
     armyupress.army.mil/Portals/7/
     online-publications/documents/
     RNGW-Unclassified-Summary-Report.
     pdf?ver=2020-03-25-122734-383.

12   See Kelly McCoy, 'The Road to Multi-
     domain Battle: An Origin Story',
     Modern War Institute at West Point,
     27 October 2017, https://mwi.usma.
     edu/road-multi-domain-battle-origin-
     story/. The original AirLand Battle
     doctrine, introduced in 1982, has
     achieved almost mythical status in US
     doctrinal-development circles as it is
     seen as having played a central role in
     the swift allied defeat of Iraqi forces in
     Kuwait in the 1991 Gulf War.

13   It is the United States, not China or
     Russia, that perceived and formulated
     the A2/AD challenge. See Mike

Pietrucha, 'Avoiding the Charge of the Light Brigade Against China', *War on the Rocks*, 22 November 2019, https://warontherocks.com/2019/11/avoiding-the-charge-of-the-light-brigade-against-china-2/.

14 US Army Training and Doctrine Command, 'The US Army in Multi-domain Operations 2028', TRADOC Pamphlet 525-3-1, p. GL–7, https://adminpubs.tradoc.army.mil/pamphlets/TP525-3-1.pdf.

15 *Ibid.*

16 Feickert, 'Defense Primer', p. 1.

17 US Army Futures Command, 'Army Futures Command Concept for Maneuver in Multi-domain Operations 2028', p. vi.

18 See *ibid.*, p. 27; and US Army Training and Doctrine Command, 'The US Army in Multi-domain Operations 2028', p. 43.

19 See John R. Hoehn, 'Joint All-Domain Command and Control (JADC2)', In Focus Brief, Congressional Research Service, 16 November 2020, pp. 1–2, https://fas.org/sgp/crs/natsec/IF11493.pdf.

20 Huba Wass de Czege, 'Commentary on "The US Army in Multi-domain Operations 2028"', Strategic Studies Institute, US Army War College, April 2020, p. xxi, https://publications.armywarcollege.edu/pubs/3726.pdf.

21 See Heather Venable, 'Paralysis in Peer Conflict? The Material Versus the Mental in 100 Years of Military Thinking', *War on the Rocks*, 1 December 2020, https://warontherocks.com/2020/12/paralysis-in-peer-conflict-the-material-versus-the-mental-in-100-years-of-military-thinking/.

22 US Joint Chiefs of Staff, 'Joint Operating Environment 2035: The Joint Force in a Contested and Disordered World', 14 July 2016, p. 15, https://www.jcs.mil/Portals/36/Documents/Doctrine/concepts/joe_2035_july16.pdf?ver=2017-12-28-162059-917. 'C3/ISR' refers to command, control, communications, intelligence, surveillance and reconnaissance.

23 *Ibid.*, p. 49.

24 See, for example, Gordon Arthur, 'Zhuhai 2016: Stealth Aircraft on China's Radar', Shephard Media, 10 November 2016, https://www.shephardmedia.com/news/digital-battlespace/zhuhai-2016-stealth-aircraft-appear-chinas-radar-s/.

25 See Alastair Luft, 'The OODA Loop and the Half-beat', The Strategy Bridge, 17 March 2020, https://thestrategybridge.org/the-bridge/2020/3/17/the-ooda-loop-and-the-half-beat; and Arend G. Westra, 'Radar Versus Stealth: Passive Radar and the Future of US Military Power', *Joint Force Quarterly*, no. 55, 4th quarter 2009, p. 142, https://apps.dtic.mil/dtic/tr/fulltext/u2/a515506.pdf.

26 For example, German armour in France in May and June 1940; and Israeli armour during the Six-Day War in 1967 and the Yom Kippur War of 1973.

27 See US Joint Chiefs of Staff, 'Doctrine for the Armed Forces of the United States', Joint Publication 1, 25 March 2013 (updated 12 July 2017), pp. i–3, https://fas.org/irp/doddir/dod/jp1.pdf.

28 See Hoehn, 'Joint All-Domain Command and Control (JADC2)', pp. 1–2; and Sherrill Lingel et al., *Joint*

All-domain Command and Control for Modern Warfare: An Analytic Framework for Identifying and Developing Artificial Intelligence Applications (Santa Monica, CA: RAND Corporation, 2020), p. 8.

29 See Hoehn, 'Joint All-Domain Command and Control (JADC2)'.

30 See Christopher G. Pernin et al., *Lessons from the Army's Future Combat Systems Program* (Santa Monica, CA: RAND Corporation, 2012), p. 84.

31 See Nick Childs, 'US Marine Corps Raises the Flag – and New Questions – on Future Force Design', IISS Military Balance Blog, 3 April 2020, https://www.iiss.org/blogs/military-balance/2020/04/united-states-marine-corps-future-force-design.

32 See James Holmes, 'Distributed Lethality: The Navy's Fix for Anti-access?', *War on the Rocks*, 19 January 2015, https://warontherocks.com/2015/01/distributed-lethality-the-navys-fix-for-anti-access/.

33 At the same time, dispersal seems somewhat at odds with a state-of-the-art layered defensive approach, given that it may be unrealistic to provide a widely dispersed force with air defences sufficient to protect it.

34 US Army Futures Command, 'Army Futures Command Concept for Maneuver in Multi-domain Operations 2028', p. 46.

35 See T.X. Hammes, 'Expeditionary Operations in the Fourth Industrial Revolution', *MCU Journal*, vol. 8, no. 1, Spring 2017, p. 96.

36 See Ben Garfinkel and Allan Dafoe, 'How Does the Offense–Defense Balance Scale?', *Journal of Strategic Studies*, vol. 42, no. 6, September 2019, pp. 736–63.

37 See Margarita Konaev, 'With AI, We'll See Faster Fights but Longer Wars', *War on the Rocks*, 29 October 2019, https://warontherocks.com/2019/10/with-ai-well-see-faster-fights-but-longer-wars/.

38 Michael Kofman, 'A Look at the Military Lessons of the Nagorno-Karabakh Conflict', Russia Matters, 14 December 2020, https://www.russiamatters.org/analysis/look-military-lessons-nagorno-karabakh-conflict.

39 See Bryan Clark, Dan Patt and Harrison Schramm, 'Mosaic Warfare: Exploiting Artificial Intelligence and Autonomous Systems to Implement Decision-centric Operations', Center for Strategic and Budgetary Assessments, 2020, p. iv, https://csbaonline.org/uploads/documents/Mosaic_Warfare_Web.pdf.

40 See Benjamin Jensen and John Paschkewitz, 'Mosaic Warfare: Small and Scalable Are Beautiful', *War on the Rocks*, 23 December 2019, https://warontherocks.com/2019/12/mosaic-warfare-small-and-scalable-are-beautiful/; and Work, 'A Joint Warfighting Concept for Systems Warfare'.

41 See Peng Liu, 'Měijūn Mǎsàikè Zhàn de 'ā Kā Liú Sī Zhī Zhǒng' [The 'Achilles Heel' of the US Army Mosaic War], 81.cn, 1 March 2021, http://www.81.cn/gfbmap/content/2021-03/01/content_283736.htm.

42 See Jason Healey, 'The Attacker Has the Advantage in Cyberspace. Can We Fix That?', The Cipher Brief, 25 March 2018, https://www.thecipherbrief.com/column_article/attacker-advantage-cyberspace-can-fix; and John B.

Sheldon, 'Cyber War: Cyberattack and Cyberdefense', *Encyclopaedia Britannica*, 25 May 2016, https://www.britannica.com/topic/cyberwar/Cyberattack-and-cyberdefense.

43 See Joshua Rovner, 'More Aggressive and Less Ambitious: Cyber Command's Evolving Approach', *War on the Rocks*, 14 September 2020, https://warontherocks.com/2020/09/more-aggressive-and-less-ambitious-cyber-commands-evolving-approach/.

44 US Joint Chiefs of Staff, 'Cyberspace Operations', Joint Publication 3-12, 8 June 2018, p. xii, https://www.jcs.mil/Portals/36/Documents/Doctrine/pubs/jp3_12.pdf.

45 See generally Rebecca Slayton, 'What Is the Cyber Offense–Defense Balance? Conceptions, Causes, and Assessment', *International Security*, vol. 41, no. 3, Winter 2016/2017, pp. 72–109.

46 See IISS, 'Cyber Capabilities and National Power: A Net Assessment', Research Paper, June 2021, https://www.iiss.org/blogs/research-paper/2021/06/cyber-capabilities-national-power; and Jacquelyn G. Schneider et al., 'Ten Years In: Implementing Strategic Approaches to Cyberspace', Newport Papers 45, US Naval War College, 2020, p. 86, https://digital-commons.usnwc.edu/cgi/viewcontent.cgi?article=1044&context=usnwc-newport-papers.

47 See Schneider et al., 'Ten Years In'.

48 See Jon R. Lindsay, *Information Technology and Military Power* (Ithaca, NY: Cornell University Press, 2020), p. 239.

49 This consideration influenced the US debate about the use of offensive cyber capabilities in Libya in 2011. See Eric Schmitt and Thom Shanker, 'US Debated Cyberwarfare in Attack Plan on Libya', *New York Times*, 17 October 2011, https://www.nytimes.com/2011/10/18/world/africa/cyber-warfare-against-libya-was-debated-by-us.html.

50 See David T. Fahrenkrug, 'Countering the Offensive Advantage in Cyberspace: An Integrated Defensive Strategy', 4th International Conference on Cyber Conflict, NATO CCDCOE, 2012, p. 206, https://ccdcoe.org/uploads/2012/01/3_4_Fahrenkrug_AnIntegratedDefensiveStrategy.pdf.

51 US Space Force, 'Spacepower: Doctrine for Space Forces', 2020, p. 21, https://www.spaceforce.mil/Portals/1/Space%20Capstone%20Publication_10%20Aug%202020.pdf.

52 *Ibid.*, p. 42.

53 See Colin S. Gray, *Weapons Don't Make War: Policy, Strategy and Military Technology* (Lawrence, KS: University Press of Kansas, 1993).

54 Andrew F. Krepinevich, Jr, 'US–China Relations in 2019: A Year in Review', Testimony Before US–China Economic and Security Review Commission, Hudson Institute, September 2019, https://s3.amazonaws.com/media.hudson.org/Krepinevich_US-China%20Relations%20in%202019%20Testimony.pdf.

55 Quoted in Valerie Insinna, 'Air Force Leaders on Space Deterrence: "At Some Point, We've Got to Hit Back"', *Defense News*, 16 April 2019, https://www.defensenews.com/space/2019/04/16/air-force-leaders-on-space-deterrence-at-some-point-weve-got-to-hit-back/.

56 See Jean-Michel Stoullig, 'Rumsfeld

Commission Warns Against "Space Pearl Harbor"', *Space Daily*, 11 January 2001, https://www.spacedaily.com/news/bmdo-01b.html; and Brandon J. Weichert, 'Why the US Is Risking a Pearl Harbor in Space', *New York Post*, 12 September 2020, https://nypost.com/2020/09/12/why-the-us-is-risking-a-pearl-harbor-in-space/.

57   See Bradley Townsend, 'Space: An Offense-dominant Environment?', *Purview*, January–March 2019, http://webcache.googleusercontent.com/search?q=cache:J8WqPS KJ9f4J:purview.dodlive.mil/files/2018/12/Townsend-Space-An-Offense-Dominant-Environment.pdf+&cd=1&hl=en&ct=clnk&gl=uk; and Brad Townsend, 'Strategic Choice and the Orbital Security Dilemma',

Strategic Studies Quarterly, vol. 14, no. 1, Spring 2020, pp. 64–90.

58   See Bleddyn E. Bowen, *War in Space: Strategy, Spacepower, Geopolitics* (Edinburgh: Edinburgh University Press, 2020), pp. 255–6.

59   See Eric W. Kaempfer, 'Army Doctrine Development: The French Experience, 1871–1914', *Army History*, no. 28, Autumn 1993, p. 15.

60   See Eugenia C. Kiesling, '"If It Ain't Broke, Don't Fix It"': French Military Doctrine Between the World Wars', *War in History*, vol. 3, no. 2, April 1996, pp. 208–23; and Peter Layton, 'Fighting Artificial Intelligence Battles: Operational Concepts for Future AI-enabled Wars', Joint Studies Paper Series No. 4, Australian Department of Defence, 2021, p. 54.

What the India–Russia Defence Partnership Means for US Policy

Sameer Lalwani and Tyler Sagerstrom

For almost two decades, the United States and India have significantly expanded and deepened defence cooperation based on mutual recognition of the rise of China. Four presidential administrations have invested in this defence partnership on a bipartisan basis, guided in part by a logic of 'strategic altruism'.[1] But in his January 2021 farewell address, Kenneth Juster, the departing US ambassador to India, warned of certain 'tradeoffs' and 'choices' that India needed to make as it sought defence capabilities from both Russia and the United States.[2] A week later, US diplomatic officials indicated that India was likely to be sanctioned under the Countering America's Adversaries Through Sanctions Act (CAATSA) if it took delivery of the advanced Russian S-400 air-defence system, a warning reiterated during Secretary of Defense Lloyd Austin III's first trip to India.[3] Indian analysts have decried such threats as pressure tactics, a 'mailed fist in a velvet glove', while retired senior political and military leaders said that such actions could jeopardise the US–India strategic partnership.[4] Since then, the US Congress – most notably Senate Foreign Relations Chairman Robert Menendez – has only grown more vocal in the insistence that India be hit with sanctions should its S-400 purchase proceed.[5]

For decades, the US has frowned upon India's defence relationship with Russia. Beyond concerns that Russian arms crowd out US weapons sales, Washington worries that India's political and economic relationship

Sameer Lalwani is Senior Fellow and Director of the South Asia Program at the Stimson Center. **Tyler Sagerstrom** is a Research Assistant in the South Asia Program at the Stimson Center.

Survival | vol. 63 no. 4 | August–September 2021 | pp. 149–182   https://doi.org/10.1080/00396338.2021.1956196

at least tacitly abets Russian 'malign' behaviour, which the US has identified as a primary global challenge.[6] Most importantly, the US government is concerned about the counter-intelligence risks that the presence of Russian systems, technicians and military personnel could limit or foreclose certain types of defence cooperation – including intelligence-sharing, technology transfers, and joint exercises and operations – that Washington would like to develop with New Delhi.

Consequently, a chorus of American voices has encouraged India to 'forget Russia', recognise it is an 'unreliable long-term defence partner' and 'phase out Russian systems', lest it lose out on large-scale defence-industrial cooperation with the US.[7] US officials perceive arms purchases as part of a strategic calculus and expect India to make a 'commitment' to a new arms supplier, even while acknowledging its need to sustain existing equipment.[8] While some have suggested that India is already 'gradually shifting' its acquisitions from Russian to American platforms, and just needs time, the US seems determined to induce the acceleration of any such shift.[9]

Americans have encouraged India to 'forget Russia'

India's relationship with Russia is likely to come under more intense scrutiny, which could damage US–India relations. The Biden administration has signalled a tougher approach to Russia than the last administration, driven by recent provocations, clashing ambitions and bipartisan congressional pressure.[10] Moreover, US strategists see India's growing demand for US military assistance after the recent border dispute with China as an appropriate spur to more sweeping changes. Most importantly, the 2017 CAATSA legislation enacted to isolate Russia compels secondary sanctions for any significant transactions with the Russian defence sector, placing the US–India defence relationship at greater risk when India takes delivery of the S-400 battalions in late 2021. Although waivers of CAATSA are permitted, they are narrowly designed merely to 'wean countries off Russian equipment' and not to effect wholesale changes in policy.[11]

Increased US pressure stems not only from a desire to punish Moscow, but also from the perception that the S-400 acquisition could be a tipping point and preclude important future US–India defence cooperation. Senior

US officials expressed 'very significant concerns' that 'if India pursued major new platforms and systems (from Russia)', it 'would put at risk anything that would be interoperable with US systems'.[12] If India deploys this advanced Russian system, they believe it could lock in Indian dependence on Russian assistance and effectively foreclose for India a wide range of defence-cooperation opportunities with the US military that Washington has been cultivating for two decades.

Recognising the complications that the India–Russia defence partnership creates for US regional strategy, American policymakers still appear to underestimate India's dependence on and commitment to its partnership with Russia, and to overestimate the United States' ability to reshape Indian preferences. While some seek to punish Russia at every turn, those who prioritise the US–India relationship and the China threat, but believe the India–Russia defence partnership is a diminishing Cold War relic, should not assume the US can alter India's strategic calculations through sanctions threats.[13]

India's relationship with Russia is largely oriented around defence trade of considerable breadth, depth, scope and durability.[14] The scale of India's Russian arms arsenal is larger than most accounts acknowledge and growing, with over $15 billion in deals signed in the past two years.[15] It is also broader than previously understood, as Russian equipment comprises an overwhelming share of each service's offensive capabilities. Russia's defence industry and scientists have supported the development of several elements of India's strategic arsenal – including nuclear submarines and advanced cruise missiles – and India expects this to continue. Shared geopolitical interests in Eurasia and in a polycentric global order further buttress India–Russia relations.

Given India's degree of dependence on and trust in the Russians, and now Indian budget limitations due to health-crises-induced economic slowdowns, US attempts to deter India–Russia arms transactions and compel India to phase out Russian systems – whether for US commercial, geopolitical or military inter-operability reasons – are unlikely to work. Even if India were inclined to transition away from Russian equipment – of which there is scant evidence – the process would stretch over decades. Consequently, the US needs to rethink and recalibrate its approach to India's defence relationship with Russia. Washington should consider holstering sanctions threats while communicating the ceiling for US technology transfers, concentrating cooperation on military domains of opportunity, developing workarounds and embracing an alternative partnership model for India.

The depth of the India–Russia arms relationship

Since the early 1960s, India has relied on Russia as its primary arms supplier.[16] The cumulative stock of Russian materiel, along with the strategic importance of these systems and the strength of India–Russia defence-technology cooperation, will persist well into the future.[17] This durable relationship is built on the large quantity of Russian arms, the breadth of purchases across military services, the depth of trusted cooperation involving local production, technology transfers, future co-development and the likely service life of Russian platforms in India's arsenal. Some have also argued that Russia's established relationships within India's Ministry of Defence and military services may afford competitive advantages to Russia's bids, as it can leverage political connections, make side deals or extend bribes.[18]

The sheer quantity of Russian kit in India's arsenal is often underestimated. Authoritative sources have placed the proportion at 60%.[19] Our estimate, based on a detailed examination of India's large weapons systems, suggests the true number is closer to 85%. Estimates cannot capture

Figure 1: **Cumulative major Indian military-equipment pieces (by national origin/decade)**

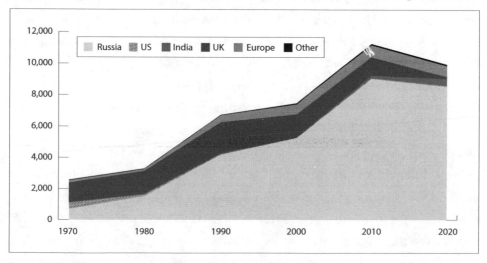

Source: IISS, *The Military Balance*, 1970, 1980, 1990, 2000, 2010 and 2020 editions

Figure 2: **Cumulative major Indian military-equipment pieces (by national origin/decade/service)**

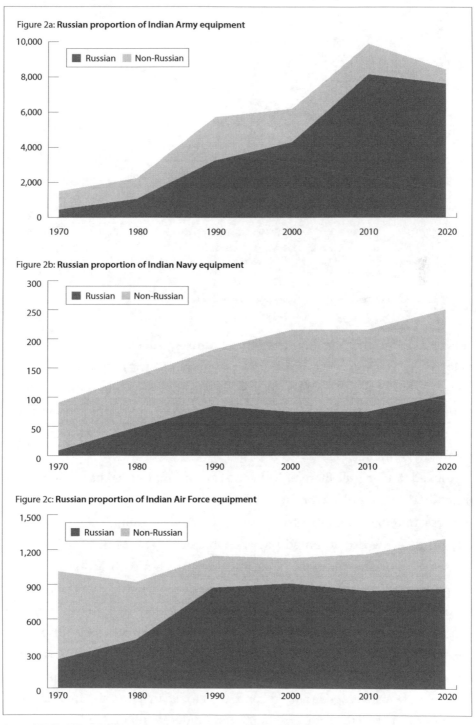

Figure 2a: **Russian proportion of Indian Army equipment**

Figure 2b: **Russian proportion of Indian Navy equipment**

Figure 2c: **Russian proportion of Indian Air Force equipment**

Source: IISS, *The Military Balance*, 1970, 1980, 1990, 2000, 2010 and 2020 editions

Figure 3: **Major Indian military equipment of Russian origin**

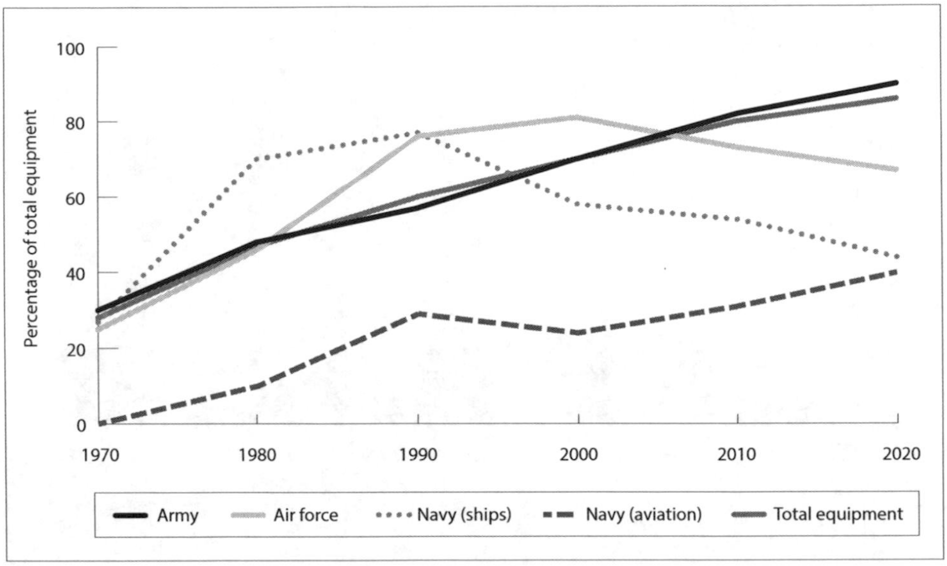

Source: IISS, *The Military Balance*, 1970, 1980, 1990, 2000, 2010 and 2020 editions

subcomponents manufactured by other countries, such as Israeli and French avionics in the Su-30MKI or American General Electric engines in the *Tejas* light combat aircraft. Nevertheless, since the Cold War the Indian Army's dependence on large Russian platforms has continued to grow. The air force has only slightly tapered its dependence. Only the Indian Navy has appreciably diversified. (See Figures 1–3.)

Indeed, the overall share of Russian arms of India's total has grown since the end of the Cold War, when it made up about 70% of India's arsenal. Despite the cessation of favourable 'friendship prices', New Delhi has continued to rely on Moscow due to broad path dependence.[20] The Ministry of Defence is used to working through the acquisitions process with Moscow. Indian operators and maintenance crews are experienced with Russian systems, such that the retraining costs of any transition would be high. Accounting and procurement procedures that discount best-value or life-cycle price also make the Russian systems appear more cost-effective than American or European ones.[21] And India fears that visible attempts to diversify away from Russia will cause Russia to leverage India's reliance on it for spare parts and maintenance support to weaken the Indian military and render it vulnerable.[22]

Table 1: **Percentage of current major Indian Army platforms by national origin**

Country of origin	Fighting vehicles and tanks (%)	Fires (%) (artillery and rocket launchers)	Air defence (%)	Army aviation (%)
Russia	98	52	100	0
US	0	1	0	0
India	2	5	0	45
US allies*	0	1	0	55
Other	0	43	0	0

*US allies include states having systems with which US systems would presumably be readily inter-operable
Source: IISS, *The Military Balance*, 2020 edition

From a straight bean count, it would appear that Russian arms dependence is concentrated within, and bolstered by, the Indian Army, India's dominant service. The army is the largest operator of Russian equipment in terms of sheer numbers as well as a percentage of total equipment. But even in the air and naval domains, India is reliant on Russian strike capabilities and has only diversified suppliers of its intelligence, surveillance and reconnaissance (ISR) and logistics platforms. In a breakdown of these platforms by type, the only exception to Russia's dominance is in aviation, which consists of mostly indigenous, French and Israeli uninhabited aerial vehicles (UAVs) and helicopters (see Table 1).

The navy and air force remain heavily dependent on Russian arms, especially for offensive and attack capabilities. While the Russian-origin share constitutes a little less than half of total Indian naval platforms, by displacement tonnage Russian ships make up 62% of the navy's total (see Table 2). Some 36% of the Indian Navy's missile cells are on Russian-origin ships, with 62% of its missile cells on indigenous platforms. Of the navy's attack capabilities, 80% of its missiles and 100% of its fighters are of Russian origin. As for power projection, India's newest carrier, the INS *Vikrant*, is principally designed to launch and recover Russian fighter aircraft such as the MiG-29K.[23] Only in naval aviation does US and allied equipment constitute a majority – a combined 53% – of platforms, notably American P-8 maritime-patrol aircraft, Israeli UAVs and British *Sea King* anti-submarine-warfare helicopters, which will soon be accompanied by American MH-60 *Seahawks*, potentially more P-8s, MQ-9 drones and intelligence, surveillance, target-acquisition and reconnaissance technology.

Table 2: **Current major Indian naval platforms and missile cells by national origin**

Country of origin	Displacement tonnage (%)	Missile cells by ship origin (%)	Missile cells by missile origin (%)	Naval aviation (%)
Russia	62	36	80	40
US	0	0	0	4
US allies	3	2	20	49
India	35	62	1	6

Source: IISS, *The Military Balance*, 2020 edition; author-compiled codebook

The Indian Air Force is similarly reliant on Russian-origin platforms and attack capabilities. Of its platforms, 67% are of Russian origin and only 27% were procured by the US or its allies (including France, Germany, Israel and the United Kingdom), and would thus be inter-operable with US systems with relative ease (see Table 3). Although India has begun to procure more aircraft from the US and its allies, most of those are ISR and transport platforms. Russia still provides the overwhelming proportion of the air force's strike capabilities. Only the ageing British *Jaguar* and French *Mirage* fighters, and the newer French *Rafale* fighters, make up a significant proportion of the air force's attack platforms. And even including the two *Rafale* squadrons of 36 fighter aircraft to be delivered by 2022, well over 80% of India's modern fighter aircraft will continue to be of Russian origin. In short, the preponderance of Indian strike capabilities – which in theory would be networked to an array of other sensor, shooter and command platforms – are of Russian origin. Even if India suddenly abandoned the S-400 for the US Terminal High Altitude Area Defense or *Patriot* systems, these would still not integrate well with much of India's fighter aircraft.[24]

Admittedly, the data presented here is a contemporary snapshot that could change over the next decade, depending on which company is

Table 3: **Current major Indian Air Force platforms by national origin**

Country of origin	All platforms (%)	Legacy attack* (%)	Modern attack** (%)	ISR/transport (%)
Russia	67	60	93	60
US	3	2	0	5
US allies	24	39	1	24
India	6	0	6	10

*Equipment designed during the Cold War **Equipment designed after the Cold War
Source: IISS, *The Military Balance*, 2020 edition

awarded the lucrative tender currently under way for the purchase of 114 new fighters. But even that could be subject to substantial delays or rollbacks like those that afflicted the previous medium multi-role combat-aircraft programme, which was intended to procure 126 fighters only to yield 36, delivered two decades later.[25]

The scope and depth of the India–Russia arms relationship is apparent not only from the quantity of Russian systems India has purchased, but also from the technical sophistication of the partnership. Russia has accommodated the Indian defence establishment's requests for local production of advanced systems, and its leaders boast of transferring sensitive, cutting-edge technology.[26] India's decision to remain largely reliant on Russia for attack capabilities is due to Russia's willingness to transfer technology for local Indian production and to allow its engineers to assist their Indian counterparts in designing some advanced Indian systems, such as the *Agni*-I short-range ballistic missile. This support is in line with India's long-term strategic objective of self-reliance in defence production. For example, Russia has a joint venture with India on the *BrahMos* cruise missile, which allowed Indian engineers to gain experience working on missile canisterisation, enhancing the indigenous development of the *Agni*-I.[27] India also appears poised to proceed with the co-development of new *BrahMos* variants, including a hypersonic anti-ship missile as well as a counter-high-value-aircraft missile.[28] Russia's multiple long-term leases of nuclear attack submarines to India demonstrate significant trust. Deep naval and strategic cooperation was also apparent in the furtive consultations Russia gave on India's nuclear-powered ballistic-missile submarine programme, including support on submarine design and reactor miniaturisation, without which former officials have said such a ship would have been 'impossible to realise'.[29] This strong support has engendered an abiding belief on India's part in the positive externalities of the partnership with Russia. The US has yet to reach such high levels of cooperation on advanced platforms.

Arvind Gupta, who recently served as India's deputy national security adviser, has noted that 'India depends on Russia and will continue to do so for several decades for its military hardware needs'.[30] Experts forecast that Indian reliance on Russian technical assistance, particularly for strategic

Figure 4: **Estimated service life of India's major Russian weapons systems**

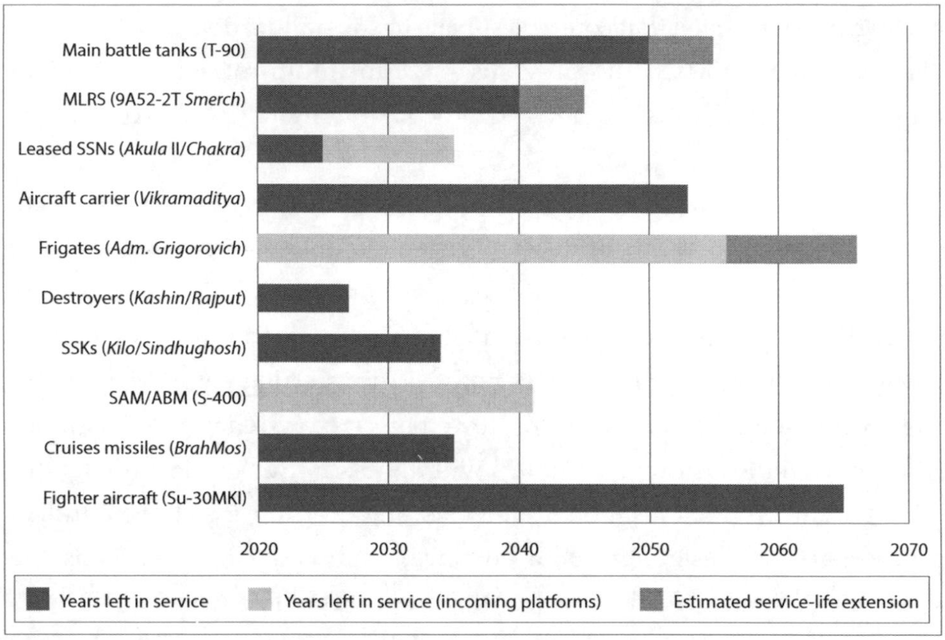

Source: IISS, *The Military Balance*, 2020 edition; author-compiled codebook

systems, will persist.[31] Russia maintains its outsize role in India's arsenal partly through coercion, leveraging the threat of cutting off India's spare parts and servicing, or selling to its rival, Pakistan. Network effects also sustain Russia's position. Any newly procured fighter aircraft over the next decade will be expected to be 'fully integrated with the Su-30MKI fighters which would be the mainstay' of the Indian Air Force for decades.[32]

The disruptive impact of the COVID-19 global pandemic is expected to impose significant budgetary pressures on India over the next decade, further constraining diversification of Indian military platforms. The 3% increase in defence spending planned for 2021 may be clever accounting rather than an indication of future trends, since the capital budget seems intended to cover existing procurements already under contract rather than to fund the acquisition of new systems.[33] Consequently, India will depend even more on extending the service life of the largely Russian platforms it has, and will be less likely to phase them out. The recently approved $2.5bn plan to purchase 33 new Su-30s and MiG-29s, and to upgrade another 59 MiG-29s – despite

Table 4: **Indian arms deals with Russia and the US (2008–20)**

	Russia				**United States**		
	Item	Total units ordered	Amount (US$ billions)		Item	Total units ordered	Amount (US$ billions)
Air force	MiG-29SMT/*Fulcrum*-F	92	2.26	Air force	C-130J-30 *Hercules*	13	2.14
	Mi-8MT/Mi-17	148	2.80		C-17A *Globemaster*-3	11	4.36
	Su-30MKI	60	2.75		AH-64E *Apache Guardian*	18	2.23
	S-400/SA-21	20	5.40		CH-47F *Chinook*	10	1.00
Army	T-90S tank	700	3.75	Army	M777 *Howitzer* guns	145	0.73
	BMP-2 IFV	149	0.14				
	Ka-226T *Sergei*	200	2.00				
Navy	Project-971I/*Akula*	1	3.00	Navy	P-8A *Poseidon*	18	6.00
	Ka-31	11–15	0.71		MH-60R *Seahawk*	25	2.60
	BrahMos ASM	216+ missiles for 15 warships	3.60				
	Adm. Grigorovich frigates	4	2.50				
Total			**28.91**	**Total**			**19.06**

Source: SIPRI Trade Register

their being suboptimal for precision air-to-ground strikes and high-altitude operations – is likely to be repeated.[34] Figure 4, based on open-source analysis and reporting, indicates that many existing or forthcoming Russian-origin systems are expected to remain in India's arsenal for several decades.

Moreover, since 2008, when the US–India defence partnership was officially consummated with the passage of the US–India civil nuclear agreement, India's arms deals with Russia have continued apace, with roughly $29bn in procurement deals, compared to only $19bn for the US (see Table 4). In 2016, Russian sources reported that the portfolio of booked contracts with India was estimated at $35bn.[35] This further ensures that advanced Russian military technology will be part of India's arsenal for at least another 20 years.

The India–Russia defence partnership is not merely a financially expedient or path-dependent relationship, but one anchored by geopolitical and even some ideological convergence.[36] Historically, Russia has strongly backed India in international forums regarding its nuclear tests, its expeditionary military operations and its position that Kashmir's political future is a strictly bilateral issue between India and Pakistan. India reciprocated by defending or refusing to condemn Soviet aggression, and more recently was silent about covert Russian transgressions in Syria, Crimea and the United Kingdom, as well as its meddling in Western elections. Today, some Indian strategists also believe that investing in ties with Russia helps preclude full Russian alignment with China, as well as any potential Russian alignment with Pakistan, and that arms purchases are among the best means of keeping Russia on India's side. Indeed, Russia's mediation efforts and its promise to speed up the delivery of 33 jets that India purchased in the early weeks of its border crisis with China in summer 2020 signalled to India its continued reliability as an arms partner.[37]

Underpinning these geopolitical alignments are shared theories of a preferred international order. In particular, India essentially agrees with Russia on the benefits of a more polycentric and multipolar world order, and seeks to promote greater Russian engagement in the Indo-Pacific even while some US strategists fear this would weaken America's global influence.[38] The international order that New Delhi and Moscow broadly prefer involves both states safeguarding their own privileged spheres of regional influence, as well as accelerating a diffusion of power so that they are effectively regarded as poles in the international system.[39] In light of these congruent visions of global order and a durable defence partnership, India is unlikely to jettison its relationship with Russia to embrace a procurement strategy dependent entirely on the US and its allies.

Implications of the India–Russia defence partnership

Russia's dominant sway over India's arsenal has significant implications for US strategists, military planners and defence suppliers. It complicates India's own military effectiveness while raising the risks of 'exploitation, theft, or actually risk of non-operability' that constrain combined operations with US forces and the prospects for joint defence-technology development.[40] The diverse origins of India's defence systems obstruct its ability to integrate its battle networks, resulting in partial, if not substantial, loss in speed, agility, efficiency and military effectiveness. The India–Russia arms partnership also poses a significant impediment to full US–India military inter-operability by potentially limiting US networking with Indian platforms of Russian origin.

Constraints on communication- and information-system links for security reasons can increase the risk of non-coordination, military friction and accidents, thereby limiting the scope of joint exercises or operations.

The Indian military's limited scope for its own joint-force integration jeopardises the role the US envisions. Connectivity between, say, India's Russian attack platforms and its US- and Israeli-origin ISR platforms is often cumbersome. Operational integration of subsystems in the *Sukhoi* programme and the *Kolkata*-class frigate has been especially troublesome.[41] A friendly-fire incident during the 2019 Balakot crisis, when an Israeli-origin defence system shot down a Russian-origin transport helicopter, was the product of both human error and work overload that stemmed from systems-integration failures.[42]

India's system-integration challenges are more pronounced at the level of 'architecture integration'.[43] For example, with the S-400, India would have little difficulty at the level of weapon integration (for example, the components in an S-400 interceptor) and platform integration (such as connecting the S-400's on-board radar and sensors to the interceptor), but the integration of the S-400 with India's broader air-defence architecture – including other missile-defence systems, radars and ISR assets, and command, control and communication networks – would prove complex, inefficient, expensive and error-prone due to technical differences in the equipment of India's diverse suppliers.[44]

Exacerbating operational problems are the political constraints that preclude linkage of Western-origin and Russian-origin systems, as in India's air-defence network. India's purchase of the S-400 poses acute inter-operability concerns, as there is a risk that it could fire on India's own Western-origin fighters. This prospect will force India to integrate platforms never meant to operate together, hampering the ability of both fighters and air defences to avoid friendly-fire incidents.[45] There is also an inter-services problem, which the appointment of an Indian Chief of Defence Staff in 2019 was intended to ameliorate, as services still do not coordinate procurements to allow for easy integration and cross-service communication between systems.[46]

Poor systems integration also lowers expectations of how India might fit into a China-balancing strategy. The persistent difficulties of platform integration into the battle network could impair India's battle management, which will theoretically demand near real-time data links connecting sensors and shooters to command and control.[47] Poor internal inter-operability ultimately compromises either the security or the speed of data and communications, which can prove decisive in modern warfare. A militarily ineffective India will frustrate US plans for creating dilemmas and complications for China in peacetime, crisis and conflict.[48]

One senior US defence official notes that, in addition to bolstering partner defence capabilities, the primary purpose of US arms exports is allied military inter-operability – 'to facilitate [partners'] ability to operate alongside the US military to address shared security challenges'.[49] Senior congressional leaders also expect Indian access to advanced US defence technologies, such as uninhabited systems (for example, drones), to enable US forces.[50] Senior Indian military officials have boasted that such 'plug and play' partner inter-operability already exists, but this contradicts most assessments.[51] Partner inter-operability requires more than just common operating platforms, but fusing information and communications in systems that can be routinely employed is increasingly essential in modern warfare.

Inter-operability is arguably a core US interest

Multinational technical inter-operability is arguably a core US interest.[52] In the information-warfare age, it may be more important for systems to communicate with one another than for troops to train with one another.[53] For example, the area where India professes the greatest interest in defence cooperation, maritime-domain awareness, requires dense, meshed sensor networks to effectively 'fuse, integrate, and distribute the resulting operational information' between partners.[54] While US allies such as Japan and Australia employ common satellite data links and electronic combat systems, sharing sensitive information across systems requires secure-communication protocols. This requirement is challenging to meet even when both militaries share the same equipment, but especially complicated when adversarial systems are involved. Interpersonal and procedural inter-operability gaps can be narrowed through training exercises and inter-military exchanges, but the financial cost and invasiveness of overhauling equipment and hardware impose limits on secure communications and systems inter-operability between militaries.

Both sides have been sensitive to the security risks of systems inter-operability. India previously barred even temporary data links to its ships during the US–India *Malabar* exercises, and flew its Russian fighter aircraft with their radars and electronic-warfare jammers turned off.[55] India's Russian platforms and systems today present a general intelligence risk to information security. A related concern is the threat to cyber security, particularly given Russia's recent aggression in this domain. The US is extremely wary of linking up to any Russian-origin networks that could incorporate malware or cyber vulnerabilities that could be exploited to disrupt future operations.

A final US worry involves the ability of the S-400 (and potentially other advanced sensor systems) to observe and collect sensitive data on fifth-generation fighters such as the F-35, especially if the two systems are co-located and operating simultaneously, and to compromise US data-link equipment through backdoors.[56] Proper functioning of the S-400's target-acquisition and engagement radars would also require sensitive data about US aircraft and UAVs that India operates to be inputted to prevent friendly fire. Turning over data on Identification Friend or Foe (IFF) transponders, Link-16 and other sensors to a system that Russian engineers may access in the future for maintenance would pose unacceptable risks and could even constitute a violation of the Arms Export Control Act.[57] The US would also have serious misgivings about linking up for tactical operations with any of India's new and advanced Russian platforms that involve sensors networked to any potential command-and-control systems, such as the Su-30 fighter, *Talwar* and *Grigorovich* frigates, *Akula* submarines and *BrahMos* missiles. With such inter-operability precluded, future joint military exercises would only contribute to socialisation rather than to actual preparation for combat.[58] Future US–India operational coordination may necessitate an alternative distributed model to allied inter-operability.

The overarching concern about deep India–Russia defence cooperation is that it could impose limits on India's procurement of sensitive military technology and on broader US–India defence-industrial integration.[59] US policymakers have voiced serious concerns about India's lax technical security protocols, which Russia's close connection to the Indian defence industry may allow it to exploit for intellectual-property theft or to disrupt US military operations.[60] Recent US policy changes have helped to ease export restrictions and technology controls, but do no more than open the door to cooperation. Actually sharing and co-developing technology require the confidence of the American defence community and industry. The introduction of advanced Russian technologies into India's command-and-control networks would likely cause the US to withhold sensitive technology for fear of compromise.[61] This would undermine India's stated goal of defence-manufacturing integration with the US from research and development to production.

Russia's close defence relationship with India thus poses two forms of risk. The first is that of active espionage. Russian systems bring with them personnel, including technicians, advisers and engineers, who could per-petrate exploitation or theft. As one US official stated candidly, 'we don't want [American technology] exposed because some Russians walking the shop floor decide to go walk away and put it in their handbag or knap-sack and take it back to Moscow'.[62] Certified-safe joint-production facilities can mitigate this risk, but these have inherent limits.[63] Some also worry that procurement corruption in the service branches and Indian Ministry of Defence could pose substantial counter-intelligence risks with respect to transferred US technologies. The second risk is that of passive espionage. It derives from the co-location of Russian-origin systems and sensors, such as the S-400, with advanced US platforms, allowing them to collect critical information.[64] Noting that both the S-400 and F-35 are effectively computer systems, one senior US defence official bluntly stated, 'you don't hook your computer to your adversary's computer'.[65]

While some US officials, such as former secretary of defense Ash Carter, have suggested that the drawbacks of India's use of Russian systems could be 'surmountable' over time, doing so is neither easy nor optimal.[66] US policy has focused on gradually 'weaning' India off its Russian reliance through diversification, largely with an eye to substituting US for Russian systems 'at all but the lowest end where strategic issues are minor (like Kalashnikovs) and the highest end where changes are difficult (like *BrahMos* and other missile systems)'.[67] But India cannot afford to procure an entirely new arsenal, given its development needs and the budgetary impacts of the COVID-19 pandemic. Even if the US offered to support such a transition through Foreign Military Financing (FMF), an Indian force with Russian technology that was sufficiently minimal and compartmentalised to allow safe and effective inter-operability would take decades to realise.

In this regard, Egypt's transition is instructive. Even after Cairo ceased cooperating with the Soviet military, a US Government Accountability Office study found that after 26 years of extraordinarily high FMF support, averaging $1.3bn annually, only about half of Egypt's military equipment had switched to that of US origin.[68] Furthermore, India would be wary of accepting an offer of comparable FMF support out of concerns that Russia would be able to leverage India's near-term reliance on spare parts, supplies and maintenance to hold it hostage until US systems were fully inducted. Moreover, India would be hesitant merely to supplant inordinate reliance on Russia with inordinate reliance on the United States. India tolerates some friction from its multi-origin systems as the price of relative strategic autonomy.

India's most prominent defence strategist, K. Subrahmanyam, noted that India's defence market was large enough that it could afford 'two lines of research and production' from both the US and Russia.[69] Furthermore, while India seeks US intelligence, diplomatic and material support, it may not foresee many contingencies in which Indian and US forces would actually fight together, thereby vitiating the need for the highest levels of hardware and software inter-operability.[70] And while New Delhi does covet US defence technology, it may consider demands for exclusivity too high and hedge by way of less complicated sources, such as Russia, France and Israel.

Easing the challenge

If the United States considers India a critical component of its Asia policy, it needs to accept that India will have a durable Russian-origin force structure and arms relationship with Russia, even as it seeks closer defence cooperation with the US to enhance its capabilities and deterrence in the broader Indo-Pacific.[71] Therefore, US sanctions are likely to backfire and unwind two decades of careful cultivation, and preclude substantive cooperation with New Delhi for years.[72] India reads the repeated public brandishing of sanctions threats as an indicator of the United States' unreliability, its disdain for India's sovereignty and its naked pursuit of defence-industry sales.[73] The imposition of sanctions would reawaken Indian memories of perceived US perfidy, as when it slapped sanctions on India over its 1998 nuclear tests, and provide ammunition to New Delhi's sceptics of the US partnership.[74]

The threat of sanctions has not deterred future transactions. Since the passage of CAATSA, India has signed new deals with Russia to purchase the S-400 and next-generation frigates, and to lease a nuclear submarine. Implementing sanctions could even provoke India into doing the very opposite of the legislation's intent and increase its weapons procurements from Russia.[75] While some fear a waiver for India would set an awkward precedent, there are good reasons to consider India a special case. Unlike Turkey, a treaty ally, India's procurement of the S-400 is not jeopardising the integrity of an already integrated multilateral alliance or compromising an existing defence supply chain, even if its choices could risk foreclosing these in the future. The S-400 was sought and approved by the Indian government years before CAATSA legislation was passed, and the US government reacted slowly and only offered an alternative once the deal was effectively concluded.[76] The Biden administration can rest assured that recent sanctions on Turkey, denial of F-35 delivery and expulsion from production chains will deter US allies from such defections. But penalising critical, non-allied swing states like India and many Southeast Asian countries for purchasing Russian arms harms US interests more than it hurts Moscow.[77] Sanctioning India–Russia defence transactions might also sacrifice valuable opportunities for the US to develop insights on Russian equipment or drive small wedges between Russia and China.[78]

More broadly, policies like CAATSA are self-defeating if they come at the expense of ensuring a favourable Asian balance of power. And sanctions or the threat thereof diminish the US–India relationship and inhibit India's ability to defend itself against China so as to strike such a balance. Obstructing India's acquisition of the S-400 in particular would undercut the key US policy

Sanctions diminish the US–India relationship

objective of enhancing Indian defensive capabilities against China: as many US defence officials and analysts acknowledge, deploying the S-400 would be a cost-efficient way for India to manage its airpower deficiencies by freeing up overstretched fighter squadrons from air-defence missions for an offensive role on its border with China.[79] CAATSA sanctions would also impede India's ability to export its *BrahMos* missile, a joint venture with Russia, to interested buyers such as the Philippines and Vietnam, which would provide them with a platform for protecting their interests in the South China Sea.[80] This would not only undermine the defence efforts of Southeast Asian nations against China, but also inhibit the South–South cooperation that weakens China's narrative of Washington instigating regional competition. The very fact that India maintains strong defence ties with Russia and eschews full alignment with the West affords it special credibility with swing-state audiences in Southeast Asia. When India challenges Chinese aggression or coercion, this is more likely to appear as an independent defence of the rules-based order rather than choosing sides in the US–China competition.

The US has several options for remedying a potentially dysfunctional policy. Firstly, the Biden administration should work to prevent the imposition of new sanctions on India. CAATSA sanctions over delivery of the S-400 system could deal a 'catastrophic' blow to the US–India relationship, especially in the wake of recent friction, such as that caused in April when the US executed a freedom-of-navigation operation in India's exclusive economic zone without seeking prior authorisation from India.[81] The same motives that led the Biden administration to recently adjust course on its Russia policy and waive sanctions on the Nord Stream 2 pipeline to remove an obstacle with European partners may be applicable here.[82] In the short term, the Biden administration could halt public sanctions threats and issue India a waiver after congressional consultation and buy-in. Given other Russian transactions in the pipeline, however, a one-off waiver will not be sufficient to allay India's anxiety, casting a shadow on the relationship.[83] In the medium term, therefore, the Biden administration should work with Congress to further modify the waiver language in CAATSA to prevent future punishment of US partners that act in the broader interests of Washington's Indo-Pacific strategy.

India's enduring arms relationship with Russia ensures that sanctions dramas will recur until the US clarifies its priorities and provides greater predictability on waiver eligibility and secondary-sanctions targeting. As Richard Verma, a former US ambassador to India, has argued, the US is more likely to shape Indian choices and alignment not through sanctions, but through 'the commercial and strategic space'.[84] If sanctions prove unavoidable, the administration should apply the lightest sanctions possible – for instance, denial of visas or loans rather than technology exports – to minimise the impact on future defence cooperation.

Secondly, the US should prioritise defence cooperation with India in the domains of greatest operational value and where Russian hardware poses the fewest obstacles. For instance, the Indian Air Force and Navy's ISR and maritime-patrol platforms are increasingly of American and US-allied origin, while most of their combat airframes are Russian. Given the United States' primary interest in the maritime domain, it should focus military assistance, joint exercises and operations on maritime reconnaissance, where there is greater opportunity for inter-operability. This would enable the US and India to use each other's reconnaissance platforms to build a common maritime operating picture and track Chinese movements in the Indian Ocean.[85]

The US could also seek to enhance other collaborative efforts outside of Russian platforms, such as strategic assessments, cyber security, intelligence-sharing and geospatial imaging. Washington could make maritime cooperation more economically attractive by using the Excess Defense Articles and FMF programmes to enhance India's maritime capacity, or by investing in infrastructure projects on India's islands through the US International Development Finance Corporation.[86] Such offers would be more palatable if framed as 'offsets' rather than 'assistance'. The US Congress could also amend the National Defense Authorization Act to allow arms sales to India to be approved on the same basis as for NATO and other key allies, allowing speedier completion of deals.[87] Since India prizes diversified procurement networks, as it evaluates bids for 114 multi-role fighters and a next-generation submarine programme, the US government should privately remind New Delhi that information-security concerns would be significantly ameliorated if the contract went to a vendor based in an allied country.

Thirdly, the US could isolate specific platforms and develop workarounds to technical and policy roadblocks that would most impair desired US–India defence cooperation, even if this involved a modicum of risk. One tack might be to confine inter-operability goals to a specific set of platforms or domains, while expanding the use of receivers or portable kits on Indian naval platforms to access the Combined Enterprise Regional Information Exchange System, a classified network through which the US can disseminate tactical data to partner militaries in a combined war-fighting environment. This would be consistent with the Pentagon's Mission Partner Environment concept, which supports information-sharing for establishing a common operational picture.[88] While it is not realistic for India to deploy the S-400 batteries as stand-alone systems, it could take certain precautions, such as turning off its radars during exercises in the area that involves American fifth-generation platforms.[89]

The US could isolate specific platforms

To address the cyber-security risks of networking with some Indian systems' interface protocols, customised 'cross-domain solutions' could be developed to connect Indian with American (as well as Australian and Japanese) tactical data links. Admittedly, this would be a costly process that would require US access to Russian-origin systems and could put India in a bind.[90] To defend against counter-intelligence risks such as theft or inadvertent sharing of technology, the US could deploy technical-security teams, as it has done to manage Pakistan's operation of the US F-16 and Chinese J-7s and JF-17s.

To reduce Indian dependence on Russian sustainment, US diplomats and defence attachés might help broker commercial maintenance relationships with non-Russian companies, perhaps from Serbia, Slovakia or Ukraine – states which India did turn to in the 1990s when Russian sustainment lines dried up after the fall of the USSR.[91] This course of action could also signal that the US is not using inter-operability concerns merely as a pretext for pushing US arms sales, though all second-best solutions would require India to accept greater transparency, access and political risk.

Fourthly, in their engagements with Indian counterparts at the strategic and technical levels, US officials should dispassionately remind India about the trade-offs of continued acquisition of Russian arms, highlighting ceilings on technology-sharing.[92] The US should make it clear that while it seeks to bolster India's ability to counter Chinese aggression and power projection, it cannot justify fully sharing its most advanced technology with a partner unless they are preparing to operate and fight together. India has not committed to broad allied inter-operability, and Indian analysts and leaders do not perceive US arms purchases as an effort to affect US–India military inter-operability.[93] Though India is unlikely to alter existing procurement deals, thus clarifying the US position could reduce the gap in expectations and possibly incentivise India to procure US and Western arms in the future.

The US could also illuminate the trade-offs in inter-operability and military effectiveness with simulations and tabletop exercises that engage a broad cross-section of India's strategic community, beyond senior military officers. While Indian officials are generally aware of the costs of India's Russian-oriented force structure to US–India inter-operability, more detailed explorations of the subject could encourage India to refine and clarify its long-term expectations for the defence partnership. For instance, India might come to appreciate that even if it is limited as to which fifth-generation platforms it can obtain from the US, it might grow comfortable with advanced fourth-generation options such as the F-21, F-18E/F or F-15E that still outfit it with significant combat power and defence-industry opportunities.

Although capability shortfalls resonate in the aftermath of Sino-Indian crises, there remains a striking lack of joint planning and strategic coordination.[94] More expansive consultations would allow Indian officials to candidly discuss their ambitions for joint planning and operations, allowing the US to right-size its own Indo-Pacific strategy around a set of realistic, mutual expectations.[95] However, the US should also earnestly promote opportunities for deeper defence-technology engagement with India in areas of limited counter-intelligence risk, such as uninhabited systems and ground sensors for ISR, and for broader cooperation in the private sector in fields such as artificial intelligence that heavily impact defence.[96]

Finally, beyond the tactical intricacies of US–India defence cooperation, the US should rethink how India fits into its defence strategy in the

Indo-Pacific, at least in the medium term. Right now, the invocation of inter-operability implicitly suggests that India is willing and able to contribute something to a US fight in the region when it is not clear that either proposition is true.[97] Rather than emphasising the United States' traditional role of providing security assurances to its regional allies and partners and demanding their contributions to a US-led fight in the region, the US might instead seek to become a convening power that organises and manages a networked Indo-Pacific security architecture of like-minded states.[98] Under such a division of labour, the US might opt to concentrate its military forces and strategic attention on the East Asian and Western Pacific theatre, indirectly encouraging India to take the lead in deterring Chinese aggression and upholding a rules-based order in the Indian Ocean region.[99] The US might look to support greater Indian leadership in military missions within the Indian Ocean that are short of war, such as maritime-domain awareness, patrols of sea lines of communication and counter-piracy. In this way, US and Indian planning could be strategically coordinated but operationally and tactically segmented.

*   *   *

In 2001, Joe Biden, then a US senator, advocated the removal of the sanctions on India that the US imposed after its 1998 nuclear tests, recognising its importance as a rising global power.[100] It would send an unfortunate message if, 20 years later, President Biden's administration in its first year in office imposed sanctions on India for far less momentous activity.

India's heavy reliance on Russian military hardware does pose a serious challenge to one vision of the US–India defence partnership that involves seamless military inter-operability and boundless defence-industrial integration. But India's Russia dependence is a reality that will not change in any meaningful time frame due to the long-standing trust and bureaucratic familiarity between the two countries, as well as the relationship's perceived cost-effectiveness, strategic benefit and geopolitical utility. Furthermore, modern Russian arms can still equip India to counter military aggression by China – an interest the United States emphatically shares. The US would do better to embrace a pragmatic version of the bilateral relationship that appreciates this reality than to fulminate over the obstacles to an arguably unrealistic vision of an idealised partnership that emulates an alliance.

The Biden administration can signal its respect for India's sovereign choices while still strengthening the US–India defence partnership and abetting a favourable balance of power in Asia through practical cooperation and burden-sharing without the assumption of broad military inter-operability. This would entail avoiding new antagonisms such as sanctions, concentrating on areas of opportunity, investing in workarounds, communicating trade-offs and embracing a more efficient division of labour. Strengthening the US–India defence relationship in a more competitive environment firstly requires political trust, which the enactment of sanctions endangers. Once shared geopolitical objectives are mutually identified, the appropriate means of technical cooperation will naturally flow from that healthy relationship. Washington's success in managing great-power competition will depend on the partners it has, not the partners it might wish to have.

Acknowledgements

The authors would like to thank Chris Bassler, Liv Dowling, Eugene Gholz, Zachary Keck, Rear Admiral (Retd) William McQuilkin, John Parachini, Benjamin Schwartz, Elizabeth Threlkeld, Robin Walker and Matthew Zweig for their feedback and advice, and Julia Lodoen for her research assistance.

Notes

[1] See Robert D. Blackwill and Ashley J. Tellis, 'The India Dividend: New Delhi Remains Washington's Best Hope in Asia', *Foreign Affairs*, vol. 98, no. 5, September/October 2019, pp. 173–83.

[2] Ambassador Kenneth I. Juster, 'Farewell Address: Ambition and Achievement in the US–India Partnership', 5 January 2021, https://in.usembassy.gov/farewell-address-by-ambassador-kenneth-i-juster-ambition-and-achievement-in-the-u-s-india-partnership/.

[3] See Jack Detsch and Robbie Gramer, 'Russian Arms Sale Clouds US–India Ties', *Foreign Policy*, 19 March 2021, https://foreignpolicy.com/2021/03/19/russia-india-defence-secretary-lloyd-austin-s-400-china-arms-sales/; and Sanjeev Miglani, 'Exclusive: India's

Friction with US Rises over Planned Purchase of Russian S-400 Defence Systems', Reuters, 15 January 2021, https://www.reuters.com/article/us-india-usa-missiles-exclusive/exclusive-indias-friction-with-u-s-rises-over-planned-purchase-of-russian-s-400-defence-systems-idUSKBN29K2DO.

4   See, for example, Anil Ahuja, 'Charting the Future of India–US Defence and Security Cooperation', DPG Policy Brief, Delhi Policy Group, 28 March 2021, https://www.delhipolicygroup.org/uploads_dpg/publication_file/charting-the-future-of-india-us-defence-and-security-cooperation-2260.pdf; Rahul Bedi, 'Why Is the US Saying India Could Face Sanctions for Buying Russian S-400 Missile Systems?', Wire, 20 January 2021, https://thewire.in/security/us-india-sanctions-caatsa-s400-russia; and Suhasini Haidar, 'Delhi Opts to Wait, Watch US Foreign Policy Shift', Hindu, 7 February 2021, https://www.thehindu.com/news/national/analysis-delhi-opts-to-wait-watch-us-foreign-policy-shift/article33770595.ece.

5   US Senate Committee on Foreign Relations, 'Menendez Urges Secretary Austin to Use Upcoming Trip to India to Discuss Democracy, Human Rights and Opposition to S-400 Missile System', press release, 17 March 2021, https://www.foreign.senate.gov/press/chair/release/menendez-urges-secretary-austin-to-use-upcoming-trip-to-india-to-discuss-democracy_human-rights-and-opposition-to-s-400-missile-system-.

6   White House, 'National Security Strategy of the United States of America', December 2017, p. 25, https://trumpwhitehouse.archives.gov/wp-content/uploads/2017/12/NSS-Final-12-18-2017-0905-2.pdf.

7   See, for example, Sadanand Dhume, 'Moscow Isn't New Delhi's Pal', Wall Street Journal, 23 July 2020, https://www.wsj.com/articles/moscow-isnt-new-delhis-pal-11595548947; Sumit Ganguly, 'To Fight China, India Needs to Forget Russia', Foreign Policy, 16 July 2020, https://foreignpolicy.com/2020/07/16/india-fighting-china-means-forgetting-russia/; and Vikram Singh, 'How to Keep the US–India Defense Relationship Moving Ahead', Defense One, 8 August 2018, http://defenceone.com/ideas/2018/08/how-keep-us-india-defence-relationship-moving-ahead/150342/.

8   See US Department of State, 'Principal Deputy Assistant Secretary for South and Central Asian Affairs Alice Wells: Discussion on India and the Indo-Pacific', remarks to the Atlantic Council, 21 May 2020, https://2017-2021.state.gov/remarks-and-releases__trashed/discussion-on-india-and-the-indo-pacific-atlantic-council/index.html; and Project for Media & National Security, 'The Hon. R. Clarke Cooper, Assistant Secretary of State for Political–Military Affairs', George Washington University School of Media and Public Affairs, Defense Writers Group, 12 September 2019, https://nationalsecuritymedia.gwu.edu/project/the-hon-r-clarke-cooper-assistant-secretary-of-state-for-political-military-affairs/.

9   See Mukesh Aghi, 'Why Punishing India on Russia Would Be a Mistake for the United States', Diplomat, 17 May

2018, https://thediplomat.com/2018/05/why-punishing-india-on-russia-would-be-a-mistake-for-the-united-states/.

10 See Jim Goldgeier, 'US–Russian Relations Will Only Get Worse', *Foreign Affairs*, 6 April 2021, https://www.foreignaffairs.com/articles/russia-fsu/2021-04-06/us-russian-relations-will-only-get-worse; and Ellen Nakashima, 'Biden Administration Imposes Significant Economic Sanctions on Russia over Cyberspying', *Washington Post*, 15 April 2021, http://washingtonpost.com/national-security/biden-to-announce-tough-sanctions-on-russia-over-cyber-spying/2021/04/15/a4c1d260-746e-11eb-948d-19472e683521_story.html.

11 'Presidential Waiver on Arms Deal with Moscow Intended to "Wean" Nations Like India Off Russian Equipment: US', *Hindu*, 6 October 2018, https://www.thehindu.com/news/international/us-sanctions-waiver-intended-to-wean-countries-like-india-off-russian-equipment-white-house/article25142648.ece.

12 Idrees Ali, 'India Not Guaranteed US Sanctions Waiver for Russian Missiles: Official', Reuters, 29 August 2018, https://www.reuters.com/article/usa-india-defence-idINKCN1LE2AW; and Nayanima Basu, 'No Blanket Waiver of CAATSA Sanctions for Buying Russian/Chinese Arms, but India Safe, Says US', *ThePrint*, 18 December 2020, https://theprint.in/diplomacy/no-blanket-waiver-of-caatsa-sanctions-for-buying-russian-chinese-arms-but-india-safe-says-us/569406/.

13 See, for example, Singh, 'How to Keep the US–India Defense Relationship Moving Ahead'.

14 For a fuller analysis, see Sameer Lalwani et al., 'The Influence of Arms: Explaining the Durability of India–Russia Alignment', *Journal of Indo-Pacific Affairs*, Special Issue, January 2021, pp. 2–41, https://media.defense.gov/2021/Jan/15/2002565540/-1/-1/1/LALWANI.PDF.

15 See Ajai Shukla, 'Two Major Russian Arms Deals Likely Next Week, Weaponry Worth $15 bn in Moscow Pipeline', *Business Standard*, 15 March 2020, https://www.ajaishukla.com/2020/03/two-major-russian-arms-deals-likely.html.

16 See Stockholm International Peace Research Institute, Importer/Exporter TIV Tables, http://armstrade.sipri.org/armstrade/page/values.php.

17 As US secretary of defense James Mattis stated: 'There are nations in the world who are trying to turn away from formerly Russian-sourced weapons and systems like this. We only need to look at India, Vietnam, and some others.' US Senate Armed Services Committee, 'Hearing to Receive Testimony on the Department of Defense Budget Posture', 26 April 2018, https://www.armed-services.senate.gov/imo/media/doc/18-44_04-26-18.pdf. See also Lalwani et al., 'The Influence of Arms'.

18 See Josy Joseph, '"Foreign Defence Companies Paid Huge Bribes to Alleged Indian Arms Dealer"', *Hindu*, 2 December 2016, http://www.thehindu.com/news/national/'Foreign-defence-companies-paid-huge-bribes-to-alleged-Indian-arms-dealer'/article16086789.ece;

and Mark Pere Madrona, 'Puno Visited Israeli Firm Blacklisted in India for Corruption', ABS-CBN News, 11 September 2012, http://news.abs-cbn.com/-depth/09/11/12/puno-visited-israeli-firm-blacklisted-india-corruption.

19   See, for example, Dipanjan Roy Chaudhury, 'More than 60–70% of India Armed Forces Equipped with Russian Origin Weapons: Indian Envoy', *Economic Times*, 11 July 2020, https://economictimes.indiatimes.com/news/defence/more-than-60-70-of-india-armed-forces-equipped-with-russian-origin-weapons-indian-envoy/articleshow/76903811.cms.

20   See Stephen P. Cohen and Sunil Dasgupta, *Arming Without Aiming* (Washington DC: Brookings Institution Press, 2010), p. 20; and Ravinder Pal Singh, 'India', in Ravinder Pal Singh (ed.), *Arms Procurement Decision Making*: *China, India, Israel, Japan, South Korea and Thailand* (Oxford: Oxford University Press, 1998), p. 64.

21   See Cara Abercrombie, 'Removing Barriers to US–India Defense Trade', Carnegie Endowment for International Peace, 10 January 2018, https://carnegieendowment.org/2018/01/10/removing-barriers-to-u.s.-india-defence-trade/ jtdk.

22   See Kartik Bommakanti, 'India–Russia Military–Technical Cooperation: Beyond Commercial Relations', ORF, 22 June 2017. The US also acknowledges this dilemma. See Project for Military & National Security, 'The Hon. R. Clarke Cooper, Assistant Secretary of State for Political–Military Affairs'.

23   See Sumit Ganguly and M. Chris Mason, *An Unnatural Partnership? The Future of US–India Strategic Cooperation* (Carlisle, PA: United States Army War College Press, 2019), p. 18.

24   See Singh, 'How to Keep the US–India Defense Relationship Moving Ahead'.

25   See Rajat Pandit, 'MMRCA Deal: India to Scrap $20 Billion Mega Project for 126 Rafale Fighter Jets', *Times of India*, 14 April 2015, https://timesofindia.indiatimes.com/india/mmrca-deal-india-to-scrap-20-billion-mega-project-for-126-rafale-fighter-jets/articleshow/46910444.cms.

26   See Ministry of External Affairs, Government of India, 'Transcript of Joint Presser by External Affairs Minister and Minister of Foreign Affairs of the Russian Federation', 6 April 2021, https://mea.gov.in/bilateral-documents.htm?dtl/33774/Transcript_of_Joint_Presser_by_External_Affairs_Minister_and_Minister_of_Foreign_Affairs_of_the_Russian_Federation_April_06_2021.

27   See BrahMos Aerospace, 'India Developing Seekers for BRAHMOS, Other Missiles: Sudhir Mishra – Part 2', press release, 27 March 2016, http://brahmos.com/pressRelease.php?id=55.

28   See Douglas Barrie, 'India's Brahmos Missile: An Added Target in the Air?', IISS Military Balance Blog, 25 September 2020, https://www.iiss.org/blogs/military-balance/2020/09/india-brahmos-missile; and H.I. Sutton, 'India Goes Hypersonic: New Missile Technology May Be Answer to China's Navy', *Forbes*, 8 September 2020, https://www.forbes.com/sites/hisutton/2020/09/08/india-goes-hypersonic-new-missile-

technology-may-be-answer-to-chinas-navy/?sh=2cc6ecb3d937.

29 Praful Bidwai, 'Sinking Billions into Nuclear Weapons', Rediff, 3 August 2009, http://news.rediff.com/column/2009/aug/03/sinking-billions-into-nuclear-weapons.htm; and Ashok Parthasarathi, 'Concern over a Pernicious Agreement', *Mainstream*, vol. 47, no. 35, 15 August 2009, http://www.mainstreamweekly.net/article1581.html.

30 Arvind Gupta, 'Introduction', in Arvind Gupta and Anil Wadhwa (eds), *India's Foreign Policy: Surviving in a Turbulent World* (Thousand Oaks, CA: SAGE, 2020), p. 6.

31 See, for example, Ashley J. Tellis, 'How Can US–India Relations Survive the S-400 Deal?', Carnegie Endowment for International Peace, 29 August 2018, https://carnegieendowment.org/2018/08/29/how-can-u.s.-india-relations-survive-s-400-deal-pub-77131.

32 See Ajit K. Dubey, 'Indian Air Force Will Focus on 1.3 Lakh Crore Deal for 114 Fighter Jets', *Live Mint*, 31 January 2021, https://www.livemint.com/news/india/indian-air-force-will-focus-on-rs-1-3-lakh-crore-deal-for-114-fighter-jets-11612086902415.html; and Benjamin E. Schwartz, 'From Inertia to Integration: Getting Serious About US–India Defense Cooperation', *American Interest*, 24 June 2019, https://www.the-american-interest.com/2019/06/24/from-inertia-to-integration-getting-serious-about-u-s-india-defense-cooperation/.

33 See Vivek Raghuvanshi, 'India Releases Details of New Defense Budget', *Defense News*, 2 February 2021, https://www.defencenews.com/global/asia-pacific/2021/02/02/india-releases-details-of-new-defence-budget/.

34 See David Axe, 'India Is Buying the Wrong Warplanes for Fighting China', *Forbes*, 19 June 2020, https://www.forbes.com/sites/davidaxe/2020/06/19/india-is-buying-the-wrong-russian-warplane-for-fighting-china/?sh=793ca6ee1281; and Sanjeev Miglani and Nigam Prusty, 'India Clears Purchase of Russian Combat Jets Worth $2.4 Billion', Reuters, 2 July 2020, https://www.reuters.com/article/us-india-china-defence-idUSKBN2432E2.

35 See, for example, 'Weapons of Mass Supply: Russian–Indian Cooperation in the Military Sphere', RIA Novosti, 2 March 2020, https://uols34sekryxy75dpuh4ztgq2a--ria-ru.translate.goog/20160728/1473076249.html.

36 For deeper analysis, see Lalwani et al., 'The Influence of Arms', pp. 7–13.

37 See Seshadri Chari, 'The Ultimate Goal of Rajnath Singh, Jaishankar's Russia Visit: Move Moscow Away from Beijing', *ThePrint*, 11 September 2020, http://theprint.in/opinion/the-ultimate-goal-of-rajnath-singh-jaishankars-russia-visit-move-moscow-away-from-beijing/500147/; and Sreeram Chaulia, 'India–Russia Friendship Is Too Pragmatic for US and China to Ruin It', RT, 11 April 2021, https://www.rt.com/op-ed/520751-russia-india-pragmatic-friendship/.

38 See Narendra Modi, 'Prime Minister's Keynote Address at Shangri La Dialogue', Ministry of External Affairs, Government of India, 1 June 2018, https://www.mea.gov.in/Speeches-Statements.htm?dtl/29943/

Prime+Ministers+Keynote+Address+at
+Shangri+La+Dialogue+June+01+2018;
and US Department of Defense, 'Indo-
Pacific Strategy Report: Preparedness,
Partnerships, and Promoting a
Networked Region', 1 June 2019, p. 12.

39 See Ashley J. Tellis, 'Non-Allied
Forever: India's Grand Strategy
According to Subrahmanyam
Jaishankar', Carnegie Endowment
for International Peace, 3 March
2021, https://carnegieendowment.
org/2021/03/03/non-allied-forever-
india-s-grand-strategy-according-to-
subrahmanyam-jaishankar-pub-83974;
and Stephen Watts et al., 'Alternative
Worldviews: Understanding
Potential Trajectories of Great-power
Ideological Competition', RAND
Corporation, 2020, pp. 8, 16.

40 See US Department of State, 'Assistant
Secretary for Political–Military Affairs
R. Clarke Cooper', special briefing,
Office of the Spokesperson, 21
November 2019, https://2017-2021.state.
gov/assistant-secretary-for-political-
military-affairs-r-clarke-cooper//index.
html; and US Department of State,
'Background Briefing on Political–
Military Affairs', special briefing, Office
of the Spokesperson, 21 November
2019, https://2017-2021.state.gov/
Background-Briefing-on-Political-
Military-Affairs/index.html.

41 See Vivek Raghuvanshi, 'India's
Auditing Agency Punches Holes
in Russian Sukhoi', *Defense News*,
21 December 2015, https://www.
defencenews.com/home/2015/12/21/
india-s-auditing-agency-punches-
holes-in-russian-sukhoi/; and Prasun
K. Sengupta, 'The Devil Always Lurks
Within the Detail', Trishul Blog, 16

March 2014, http://trishul-trident.
blogspot.com/2014/03/the-devil-
always-lurks-within-detail.html. A
senior Indian defence analyst told
one of the authors that the Indian
Air Force so lacks confidence in
the 'Frankenstein' Su-30 that it was
assigned an escort rather than a
payload-delivery mission in the 2019
Balakot strike.

42 See 'Elections Over, IAF Moves to
Confirm "Friendly Fire" Brought
Down Budgam Chopper', Wire, 21
May 2019, https://thewire.in/security/
iaf-chopper-friendly-fire-criminal-
charges. Indian defence analyst Abhijit
Iyer-Mitra reinforced this assessment in
a conversation with one of the authors.

43 Peter J. Dombrowski, Eugene Gholz
and Andrew L. Ross, 'Military
Transformation and the Defense
Industry After Next', *Newport
Papers*, no. 18, 2003, available at
http://digital-commons.usnwc.edu/
newport-papers/36/.

44 Peter A. Wilson and John V. Parachini,
'Russian S-400 Surface-to-air Missile
System: Is It Worth the Sticker
Price?', RAND Blog, 6 May 2020,
https://www.rand.org/blog/2020/05/
russian-s-400-surface-to-air-missile-
system-is-it-worth.html.

45 See Abhijit Iyer-Mitra, 'What Makes
S-400 a Politically Savvy Deal, but
Hardly a Game Changer', *Business
Standard*, 4 October 2018, http://
www.business-standard.com/article/
economy-policy/what-makes-s-400-a-
politically-savvy-deal-but-hardly-a-
game-changer-118100400668_1.html.

46 See, for example, Vivek Raghuvanshi,
'India and France to Finalize $8.9
Billion Deal for 36 Rafales', *Defense*

News, 19 April 2016, https://www.
defencenews.com/air/2016/04/19/
india-and-france-to-finalize-8-9-
billion-deal-for-36-rafales/; and Anit
Mukherjee, *Absent Dialogue: Politicians,
Bureaucrats, and the Military in India*
(New York: Oxford University Press,
2020), p. 165.

47 See Christian Brose, *The Kill Chain:
Defending America in the Future of High-
tech Warfare* (New York: Hachette,
2020), pp. 145–50.

48 See Ely Ratner et al., 'Rising to the
China Challenge: Renewing American
Competitiveness in the Indo-Pacific',
Center for a New American Security,
December 2019, pp. 8, 20, https://
s3.us-east-1.amazonaws.com/files.
cnas.org/documents/CNAS-Report-
NDAA-final-6.pdf?mtime=2020011613
0752&focal=none.

49 Abercrombie, 'Removing Barriers to
US–India Defense Trade'.

50 See Vishnu Som, 'U.S. May Block
Sale of Armed Drones as India Is
Buying Arms from Russia', NDTV,
29 May 2018, https://www.ndtv.com/
india-news/s-400-missile-deal-us-may-
block-sale-of-predator-drones-as-india-
is-buying-arms-from-russia-1858958.

51 See Snehesh Alex Philip, 'Quad
Navies Can Come Together if Needed
in Almost "Plug and Play" Manner,
Navy Chief Says', *ThePrint*, 14 April
2021, https://theprint.in/defence/
quad-navies-can-come-together-if-
needed-in-almost-plug-and-play-
manner-navy-chief-says/639988/.

52 See Christopher G. Pernin et
al., *Targeted Interoperability: A
New Imperative for Multinational
Operations* (Santa Monica, CA: RAND
Corporation, 2019), pp. 43–5.

53 Author discussion with former US
intelligence and defence official, 11
December 2020.

54 S. Paul Kapur and William C.
McQuilkin, 'Preparing for the Future
Indian Ocean Security Environment:
Challenges and Opportunities for
the Indian Navy', in Sushant Singh
and Pushan Das (eds), *Defense Primer
2017* (New Delhi: Observer Research
Foundation, 2017), pp. 59–64.

55 See Sanjeev Miglani, 'Indian Navy
the Odd Man Out in Asia's "Quad"
Alliance', Reuters, 22 November 2017,
https://www.reuters.com/article/us-
india-usa-quad/indian-navy-the-%20
odd-man-out-in-asias-quad-alliance-
idUSKBN1DM0UB.

56 See Kyle Rempfer, 'Here's How F-35
Technology Would Be Compromised
if Turkey Also Had the S-400 Anti-
aircraft System', *Air Force Times*, 5
April 2019, https://www.airforcetimes.
com/news/your-military/2019/04/05/
heres-how-f-35-technology-would-be-
compromised-if-turkey-also-had-the-
s-400-anti-aircraft-system/.

57 See 'Russian S-400 System Requires
Friendly Aircraft Data to Identify
Friend or Foe', Defense World, 16
May 2019, http://www.defenceworld.
net/news/24786/Russian_S_400_
System_Requires_Friendly_Aircraft_
Data_to_Identify_Friend_or_Foe#.
YCcQ1c9KjAN.

58 See Ganguly and Mason, *An Unnatural
Partnership?*, p. 50.

59 See US Senate Committee on
Foreign Relations, 'Menendez Urges
Secretary Austin to Use Upcoming
Trip to India to Discuss Democracy,
Human Rights and Opposition to
S-400 Missile System'.

60 See Schwartz, 'From Inertia to Integration'.

61 See Cara Abercrombie, 'Realizing the Potential: Mature Defense Cooperation and the US–India Strategic Partnership', *Asia Policy*, vol. 14, no. 1, January 2019, p. 139.

62 US Department of State, 'Background Briefing on Political–Military Affairs'.

63 See Schwartz, 'From Inertia to Integration'.

64 See Tellis, 'How Can US–India Relations Survive the S-400 Deal?'

65 Idrees Ali and Phil Stewart, 'Exclusive: US May Soon Pause Preparations for Delivering F-35s to Turkey', Reuters, 21 March 2019, https://www.reuters.com/article/us-usa-turkey-defence-exclusive/exclusive-us-may-soon-pause-preparations-for-delivering-f-35s-to-turkey-idUSKCN1R20AY.

66 Kurt Campbell and Richard Verma, 'Ash Carter', interview, Tea Leaves Podcast, 16 April 2018, http://theasiagroup.com/ash-carter/; and 'Presidential Waiver on Arms Deal with Moscow Intended to "Wean" Nations like India off Russian Equipment: US'.

67 Singh, 'How to Keep the US–India Defense Relationship Moving Ahead'.

68 See US Government Accountability Office, 'Report to the Committee on International Relations, House of Representatives: Security Assistance – State and DOD Need to Assess How the Foreign Military Financing Program for Egypt Achieves US Foreign Policy and Security Goals', GAO-06-437, 11 April 2006, p. 8, https://www.gao.gov/assets/gao-06-437.pdf.

69 K. Subrahmanyam, 'Vote of Thanks at the National Seminar on Defence Acquisition', *Journal of Defence Studies*, vol. 4, no. 1, January 2010, pp. 12–14. The authors have heard the same idea expressed in US–India Track Two discussions.

70 See Rajesh Rajagopalan, 'Fighting to Balance: China and the Purpose of the India–US Partnership', CSDR, Special Issue I, Policy Paper III, November 2020, pp. 1–11, https://csdronline.org/upload/user/RajeshRajagopalan_FightingtoBalance_CSDR.pdf.

71 See US Department of State, 'A Free and Open Indo-Pacific: Advancing a Shared Vision', 4 November 2019, p. 9, https://www.state.gov/wp-content/uploads/2019/11/Free-and-Open-Indo-Pacific-4Nov2019.pdf.

72 See Niharika Mandhana, 'Russia Missile Deal Puts India in US Sanctions Crosshairs', *Wall Street Journal*, 21 November 2018, https://www.wsj.com/articles/russia-missile-deal-puts-india-in-u-s-sanctions-crosshairs-1538586974.

73 See Kashish Paripiani, Nivedita Kapoor and Angad Singh, 'India's Purchase of the S-400: Understanding the CAATSA Conundrum', Special Report no. 129, Observer Research Foundation, February 2021, pp. 16–17, http://orfonline.org/wp-content/uploads/2021/02/ORF_SpecialReport_129_CAATSA1.pdf.

74 See Center for a New American Security, 'Special Event: Maintaining the Momentum: US–India Relations Under the Biden Administration', panel discussion, Washington DC, 18 March 2021, https://www.cnas.org/events/special-event-the-india-opportunity.

75 See Dimitri Simes, 'Indian Arms Market Heats Up as a US–Russia Battleground', *Nikkei Asia*, 27 March 2020, http://asia.nikkei.com/Politics/International-relations/Indian-arms-market-heats-up-as-a-US-Russia-battleground; and Todd Young, 'Sanctioning India Would Spoil the Quad', *Foreign Policy*, 12 April 2021, https://foreignpolicy.com/2021/04/12/united-states-india-quad-china-russia-s-400-caasta-waiver-biden-modi/.

76 See Vivek Raghuvanshi, 'India Clears Purchase of S-400 AD System for $4.5 Billion', *Defense News*, 17 December 2015, https://www.defensenews.com/pentagon/2015/12/17/india-clears-purchase-of-s-400-ad-system-for-4-5-billion/; and Schwartz, 'From Inertia to Integration'.

77 Several senior US officials have articulated this judgement to the authors, off the record. Former US ambassador to India Kenneth Juster has stated it on the record. See Center for a New American Security, 'Special Event'.

78 See Andrea Kendall-Taylor and David Shullman, 'China and Russia's Dangerous Convergence', *Foreign Affairs*, 3 May 2021, https://www.foreignaffairs.com/articles/china/2021-05-03/china-and-russias-dangerous-convergence.

79 See Schwartz, 'From Inertia to Integration'. One of the authors has participated in tabletop exercises in which former US military officers and defence officials have explicitly made this case for the S-400's utility in India's arsenal.

80 See Anil Ahuja, 'Charting the Future of India–US Defence and Security Cooperation', Delhi Policy Group, 28 March 2021, https://www.delhipolicygroup.org/publication/policy-briefs/charting-the-future-of-india-us-defence-and-security-cooperation.html#_ftnref7.

81 See, for example, Vikram Mahajan, 'India–US Defence Deals: Why CAATSA Should Be Avoided', *Economic Times*, 9 August 2019, https://economictimes.indiatimes.com/news/defence/india-us-defence-deals-why-caatsa-should-be-avoided/articleshow/70611630.cms.

82 See 'Nord Stream 2: Biden Waives US Sanctions on Russian Pipeline', BBC, 20 May 2021, http://bbc.com/news/world-us-canada-57180674.

83 One senior Indian general described it as the 'sword of Damocles'. See Rahul Bedi, 'As Trump Goes, Indian Military Wonders if Biden Will Bell the CAATSA', Wire, 23 December 2020, https://thewire.in/security/donald-trump-biden-india-russia-caatsa-defence.

84 Center for a New American Security, 'Special Event'.

85 Admiral Harry Harris, as commander of the US Pacific Command, acknowledged that some of this joint tracking was happening. See Ajai Shukla, 'US Pacific Commander Admits US–India Jointly Tracking Chinese Submarines', *Business Standard*, 19 January 2017, https://www.ajaishukla.com/2017/01/us-pacific-commander-admits-us-india.html.

86 See William C. McQuilkin, 'It's Later than You Think: Time to Get Another Gear in the India–US Strategic Partnership', Hudson Institute, 30 October 2020.

87 We thank Zachary Keck for this suggestion. See also Pranab Dhal Samanta, 'Bill Moved in US Senate to Bring India on a Par with NATO Allies', *Economic Times*, 16 June 2019, https://economictimes. indiatimes.com/news/defence/ bill-moved-in-us-senate-to-bring-india-on-a-par-with-nato-allies/ articleshow/69816875.cms.

88 See Vishnu Som, 'How Top-secret US System Will Allow India to Track Chinese Submarines', NDTV, 6 September 2018, https://www.ndtv. com/india-news/how-top-secret-us-system-will-allow-india-to-track-chinese-submarines-1912315; and US Department of Defense, 'DoD's Mission Partner Environment: Information System (MPE-IS)', Chief Information Officer, https://dodcio. defense.gov/In-the-News/MPE/.

89 See Rempfer, 'Here's How F-35 Technology Would Be Compromised if Turkey Also Had the S-400 Anti-aircraft System'.

90 See Huma Siddiqui, 'Interoperability of India, US Naval Ships: Tactical Data Inter-linking to Be Discussed at 2+2 Dialogue', *Financial Express*, 10 December 2019, https://www. financialexpress.com/defence/ interoperability-of-india-us-naval-ships-tactical-data-inter-linking-to-be-discussed-at-22-dialogue/1790119/.

91 We thank John Parachini for this idea. See Deepa Ollapally, 'Indo-Russian Strategic Relations: New Choices and Constraints', *Journal of Strategic Studies*, vol. 25, no. 4, 2002, pp. 135–56.

92 Ashley Tellis has noted that 'the United States needs to … alert India to the complications that its choices make'. Milan Vaishnav, 'Ashley J. Tellis on America's "India Dividend"', Grand Tamasha, podcast interview, 8 October 2019, https://grand-tamasha.simplecast.com/episodes/ ashley-j-tellis-on-americas-india-dividend-h__Myfl4.

93 We have observed this over years of Track Two discussions. See also Paripiani, Kapoor and Singh, 'India's Purchase of the S-400'.

94 See remarks by former US ambassador to India Kenneth Juster in Center for a New American Security, 'Special Event'.

95 For more on adjusting expectations, see Sameer Lalwani and Heather Byrne, 'Great Expectations: Asking Too Much of the US–India Strategic Partnership', *Washington Quarterly*, vol. 42, no. 3, Fall 2019, pp. 41–64.

96 See Andrew Imbrie et al., 'Agile Alliances: How the United States and Its Allies Can Deliver a Democratic Way of AI', Center for Security and Emerging Technology, Georgetown University, February 2020, http:// cset.georgetown.edu/research/agile-alliances/; Dan Markey, 'Preparing for Heightened Tensions Between China and India', Contingency Planning Memorandum Update, Center for Preventive Action, Council on Foreign Relations, 19 April 2021, https://www. cfr.org/report/preparing-heightened-tensions-between-china-and-india; and Vikram J. Singh and Joe Felter, 'How SecDef Austin Can Make the Most of His India Visit', Defense One, 18 March 2021, https://www. defenseone.com/ideas/2021/03/ how-us-can-make-most-austins-visit-india/172771/.

97 On American expectations of India,

see, for example, former US national security advisor H.R. McMaster's remarks in 'Ex-Trump National Security Advisor Urges "A Different Approach" to China', NPR, 23 April 2021, https://www.npr.org/transcripts/990088380. On India's willingness, see Rajagopalan, 'Fighting to Balance'. On India's ability, see Ganguly and Mason, *An Unnatural Partnership?*, p. 49.

98 See Richard Fontaine et al., 'Networking Asian Security: An Integrated Approach to Order in the Pacific', Center for a New American Security, June 2017, https://s3.us-east-1.amazonaws.com/files.cnas.org/documents/Networking_Asian_Security_finalc.pdf?mtime=201706191 53411&focal=none.

99 See Ashley Tellis, 'Waylaid by Contradictions: Evaluating Trump's Indo-Pacific Strategy', *Washington Quarterly*, vol. 43, no. 4, Winter 2021, pp. 123–54.

100 See George Gedda, 'Biden Pushes End to India Sanctions', Associated Press, 27 August 2001, https://apnews.com/article/7db49bd4371acb8b387e8a46f81f6b40.

The Iran Nuclear Deal and Sanctions Relief: Implications for US Policy

Esfandyar Batmanghelidj and Mahsa Rouhi

President Joe Biden claimed that there was a 'smarter way to be tough on Iran' during the 2020 US election campaign, and has made returning to the Joint Comprehensive Plan of Action (JCPOA) – that is, the Iran nuclear deal – a foreign-policy priority in his first few months in office.[1] Following a stalemate over which side would move first, negotiations began in May 2021, though without direct talks between American and Iranian officials. A fundamental challenge was how to address Iran's demand for sanctions relief. Iran's leaders have expressed scepticism that the Biden administration is willing to 'verifiably' lift sanctions, which they consider a requirement of the JCPOA.

Their scepticism was understandable: there are efficient and effective means of imposing sanctions, but unwinding them is far more difficult, as trade and investment can lag long after the formal implementation of sanctions relief. This asymmetry will continue to impede US engagement with Iran. More broadly, it potentially undermines the utility of sanctions as a tool of foreign policy, particularly in achieving non-proliferation objectives.

Esfandyar Batmanghelidj is the founder and CEO of the Bourse & Bazaar Foundation, a think tank committed to economic diplomacy, economic development and economic justice in the Middle East and Central Asia, and a Visiting Fellow at the European Council on Foreign Relations. He is also a core member of the Swiss Network for International Studies-funded project 'When Money Can't Buy Food and Medicine', which examines the impact of sanctions on humanitarian trade. **Mahsa Rouhi** is a Research Fellow for Iran, the Levant and Turkey at the Institute for National Strategic Studies at the National Defense University and an Associate Fellow at the IISS. The analysis and conclusions presented in this article are based on her individual research and do not necessarily represent the policies or perspectives of the National Defense University, the US Department of Defense or the US government.

Survival | vol. 63 no. 4 | August–September 2021 | pp. 183–198   https://doi.org/10.1080/00396338.2021.1956192

Agreements such as the JCPOA require sustained compliance. In order to incentivise it, target countries need credible assurance that full compliance guarantees sustained relief.

Sanctions are often seen as an alternative to the use of military force in pursuit of specific policy objectives such as non-proliferation. The United States has devoted more resources than any other power to developing sanctions as a core foreign-policy tool, leveraging the dominant position of the US dollar in the global economy. But sanctions are not a panacea. They impose costs on the targeting as well as the targeted party, which limits their utility. To maximise it, sanctions should be tailored to producing specific policy outcomes, such as nuclear non-proliferation, and not used merely to punish the target or score domestic political points. In the Iranian context, this means ensuring that lifting sanctions will lead to substantial economic relief.

Sanctions and the JCPOA

Sanctions relief under the JCPOA fell short in several areas. Ambiguous guidelines, limited outreach to businesses, insufficient licences and exemptions, and a lack of coordination with third countries made it prohibitively difficult and expensive for most companies to engage in trade or investment in the Iranian market. Companies were critically hampered by the reluctance of banks to process Iran-related transactions due to their perceptions of political, as opposed to mere commercial, risk. Trade did rebound following the lifting of JCPOA-related US and EU sanctions on Iran in January 2016, as an increase in oil exports led quickly to 13.4% economic growth. But no significant investments materialised, hindering prospects for sustained growth. Many key investment contracts floundered because of a lack of financing facilities and general uncertainty.[2]

In May 2018, the US withdrew from the nuclear deal and unilaterally reimposed sanctions. Rather than succumb to the Trump administration's 'maximum pressure' campaign, Iran ramped up uranium enrichment, shortening a one-year breakout time to about three months as of March 2021.[3] Without prospects for meaningful sanctions relief, Iran's strategic cost–benefit calculations are likely to disfavour a revived agreement.[4] To improve prospects for a diplomatic breakthrough, the United States should consider measures for unwinding sanctions expeditiously and equitably.

The JCPOA serves as an important case study of the asymmetry of means in sanctions policy, applicable to US non-proliferation policy in general. Without potent means to deliver effective sanctions relief, arms-control agreements providing it in exchange for verified steps to reduce proliferation are liable to be less durable. This article is not intended to assess whether sanctions are a good or bad foreign-policy tool, or to discuss their legal and ethical status. Rather, we assume that sanctions will remain a significant tool of US non-proliferation policy and identify the inability to effectively lift them as a factor that undermines their usefulness.

Relief versus targeting

Over the last two decades, as sanctions have become a fundamental tool of American foreign policy, analysts and policymakers have primarily examined how to target them effectively against specific individuals, entities and sectors. David Cortright and George Lopez have been particularly influential in developing the concept of 'smart sanctions', which are intended to mitigate the kind of devastating humanitarian damage caused by the application of broad sanctions on Iraq in the 1990s.[5] Sanctions have remained popular policy tools owing to the widespread perception that they can be selectively targeted and discriminate in their effects. It remains less clear, however, that smart sanctions can be effectively lifted. If not, even smart sanctions would preclude meaningful sanctions relief.

Sanctions relief in Iran under the Obama administration was disappointing, as continued legal ambiguity and the hesitancy of banks to support Iran-related transactions stymied foreign investment. The subsequent reimposition of sanctions by the Trump administration has led to escalatory exchanges that brought the US and Iran to the brink of war.[6] In addition, it has led Iran to forge closer alliances with Russia and China, increasing their presence in the Persian Gulf region. Thus, the failure to provide durable sanctions relief has intensified great-power competition and increased risks of military conflict in addition to visiting economic costs on Iran, the US and many other states.

Clearer objectives and mechanisms for sanctions relief would produce better outcomes. Richard Nephew notes that 'sanctioners should anticipate the problems of sanctions relief if they seek to use sanctions to achieve a policy goal', but his proposed solutions to these problems are limited.[7] They include greater clarity with respect to objectives to head off disputes with the target country; more extensive outreach to the private sector; and patience on the part of both the sanctioning party and the target as to the implementation of relief. With respect to the latter, Nephew notes that in 2014, 'the initial release of Iranian restricted assets that, though scheduled and covered with explicit letters of comfort to the associated financial institutions, did not take place as promised'. He observes that at first 'Iranian authorities assumed that the United States was deliberately interfering with implementation as a means of damaging Iranian economic interests'. Nevertheless, he continues, 'over time, Iranian officials began to trust, if not the overall intent of the United States, at least the intent of those officials struggling to solve the problems that emerged'.[8]

Patience, trust and clear expectations, fostered by better targeting and political communication, are necessary but not sufficient conditions of a successful sanctions regime. Overcoming the structural asymmetry between imposing and lifting sanctions is also key, and calls for fair and enforceable verification mechanisms.[9]

The US should consider developing the mechanisms and institutions necessary to implement effective sanctions relief and to ensure that these mechanisms and institutions are considered credible by the target country. In recent years, senior American and European officials have increasingly highlighted deficiencies in the implementation of sanctions relief, especially in the case of Iran. These officials have observed that while governments can move to lift sanctions, eliminating legal barriers to trade and investment, they have highly limited capacities to obligate or encourage the private sector to re-engage. To date, policymakers have primarily sought to address this problem by increasing outreach to the private sector, clarifying how parties can re-engage with Iran without exposing themselves to any lingering sanctions risks. But this approach eases only some of the disincentives to re-engagement.

Sanctions tend to be more effective when (1) the goal is clear and modest; (2) the target is economically and politically weaker; (3) sanctions are imposed decisively; and (4) they do not work inordinate damage to American interests.[10] To ensure sanctions can be effectively lifted and thereby remain an effective foreign-policy tool, policymakers can follow several guidelines.

Set clear and modest goals

In general, sanctions are imposed to meet two kinds of objectives: to stop a particular activity by the target country and to satisfy domestic audiences. The second aim has become particularly relevant since the end of the Cold War. Meghan O'Sullivan has noted that lobbyists were able to shift domestic narratives and that the absence of the Soviet threat provided an opening for their arguments.[11] But domestic political dynamics often make it impossible to forge consensus on sanctions objectives. If domestic political posturing is a prime motivating factor for sanctions, the target state is obliged to weigh its response accordingly. It needs to be attuned to the possibility that domestic constituencies supporting sanctions may 'move the goalposts' to undermine sanctions relief.

Some sanctions are designed to punish a country for a specific act, force it to change its behaviour and signal that similar actions would produce similar consequences in the future. For instance, in 1979, when the US imposed sanctions on Iran for taking American hostages, it was clear to all parties that these were in response to the Americans' detention, and that, unless the hostages were released, the sanctions would remain in place. The Iranians released the hostages in 1981 and sanctions were lifted.

The Trump administration did not make the goal of reimposed sanctions clear to Iran. Restoring all sanctions that had been lifted under the terms of the nuclear deal and designating more than 1,500 additional Iranian individuals and entities for sanctions, the administration made 12 demands that Iran would have to meet in order for sanctions to be lifted. These included not only changes to its nuclear programme but also fundamental changes to Iran's approach to regional security – particularly by ending support for non-state partners such as Hamas and Hizbullah. Given their radically expanded scope, the demands were widely seen as unrealistic and unacceptable terms of surrender, and summarily dismissed by Iranian officials. Iran's foreign minister issued his own list of 15 demands for changes in US behaviour.[12] The view in Tehran was that the American demands were designed to be impossible to meet, were meant simply to signal the administration's maximalist approach to gratify domestic US audiences and at the same time masked the United States' real goal – namely, regime change.[13] It remained at best unclear whether a deal could be reached short of Iran's comprehensive compliance.

Recognise sanctions-relief failure as a security threat

Sanctions can harm US strategic interests if they result in military escalation or place undue strain on US relationships with allies, partners and great-power competitors. Iranian political leaders described American 'economic terrorism' and acts of 'economic war'.[14] Senior Trump administration officials did little to hide the essentially bellicose intentions behind their sanctions, as illustrated by the infamous 'sanctions are coming' poster produced by the White House, comparing Donald Trump's maximum-pressure policy to the threat of war depicted in the TV series *Game of Thrones*. Applied alongside maximalist demands with confusing or unrealistic objectives, sanctions are likely to make a target country more inclined to engage in the use of force than diplomacy.

In this context of maximum pressure – and in contrast to the salutary run-up to the JCPOA, when Iran believed there could be prospects of long-term relief and a shift in relations – Iranian leaders increasingly felt there was little left to lose from defiance. Despite its outdated conventional military capabilities, Tehran was able to leverage its regional proxy network and missile capabilities to disrupt oil shipments in the Gulf by attacking Saudi oil facilities at Abqaiq.[15] This only reinforced the United States' scepticism about Iran's intentions, increased the potential for escalation and reduced regional stability.

The United States' secondary sanctions also have had significant extra-territorial effects. The Kiel Institute recently calculated that the GDP loss experienced by the European Union due to sanctions was $29.5 billion.[16] Notwithstanding the relative powerlessness of other countries against

American economic assertiveness, the Trump administration's unilateral approach has involved significant political costs. EU president Jean-Claude Juncker registered the perception that the US 'no longer wants to cooperate with other parts of the world'.[17] Sanctions also kindled European legal and institutional efforts to sustain the nuclear deal's viability after the US withdrawal.[18] European policymakers revived the so-called 'blocking regulation', which in theory prohibits EU companies from complying with foreign sanctions laws. In practice, however, companies can often point to other reasons for withdrawing from a market, and they did.[19] The revival of the blocking regulation was therefore a largely symbolic move. But EU-wide support for somehow resisting secondary sanctions did help build consensus behind bolstering Europe's economic sovereignty in the long term.

Subsequent efforts included the creation of a novel special-purpose vehicle, called the Instrument in Support of Trade Exchanges (INSTEX), which was intended to relax banks' unwillingness or reluctance to engage in transactions with Iranian financial institutions due to US secondary sanctions. INSTEX would make payments to European exporters on behalf of Iranian importers, netting those liabilities against payments made by its Iranian counterpart, the Special Trade and Finance Instrument, to Iranian exporters on behalf of European importers. In this way, no payment would have to be made between the European and Iranian financial systems. But the first reported INSTEX transaction was not completed until March 2020, and involved the transfer of medical goods from Europe to Iran, largely in response to the nascent global COVID-19 pandemic.[20] INSTEX failed to facilitate any significant trade in the two years following Trump's withdrawal from the nuclear deal. But the development of INSTEX did attune European policymakers to the ways in which US secondary sanctions affected the commercial operations of European companies and the long-term need to mitigate them.

China and, to a lesser extent, Russia also examined methods to counteract US sanctions, fearing that they too could become targets. The two countries explored the wider adoption of Russia's System for Transfer of Financial Messages, a Russian alternative to the globally dominant SWIFT payments-messaging system, which, although headquartered in Belgium, was compelled to cut off Iranian banks in 2012 under American pressure. But despite Beijing's strident opposition to American 'bullying', Chinese firms exhibited a degree of risk aversion similar to that of European firms to staying in Iranian markets.[21] Notably, Bank of Kunlun, the key Chinese bank in bilateral trade with Iran, which had been designated by the Obama administration for directly flouting pre-JCPOA sanctions, revised its policies, informing clients that it would only process payments for trade not subject to US secondary sanctions.[22] Even so, while Chinese imports of Iranian oil did fall significantly in the face of US sanctions, they did not drop to zero, as China sustained imports in part by routing purchases through third countries such as Malaysia. Overall, Iran continued to export a million barrels of oil per day after Trump's withdrawal from the nuclear deal. Although Iranian officials remained disappointed, the Chinese have helped Iran use cryptocurrency systems to circumvent US sanctions.[23] Europe, Russia and China didn't compensate for the economic impact of US withdrawal, but they did mitigate it and diminish US leverage. For the sake of preserving US economic primacy, Washington would do well to reconsider secondary sanctions in light of their unintended costs and consequences.

Avoid layering designations

The layering of sanctions designations was arguably the most cynical aspect of the Trump administration's sanctions policy. Not only were sanctions applied in such a way as to make it impossible for the target country to change its behaviour to benefit from sanctions relief, but, in the final year of the administration, a concerted effort was made to preclude future administrations from relaxing or lifting sanctions even in the event of resumed Iranian compliance with the JCPOA. Under the so-called 'sanctions wall' erected by the Trump administration, entities designated under nuclear sanctions were also designated under new authorities based on terrorism and human-rights violations.

This dispensation did not meaningfully increase US national security, as the additional designations did not establish new financial penalties for entities already isolated from the global financial system. For example, the new sanctions roll-out included designating the Central Bank of Iran and other financial institutions as terrorist organisations. But the Central Bank had been sanctioned for at least 20 years, and the move served only to remove certain exceptions that facilitated the delivery of food, medicine and medical devices to Iran, doing precious little to further hinder the militant organisations that concerned the United States – namely, the Islamic Revolutionary Guard Corps and Hizbullah.[24] To Iran, the JCPOA had been not only relief from nuclear sanctions but also an 'invitation back to the international economic community'.[25] By effectively cancelling that invitation and increasing Iranian resistance, the sanctions wall diminished international security.

One lesson is that, in general, sanctions relief warranted by a behaviour change in one area should not be inhibited if there is a lack of progress in another area. For example, if it is necessary for US policymakers to lift sanctions on the Central Bank of Iran in order to achieve a non-proliferation objective, a terrorism designation should not impede such a move, so long as it can be demonstrated that the lifting of nuclear-related sanctions on the bank has a neutral impact on US policy goals related to terrorism. The Biden administration seems to have absorbed this general lesson, having indicated a willingness to lift sanctions that were inconsistent with the terms of the nuclear deal. Admittedly, however, it would be politically difficult for the administration to remove counter-terrorism designations outright.

Introduce default sunsets

Policymakers should consider exploring whether sanctions should be subject to time limitations, often called sunsets, that would require designations to be renewed in order to remain in force.[26] Sunsets have been used in the context of multilateral sanctions imposed by the UN Security Council. But they have not become standard components of multilateral sanctions policy, in part due to opposition from the United States.

Including sunsets within sanctions programmes would mandate an inter-agency review as to whether sanctions were achieving their intended goals or creating unintended and counterproductive new risks. This review process could also provide an opportunity for congressional leaders to weigh in on the justifications of the renewal and the consistency of the sanctions imposed by the executive branch with underlying legislation. Moreover, the pendency of the sanctions-renewal process would incentivise a non-compliant sanctions target to change its behaviour so as to preclude renewal. Such a system would reduce the political burden on both the sanctioning and the sanctioned party, insofar as lifting sanctions is a more significant political act than merely allowing them to expire.

Reorganise the sanctions bureaucracy

One of the most obvious structural problems bedevilling sanctions relief is that the same entities responsible for imposing sanctions are given the responsibility for lifting them. In March 2016, just a few months after the US lifted secondary sanctions on Iran, then-treasury secretary Jack Lew gave a major speech on the future of US sanctions policy, emphasising that the US 'must be prepared to offer sanctions relief if we want countries to change their behavior'. At stake was the 'credibility' of the US and the 'ability to use sanctions to drive policy change'. Notably, Lew did not address the political willingness to offer sanctions relief but rather focused on practical preparations for sanctions relief. He referred to the 'widespread global outreach' being undertaken 'to help governments and businesses understand the sanctions relief provided'.[27] But the adequacy of that outreach was part of the problem.

The US government soon realised that non-US banks remained reluctant to facilitate Iran-related transactions, even after the lifting of sanctions made those transactions permissible. Companies that had sought to resume or expand trade with Iran were finding it difficult to make payments, imperilling the economic relief promised to Iran under the JCPOA. In May 2016, then-secretary of state John Kerry travelled to London to meet collectively with senior executives from some of the world's largest banks to reassure them that they no longer faced legal and reputational risks for engaging with Iran.[28] Kerry's meeting did not go well. Stuart Levey, chief legal officer of HSBC and former under secretary of the treasury for terrorism and financial intelligence, subsequently penned an op-ed in the *Wall Street Journal* stating that his bank would not be engaging in business with Iran and noting that US financial institutions were still barred from engaging in most Iran-related business because of 'financial-crime risks' posed by the Iranian financial system.[29] Levey also pointed to the 'irony' that, from his perspective, Kerry's message reflected more a change in US policy than one in Iranian policy. The Obama administration would never manage to get major banks on board with processing Iranian transactions, although there were some indications that with more time, banks may have been convinced to do more business with Iran at the behest of major clients. Six months later, the election of Donald Trump, who had promised during his campaign to tear up the Iran nuclear deal, ensured that they would refrain from doing so. Iran was the latest case in a long line of countries for which sanctions relief had proven 'controversial, complicated and halting'.[30]

The failure of the Obama administration to mobilise an appreciable contingent of companies and banks to take advantage of sanctions relief made it easy for the Trump administration to reimpose sanctions. To reduce the likelihood of such failures in the future, Congress could explore the creation of a dedicated office within the US Department of the Treasury responsible for the implementation of sanctions relief. This office would work closely with the Office of Foreign Assets Control but would have the distinct mission of maximising the effectiveness of US sanctions relief through guidance and outreach activities. Officials from the new body would engage with private companies and banks to explain to them the implications of sanctions relief for their businesses, articulate its benefits to the companies themselves as well as the US financial system and economy, and reinforce the US commitment to sanctions relief.

To maximise the efficacy of sanctions relief, the US government would also have to consider cultivating connections between the private sector and target parties. Following the implementation of the JCPOA, Boeing's agreements to sell aircraft to two Iranian carriers, Iran Air and Aseman, for $20bn was presented as an example of both the provisional US commitment to the regeneration of the Iranian economy and the economic benefits that could flow back to the US. But despite Boeing's lobbying clout and the direct involvement of the US Treasury, which provided Boeing with the necessary licences, the deal floundered, mainly due to the reluctance of lenders to provide the Iranian airlines substantial credit or process simple payments from Iran. The Obama administration could have mobilised the US Export–Import Bank to provide the required short-term credit and reassure prospective commercial lenders of firm federal backing.[31] But congressional pushback and a legal interpretation that the bank was barred from engaging with Iran so long as the country was identified by the US as a state sponsor of terror prompted Boeing to back away from the deal.[32]

In implementing sanctions relief in the future, the US government should consider looking to the US Export–Import Bank or perhaps the international financial institutions to provide financing when commercial banks remain wary. It might also be worth investigating the feasibility of a new federal institution purpose-built to facilitate sanctions relief. In addition, the US should consider extending grants, technical assistance and other programmatic support to the targeted country in order to accelerate the return of private-sector business activity.

Create a multilateral framework for verification

The decision to lift sanctions is typically tied to a specific foreign-policy or national-security goal, and very often these goals pertain to non-proliferation. To benefit from sanctions relief, the target country is expected to verifiably reduce or cease activities that pose a proliferation threat. This is the quid pro quo at the heart of the JCPOA. Under the agreement, Iran's compliance with restrictions on its nuclear programme are forensically verified by the International Atomic Energy Agency. But there is no third party empowered or tasked to verify whether the countries that imposed sanctions have lifted them in accordance with the agreement. As the Biden administration began its efforts to re-enter the JCPOA, verification of sanctions relief emerged as a key Iranian demand.

In a February 2020 speech, Ayatollah Sayyid Ali Khamenei, Iran's Supreme Leader, insisted that sanctions relief take place 'in practice' and not just 'on paper', suggesting that improved guidance and outreach would be insufficient. Particularly after the fraught experience of sanctions relief following the implementation of the JCPOA in 2016 and the ambiguities that any new sanctions relief will inevitably involve, Iranian officials will likely need to see a more tangible and institutionally consolidated means of realising sanctions relief to remain satisfied with a renewed agreement. Verification will also be important to third countries that have supported a multilateral sanctions campaign in which US sanctions provided the main source of economic coercion.

To ensure the effectiveness of sanctions relief, the target country, third countries and financial institutions should be able to turn to a body empowered to monitor and report on the extent to which political and structural factors – some associated with one state, others more systemic – are impeding or facilitating the lifting of sanctions. Such a body would enable these interested parties to better inform their risk assessments with regard to commercial and financial transactions, and identify sanctions-related matters requiring clarification or diplomatic attention. It would make sense for this body to be part of the UN system, perhaps initially as a panel of experts and eventually as a dedicated agency. A UN verification capacity could prove important to the integrity not only of the JCPOA, but also of future political and legal arrangements involving Cuba, North Korea, Syria and Venezuela.

*   *   *

Sanctions have become an American policy tool of choice, particularly to address non-proliferation concerns. They have evolved considerably since the 1990s, but so far policymakers have not established a satisfactory way of lifting sanctions when they have achieved their intended aim. The Biden administration's struggles to re-enter the Iran nuclear deal show that inadequate sanctions policy cannot be neatly remedied after the fact. Rather, effective sanctions relief must be considered and secured along the lines suggested here as a sanctions policy is being devised and initiated.

The Biden administration is now undertaking an extensive review of sanctions policy in part to ensure the long-term efficacy of sanctions as an instrument of statecraft.[33] Such a review must contend with the clear challenges of US policy in the area of sanctions relief and recognise that lifting sanctions is as crucial as imposing them in an effective sanctions programme.

Notes

1   'Joe Biden: There's a Smarter Way to Be Tough on Iran', CNN, 13 September 2020, https://edition.cnn.com/2020/09/13/opinions/smarter-way-to-be-tough-on-iran-joe-biden/index.html.

2   World Bank, 'Iran's Economic Outlook – October 2017', October 2017, https://www.worldbank.org/en/country/iran/publication/iran-economic-outlook-october-2017.

3   See Kelsey Davenport and Julia Masterson, 'Restoring the Nuclear Deal with Iran Benefits US Nonproliferation Priorities', Arms Control Association, 15 March 2021, https://www.armscontrol.org/issue-briefs/2021-03/restoring-nuclear-deal-iran-benefits-us-nonproliferation-priorities.

4   Iran has also faced three years of economic recession, prolonged by the COVID-19 pandemic, following the reimposition of US secondary sanctions. US sanctions hit export revenues, thrusting the country into a balance-of-payments crisis. Iranian officials were largely unable to dip into reserves to ease pressure on the currency, leading to sharp devaluation. Inflation rose, putting pressure on households as everyday goods, including food and medicine, became more expensive, and in the case of imported goods, scarcer. Reduced consumption saw factories scale back, exacerbating Iran's already high rates of chronic unemployment. Perhaps most consequentially, millions of Iranians were pushed into poverty. Today, as Iran's economy begins to recover from its long and painful downturn, many households are being left behind, their fortunes irrevocably changed. Having weathered the storm for years, however, the Iranian government is not likely to relax its insistence on meaningful sanctions relief. For more on the human costs of sanctions, see Joy Gordon, *Invisible War: The United States and the Iraq Sanctions* (Cambridge, MA: Harvard University Press, 2012); Erica S. Moret, 'Humanitarian Impacts of Economic Sanctions on Iran and Syria', *European Security*, vol. 24, no. 1, February 2014, pp. 120–40; and Tara Sepehri Far, '"Maximum Pressure": US Economic Sanctions Harm Iranians' Right to Health', Human Rights Watch, 29 October 2019, https://www.hrw.org/report/2019/10/29/maximum-pressure/us-economic-sanctions-harm-iranians-right-health.

5   See David Cortright and George A. Lopez (eds), *Smart Sanctions: Targeting Economic Statecraft* (New York: Rowman & Littlefield Publishers, 2002).

6   See Mahsa Rouhi, 'Will Iran Follow North Korea's Path and Ditch the NPT?', *Foreign Policy*, 16 March 2020, https://foreignpolicy.com/2020/03/16/will-iran-follow-north-korea-path-ditch-npt-nuclear-bomb/.

7   Richard Nephew, 'The Hard Part: The Art of Sanctions Relief', *Washington Quarterly*, Summer 2018, pp. 63–77, 75.

8   *Ibid.*, p. 75.

9   See White House, 'Statement by the President on Iran', 14 July 2015, https://obamawhitehouse.archives.gov/the-press-office/2015/07/14/

statement-president-iran; and Ali
Khamenei, 'If They Want Iran to
Resume Its JCPOA Commitments,
the US Has to Remove All Sanctions',
Khamenei.ir, 7 February 2021, https://
english.khamenei.ir/news/8363/
If-they-want-Iran-to-resume-its-
JCPOA-commitments-the-US-has.

10 See Kimberly Ann Elliott, Gary
C. Hufbauer and Barbara Oegg,
'Sanctions', Library of Economics and
Liberty, https://www.econlib.org/
library/Enc/Sanctions.html.

11 Meghan L. O'Sullivan, *Shrewd
Sanctions: Statecraft and State Sponsors
of Terrorism* (Washington DC:
Brookings Institution Press, 2003).

12 See 'Zarif Responds to Pompeo's
Demands', United States
Institute of Peace, 21 June 2018,
https://iranprimer.usip.org/
blog/2018/jun/21/zarif-responds-
pompeo%E2%80%99s-demands.

13 See Jon B. Wolfsthal and Julie Smith,
'Pompeo's Iran Plan Is a Pipe Dream',
Foreign Policy, 21 May 2018, https://
foreignpolicy.com/2018/05/21/
pompeos-iran-nuclear-plan-is-a-pip-
dream-trump/.

14 See, for example, Aime Williams and
Najmeh Bozorgmehr, 'Iran's Rouhani
Accuses US of "Merciless Economic
Terrorism"', *Financial Times*, 25
September 2019.

15 See Verity Ratcliffe, Julian Lee
and Javier Blas, 'Why the Strait of
Hormuz Is a Global Flashpoint',
Washington Post, 13 January 2021;
Mahsa Rouhi, 'Whatever Iran's Role
in the Saudi Attack, the Regional
Status Quo Is Unsustainable',
Guardian, 18 September 2019; and
Hadi Ajili and Mahsa Rouhi, 'Iran's

Military Strategy', *Survival*, vol. 61,
no. 6, December 2019–January 2020,
pp. 139–52.

16 See Sonali Chowdhry et al., 'The
Economic Costs of War by Other
Means', Kiel Policy Briefs no. 147,
Kiel Institute for the World Economy,
October 2020.

17 David Koenig, 'Sanctions on Iran
Could Cost US, European Companies
Billions', Associated Press, 9 May
2018, https://apnews.com/article/
donald-trump-financial-markets-
ap-top-news-germany-france-
2d65918e1f2c414289cd9429058ced9b.

18 See 'France Urges Europe to Push
Back Against "Unacceptable" US
Sanctions on Iran', *France 24*, 5
December 2018, https://www.france24.
com/en/20180511-iran-france-usa-
europe-business-push-back-against-
unacceptable-sanctions-nuclear-trump.

19 See Ellie Geranmayeh and Esfandyar
Batmanghelidj, 'How Europe Can Block
Trump', *Foreign Policy*, 16 May 2018.

20 See 'Europe and Iran Complete
First INSTEX Deal Dodging US
Sanctions', Deutsche Welle, 21 March
2020, https://www.dw.com/en/
europe-and-iran-complete-first-instex-
deal-dodging-us-sanctions/a-52966842.
See also Mark Fitzpatrick, 'Sanctioning
Pandemic-plagued Iran', *Survival*, vol.
62, no. 3, June–July 2020, pp. 93–102.

21 See Huizhong Wu and Humeyra
Pamuk, 'China Criticizes New
US Sanctions over Iranian Oil
Deals', Reuters, 25 September 2019,
https://www.reuters.com/article/
us-iran-nuclear-usa/china-criticizes-
new-u-s-sanctions-over-iranian-oil-
deals-idUSKBN1WA1M6.

22 See Maziar Motamedi, 'Policy

Change at China's Bank of Kunlun Cuts Iran Sanctions Lifeline', Bourse & Bazaar, 2 January 2021, https://www.bourseandbazaar.com/articles/2019/1/2/policy-change-at-chinas-bank-of-kunlun-cuts-sanctions-lifeline-for-iranian-industry.

23 See Enrique Dans, 'A Parallel Financial System Is Being Created and It's Going To Be a Problem', EnriqueDans, 2 August 2019, https://medium.com/enrique-dans/a-parallel-financial-system-is-being-created-and-its-going-to-be-a-problem-347e1d09cbf3; and Thomas Erdbrink, 'How Bitcoin Could Help Iran Undermine US Sanctions', *New York Times*, 29 January 2019.

24 See Brian O'Toole, 'Iranian Central Bank Designation: What Does It Mean?', Atlantic Council, 20 September 2019, https://www.atlanticcouncil.org/blogs/new-atlanticist/iranian-central-bank-designation-what-does-it-mean/.

25 Karen DeYoung et al., 'US Willing to Lift Sanctions Imposed on Iran by Trump that Are "Inconsistent" with 2015 Nuclear Deal, Senior Biden Administration Official Says', *Washington Post*, 10 April 2021.

26 See Kristen E. Boon, 'Terminating Security Council Sanctions', International Peace Institute, April 2014, https://www.ipinst.org/wp-content/uploads/publications/terminating_security_council_sanctions.pdf.

27 US Department of the Treasury, 'Remarks of Secretary Lew on the Evolution of Sanctions and Lessons for the Future at the Carnegie Endowment for International Peace', 30 March 2016, https://www.treasury.gov/press-center/press-releases/pages/jl0398.aspx.

28 See Wu and Pamuk, 'China Criticizes New US Sanctions Over Iranian Oil Deals.'

29 Stuart Levey, 'Kerry's Peculiar Message About Iran for European Banks', *Wall Street Journal*, 12 May 2016.

30 Nephew, 'The Hard Part', p. 63.

31 See Christopher Lawrence, 'Making Peace with Iran and North Korea Could Be Good for US Workers', *Foreign Policy*, 25 March 2021.

32 See Vicki Needham, 'Boeing Tells Lawmakers Sale of Planes to Iran Well-known Part of Nuclear Agreement', *Hill*, 23 June 2016, https://thehill.com/policy/finance/284705-boeing-tells-lawmakers-sale-of-planes-to-iran-well-known-part-of-nuclear.

33 See Mengqi Sun, 'Biden Administration's Review of Sanctions Programs Could Take Months, White House Official Says', *Wall Street Journal*, 2 March 2021.

The US–Mexico Border: Asylum, Fear and Trump

Russell Crandall

The Dispossessed: A Story of Asylum at the US–Mexican Border and Beyond
John Washington. London: Verso, 2020. £16.99. 352 pp.

Growing up in the provincial district of Usulután, El Salvador, in the coastal town of Corral de Mulas, Arnovis Guidos Portillo was one of the lucky children who owned sandals, as shoes were a rare and expensive commodity. His home was a one-room, dirt-floored hut without electricity, with goats roaming out front. Young Portillo worked alongside his father, leading oxen to plough the family's small plot of land for beans, corn and other crops. Before long, he was able to single-handedly seed a 50-acre field, earning him $12, of which $10 would be handed over to his family. Portillo earned some extra money by acting as a scarecrow for his grandfather and working nights at a sea-turtle hatchery, which paid him $180 per month. Though Portillo's economic prospects were limited, he was more than satisfied with his life in the small hamlet, where he and his parents would relax in hammocks, take in the evening's warm ocean breeze, eat the national dish of *pupusas* and enjoy each other's company.

This all changed in 2016. Now 20-year-old Portillo had become a talented football player participating in the small but competitive local league.

Russell Crandall is a professor of American foreign policy and international politics at Davidson College in North Carolina, and a contributing editor to *Survival*. His latest book is *Drugs and Thugs: The History and Future of America's War on Drugs* (Yale University Press, 2020).

Survival | vol. 63 no. 4 | August–September 2021 | pp. 199–208 https://doi.org/10.1080/00396338.2021.1956199

During a game, he accidently collided with an opposing player, El Monkey, whose brother was a *palabrero* (chief) of the local Barrio 18 gang. Within days, Portillo was subjected to death threats ('*sos tumba*' – literally, 'you are a tomb'). Simultaneously, Mara Salvatrucha (MS-13), the arch-enemy of Barrio 18, offered to enlist and protect him. It was common knowledge that rejecting an 'invitation' by MS-13 would have deadly consequences. The power and influence of both these gangs should not be underestimated; they effectively constitute the ruling class, and use surveillance and violence to achieve their ends. Menaced by both Barrio 18 and MS-13, Portillo knew the only way to ensure his safety was to leave El Salvador.

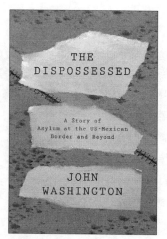

In his impassioned and essential *The Dispossessed*, journalist and activist John Washington vividly chronicles Portillo's life and the hardship that he has endured: 'The end of Arnovis's ulna cracking against El Monkey's molars: and then two years of flight, Arnovis chased and detained by the merciless men-hunters, trying three times to enter the United States, twice deported, his daughter taken from him, lingering years of dread and occasional moments of panic' (p. 27).

In what he later develops into a condemnation of contemporary neoliberal globalisation, Washington explains that Arnovis, like countless others from the Northern Triangle (comprising El Salvador, Guatemala and Honduras), never wanted to leave his homeland. Rather, he was forced out:

[Portillo] never wanted to take the one-way 'highway' out of Corral. He had wanted to finish building his house, add another room, work for his plot of land, and harvest his corn and beans and cashews for his family. He had wanted to fish, watch his daughter grow up, and hang in his hammock in the evenings or stroll down the street to visit his neighbors. Sometimes, he told me, when he was in flight – in a detention center or on the top of a train – he would think about what he would be doing if he were back at home. I would be together with my family, he said, relaxing after work, maybe watching television. That was the life he wanted. It was not the one he got. (p. 81)

Through telling his story, Washington charts how the United States (and the West in general) has eviscerated asylum protections for the world's most vulnerable people, focusing on the Trump administration's immigration policies and the converging fears at play that have resulted in asylum seekers falling between the cracks of state succour – namely, the 'instigating fear that pushes people to flee their country' and the 'receiving population's fear that propels them to slam the door'. The result, the author laments, is a 'global crisis of homelessness' (p. 15) and, in the case of those from Central America and Mexico, 'a new American diaspora'.

Detained and deported

'*La Bestia*' ('The Beast') is the infamous system of freight rail to which migrants, overwhelmingly from Central America and the southern Mexican states, 'cling to get a free but dangerous and sometimes deadly ride north' (p. 85). Astonishingly, Portillo reckons that he has ridden it no fewer than four times. On his trips northbound, he observed that his *coyotes* (smugglers) would habitually consume alcohol and drugs: 'They'd pound cheap beers and gas station mezcal and then get high, and all the migrants would watch them nervously, not knowing where the ribaldry would lead' (p. 86). Washington does not hide his indignation:

> But why does an asylum seeker even need to crawl onto the top of a freight train, gain the trust of a coyote, swim across a swift river, walk through the jungle or the desert, and languish for days with little food in a cramped safe house run by murderous young men? Isn't there a more orderly and safer way to ask the United States for protection? (p. 86)

Portillo's two trips to plead for asylum ended with deportation, from Mexico and Louisiana respectively. 'It's hard to hide here', he says of his home town. 'Everyone knows you.'[1] Undaunted by his previous failures, he then tried a third time with his six-year-old daughter, Meybelin, hoping to reach his brother who resided in Kansas.

On 26 May 2018, having spent more than a week trying to cross the US–Mexico border, Portillo and Meybelin 'boarded a raft, floated the Rio Grande, and walked into the scrub' outside of Hidalgo, Texas, where he requested asylum at a regional US Customs and Border Protection facility. He and his daughter were initially treated well, he recalled. But the next day, Meybelin, sobbing and screaming, was forcibly taken from him in accordance with the Trump administration's new family-separation strategy – part of a 'zero tolerance' policy whereby everyone crossing the border was prosecuted. *Washington Post* journalist Joshua Partlow was there, reporting the scene:

> Arnovis Guidos Portillo remembers the authorities in green uniforms telling him that this would only be temporary … They told him that [Meybelin] should really go with them, he recalled. The holding cell was cold, he said he was told, and the child was not sleeping well. Don't worry, he was assured, she would take the first bus, and he would follow soon … 'What's best is we take her to another place,' he recalled a U.S. official telling him.[2]

Portillo had no news of where they had taken Meybelin. He pleaded guilty to the charge of illegally entering the US and was transferred to an Immigration and Customs Enforcement detention centre in Texas. Though he initially refused to sign a document approving his own deportation, hoping that remaining in the facility would bring about a reunion with Meybelin, after ten days he despondently signed it and his deportation to El Salvador ensued, while his daughter remained somewhere behind.

The family-separation policy ignited a firestorm of criticism around the world, and in late June 2018 US president Donald Trump signed an executive order ending the practice – more than two months after the policy officially began. A federal judge ordered the 2,000 affected families to be reunited. Meybelin, who had been detained in a migrant shelter, was returned to El Salvador and reunited with her father after their month-long separation.[3] Yet, as recently as autumn 2020, 545 separated children remained 'unreachable', as described by the US government.[4]

Honeypots and havens
According to Washington, there is a 'reductive and false dichotomy' between 'bona fide' asylum seekers and 'bogus' migrants, the latter of whom

are attracted to the economic benefits of the 'pull' country. He criticises Alexander Betts and Paul Collier, two influential British scholars, for their view that 'migrants [are] lured by hope; refugees [are] fleeing fear. Migrants hope for honeypots; refugees need havens' (p. 47).[5] Rather, there is 'much bleeding, leapfrogging, and catalysis' between the two, as shown by the case of Portillo: perhaps with a higher wage at the sea-turtle hatchery, he might have been able to move elsewhere within the country and escape the gangs' reach. 'Living hand to mouth, however, he would have only been able to afford to move somewhere equally overrun by gangs, where he would have been quickly identified and newly targeted' (p. 47). Boiling the issue down to a dearth of economic opportunities seems obvious at first, but is nonetheless valid – especially given the connection between local economic issues and global capitalist interests: 'The first cause of the crisis is ongoing transnational corporate capitalist and neocolonial despoilment … that upheaves countries and unroots their people' (p. 49).

The Dispossessed contends that the concept of asylum is straightforward: 'Someone comes to your door because they are in danger, because they are afraid. You open your door, and you share your roof.' Yet complicating this is a mixture of fears, explains Washington – some stemming from the prospect of imminent physical danger, some part of a more generalised climate of persecution, some fears imaginary, some unrealised and others that 'send you to your grave' (p. 6). The legal basis of asylum is even more complex. Throughout the book, the author traces the history of immigration law and policy, from which we learn that the 1951 United Nations Refugee Convention established the first global definitions of 'refugee' and 'asylum seeker', the former being someone who,

> owing to a well-founded fear of being persecuted for reasons of race, religion, nationality, membership of a particular social group or political opinion, is outside the country of his nationality and is unable, or, owing to such fear, unwilling to avail himself of the protection of that country; or who, not having a nationality and being outside the country of his former habitual residence as a result of such events, is unable or, owing to such fear, is unwilling to return to it. (p. 7)

As the US government sees it, an asylee is someone who meets the definition of a refugee but is already in the US, including at a port of entry. Although Washington emphasises that fear is a necessary criterion for the granting of asylum, the UN language is predicated on fear of oppression by the state. Yet for Central Americans and Mexicans, who constitute a significant share of today's US asylum seekers, it is non-state actors that they fear and flee from.

The author also describes how the process to enter the United States has changed over the years. Refugees submit their case from their native soil or interim resettlement locale in order to obtain refugee status. The US accepts a limited number of refugees from each region – for Latin America in 2018 it was 1,500, but fewer than 1,000 were actually approved. By contrast, there is no ceiling for the number of asylees. While the author does not provide evidence of a direct causal relationship, he is convinced that the ever-shrinking refugee limits have driven migrants to seek asylum instead. According to the US Department of Homeland Security, in 2017, 107,394 people from El Salvador, Honduras and Guatemala alone applied for asylum, more than double the rate of the two prior years. Between 2013 and 2015, the Northern Triangle nations had generated more asylum cases than the previous 15 years combined.[6] About a decade ago, around 1% of border-crossing migrants pleaded asylum, compared with 33% in 2018.[7]

Fear and persecution

Washington was surprised by the number of Salvadoran deportees with whom he spoke that felt discriminated against by their communities since returning home – for example, due to the assumption that they had committed crimes in the US. Such presumptions fuelled the vicious cycle of worse employment prospects, poorer and more violent barrios, and increased gang threats, driving even more Salvadorans to seek asylum. Washington acknowledges that this fear of persecution can be legitimate, exaggerated or fabricated, but also that it remains the 'only currency besides actual currency (wealth) that will buy you entrance into the United States and other so-called developed countries. And migrants know it; that fear is their ticket. And so they claim it' (p. 49). The author elaborates: 'For asylum seekers, originally displaced through violence or persecution, refugee protocols demand they tell a story in order to find a new home' (p. 50).

But this does not prevent countries answering 'claims of fear by claiming their own fear', and thus not offering help to, or even targeting, asylum seekers (p. 49). In the case of the United States, Trump, during a speech to police officers in 2017, used MS-13 violence in Long Island, New York, to justify his administration's immigration policy:

> They kidnap, they extort, they rape and they rob. They prey on children. They shouldn't be here. They stomp on their victims. They beat them with clubs. They slash them with machetes, and they stab them with knives. They have transformed peaceful parks and beautiful quiet neighborhoods into blood-stained killing fields. They're animals.[8]

By the end of 2019, the administration had fully established a new policy of 'metering', or turning away, asylum seekers. It also implemented the Migrant Protection Protocols, which effectively forced asylum seekers to remain on the Mexican side of the border before having their hearing in a US court at a later date (p. 113). In less than a year, more than 66,000 asylum-seeking migrants, one-third of them children, had been sent to Mexico; some migrants waited for over a year for their hearings, during which time they lived in poor sanitary conditions in de facto refugee camps rife with gang activity, and were barred from working in Mexico. According to one Guatemalan woman who lived in a border camp: 'They don't secure us, we can't bathe, they don't have food, they treat us like dogs' (p. 114). And that was before the COVID-19 pandemic. Human Rights First reported that, as of the end of 2020, there were more than 1,313 reported cases of kidnapping, rape, torture, murder and other violent crimes against migrants waiting in Mexico.[9] The absence of any protection for these migrants has prompted critics to dub the programme the 'Migrant *Persecution* Protocols' (p. 113).

*　　　*　　　*

The Dispossessed calls not only for a complete overhaul of global capitalism, which the author holds responsible for increasing refugee claims, but for those in asylum-seeker host countries to put aside their own prejudices and fears. Surprisingly, Washington does not address the so-called 'open border' approach – 'Free to Move, Free to Stay' – pushed by the left wing of the US Democratic Party, intended to make amends for long-standing US racism.[10] Nor does he engage with other arguments, such as that of *New York Times* columnist Thomas Friedman, who contends that restricting migration at the US–Mexico border can be moral and necessary, but only if the wall has a 'big gate'.[11]

While Washington's book is an urgent account of Trump's most damaging policies, the election of Joe Biden offers a more optimistic outlook. Amid his many executive orders upon assuming office, Biden ordered an immediate halt to the construction of Trump's infamous border wall and terminated the 'national emergency' declared by the former president in February 2019, which diverted billions of dollars to border security, mainly from the Department of Defense. In January 2021, the Department of Homeland Security announced that it was pausing deportations for 'certain noncitizens' for 100 days as it reviewed its immigration-enforcement system.[12]

Perhaps most importantly, on his first day as president, Biden promised to 'reset the policies and practices for enforcing civil immigration laws' as part of a wider policy shift aimed at balancing issues of national security with an appreciation for the contribution of immigrants.[13] Whether this results in tangible changes that materially affect the lives of those attempting to reach safety in the US remains to be seen.

Notes

1   Joshua Partlow, 'U.S. Officials Separated Him from His Child. Then He Was Deported to El Salvador', *Washington Post*, 23 June 2018, https://www.washingtonpost.com/world/the_americas/u-s-officials-separated-him-from-his-child-then-he-was-deported-to-el-salvador/2018/06/23/37b6940a-7663-11e8-bda1-18e53a448a14_story.html. See also Anna Catherine Brigida, 'Salvadoran Deportee Finally Reunited with His Separated Daughter', *Washington Post*, 29 June 2018, https://www.washingtonpost.com/world/salvadoran-deportee-finally-reunited-with-his-separated-daughter/201

8/06/29/273b6a86-7b24-11e8-ac4e-421ef7165923_story.html.

2   Partlow, 'U.S. Officials Separated Him from His Child'.

3   See Brigida, 'Salvadoran Deportee Finally Reunited with His Daughter'.

4   'Why Hundreds of Migrant Children Remain Separated from Their Parents', PBS NewsHour, 21 October 2020, https://www.pbs.org/newshour/show/why-hundreds-of-migrant-children-remain-separated-from-their-parents; and Richard Gonzales, 'Trump's Executive Order on Family Separation: What It Does and Doesn't Do', NPR, 20 June 2018, https://www.npr.org/2018/06/20/622095441/trump-executive-order-on-family-separation-what-it-does-and-doesnt-do.

5   See Alexander Betts and Paul Collier, *Refuge: Transforming a Broken Refugee System* (London: Allen Lane, 2017).

6   See Office of Immigration Statistics, US Department of Homeland Security, 'Annual Flow Report: Refugees and Asylees', March 2019, https://www.dhs.gov/sites/default/files/publications/Refugees_Asylees_2017.pdf; United Nations High Commissioner for Refugees, 'Global Trends: Forced Displacement in 2017', 2017, https://www.unhcr.org/5b27be547.pdf; and Maureen Meyer and Elyssa Pachico, 'Fact Sheet: U.S. Immigration and Central American Asylum Seekers', Washington Office on Latin America, February 2018, https://www.wola.org/analysis/fact-sheet-united-states-immigration-central-american-asylum-seekers/.

7   See US Customs and Border Protection, 'Claims of Credible Fear Increase in Fiscal Year 2018', 10 December 2018, https://www.cbp.gov/newsroom/national-media-release/claims-credible-fear-increase-fiscal-year-2018; Adam Isacson, 'The U.S. Government's 2018 Border Data Clearly Shows Why the Trump Administration is on the Wrong Track', Washington Office on Latin America, 9 November 2018, https://www.wola.org/analysis/us-government-2018-border-data-trump-immigration-asylum-policy/; Nick Miroff, 'At Mexico Border, US Sees Surge in Migrants Claiming Fear of Harm in Home Countries', *Washington Post*, 10 December 2018, https://www.washingtonpost.com/world/national-security/at-the-us-mexico-border-us-sees-big-increase-in-migrants-claiming-fear-of-deportation/2018/12/10/37d7eb70-fca8-11e8-862a-b6a6f3ce8199_story.html; and Emma Platoff et al., 'While Migrant Families Seek Shelter from Violence, Trump Administration Narrows Path to Asylum', *Texas Tribune*, 10 July 2018, https://www.texastribune.org/2018/07/10/migrant-families-separated-border-crisis-asylum-seekers-donald-trump/.

8   'The Federal Government May Inadvertently Be Helping MS-13 to Recruit', *The Economist*, 3 August 2017, https://www.economist.com/united-states/2017/08/03/the-federal-government-may-inadvertantly-be-helping-ms-13-to-recruit.

9   Human Rights First, 'Delivered to Danger', https://www.humanrightsfirst.org/campaign/remain-mexico; and Alexandra Villareal, 'Rapes, Murders … and

Coronavirus: The Dangers US Asylum Seekers in Mexico Must Face', *Guardian*, 23 March 2020, https://www.theguardian.com/us-news/2020/mar/23/us-mexico-immigration-coronavirus-asylum.

10 See Jason DeParle, 'The Open Borders Trap', *New York Times*, 5 March 2002, https://www.nytimes.com/2020/03/05/sunday-review/democrats-immigration.html.

11 Thomas L. Friedman, 'We Need a High Wall with a Big Gate on the Southern Border', *New York Times*, 13 April 2021, https://www.nytimes.com/2021/04/13/opinion/immigration-border-wall.html.

12 US Department of Homeland Security, 'Acting Secretary of DHS Directs a Review of Immigration Enforcement Practices and Policies', press release, 20 January 2021, https://www.dhs.gov/news/2021/01/20/acting-secretary-dhs-directs-review-immigration-enforcement-practices-and-policies.

13 See White House, 'Executive Order on the Revision of Civil Immigration Enforcement Policies and Priorities', 20 January 2021, https://www.whitehouse.gov/briefing-room/presidential-actions/2021/01/20/executive-order-the-revision-of-civil-immigration-enforcement-policies-and-priorities/.

Book Reviews

Politics and International Relations
Steven Simon

You Say You Want a Revolution? Radical Idealism and Its Tragic Consequences
Daniel Chirot. Princeton, NJ: Princeton University Press, 2020.
£25.00/$29.95. 192 pp.

The Beatles' anthem appropriated by Professor Daniel Chirot for the title of his valuable book valorises bourgeois moderation. There is something to be said for this, unless of course you think your position is hopeless and that modest reforms are irrelevant. Given the temper of the times, the author's recapitulation of a wide range of revolutions and their outcomes could not be more useful. Although he does not necessarily break new ground, he synthesises the conditions that favour the outbreak of revolution, the dynamics of revolution and the reasons why it is so often true that radicals dominate the new regime with disastrous results. Comparing the American, French, Mexican, Russian, German and Iranian revolutions, and with reference to a few others that don't loom quite as large, he argues that revolutions germinate where elites fail to grapple with serious problems. They become more likely where elites not only fail to solve – or to be seen as solving – such problems, but also fail to take radical opponents seriously. This could result from the apparent clownishness of radical proposals and behaviour, or because elites are convinced that the radicals can be co-opted or controlled. Moderates who are alive to the failure of elites to take popular grievances seriously try to bridge the gap and wind up facilitating revolutionary action. Rejected by their establishment peers, they are objects of radical revolutionary suspicion. Isolated, they are picked off or marginalised by their erstwhile allies among the revolutionaries.

Survival | vol. 63 no. 4 | August–September 2021 | pp. 209–215   https://doi.org/10.1080/00396338.2021.1956201

Once in power, the radicals realise that the new society they sought to create is unachievable by inspiration and begin to rely on force to bring society into line with the revolutionary ideals. Their elimination of the moderate opposition, imposition of censorship and reliance on propaganda incubate corruption, decadence and, ultimately, conditions that are a good deal worse than those that triggered revolt to begin with.

Some revolutions, like the American one, do not conform to this model. In that case, elite accommodation at the outset ensured that the problem of slavery would be papered over. But, as Chirot points out, the catastrophically violent phase of the revolution was just put off until 1861. The French Revolution not only destroyed the moderates, but led to Napoleon Bonaparte's coup and dictatorship, and a series of foreign wars that killed a million French citizens and many more Europeans of other countries and empires. Chirot asks, was this really worth the destruction of the old regime?

Although the resonances of his argument for the polarised politics and legislative paralysis in the United States are palpable, Chirot acknowledges but does not explore them. As I write this review, my appreciation for the author's lucid analysis and straightforward prose is only getting deeper. This is an essential book.

Bullets Not Ballots: Success in Counterinsurgency Warfare
Jacqueline L. Hazelton. Ithaca, NY: Cornell University Press, 2021. $39.95. 220 pp.

The phrase 'hearts and minds' has a short and undistinguished history in American discourse. According to specialists who track these things, it was first used on the floor of the Senate to endorse humanitarian programmes. It was popularised by a documentary of that name which savaged William Westmoreland, the US military commander during Lyndon Johnson's Vietnam surge. The film juxtaposed clips of wailing North Vietnamese survivors of bombing raids with those of the seersucker-clad commander explaining that Asians do not value life as much as Americans do. But the epigram was served best by a brilliant variation attributed to several authors: 'If you've got them by the balls, their hearts and minds will follow.'

Jacqueline Hazelton, a professor at the US Naval War College, has gone one essential step further in this marvellous book. In her view, it is more like no one gives a damn about hearts and minds, and for good reason. This is not, of course, her normative judgement. Indeed, she observes that 'what succeeds in counterinsurgency is uglier, costlier in lives, more remote from moral or ethical considerations' and that her book 'is not a prescription for counterinsurgent success', adding that she does 'not advocate implementation of [her] findings'

(p. 2). But one of the refreshing things about her comparative study of counter-insurgency campaigns is the absence of either lamentation or cheerleading.

Based on her scrutiny of six counter-insurgency campaigns in widely different regions and time frames – the British in Malaya (1946–57), the US in Greece (1946–49), the US in the Philippines (1946–54), the British in Oman (1965–76), the US in El Salvador (1979–92) and the Turks versus the Kurdistan Workers' Party (1984–99) – she concludes that insurgencies are not defeated by a government's willingness and ability to compete for the loyalty of populations through social services, economic development or opportunities for political participation. The winning formula, it turns out, is the use of force and the co-optation of elites to secure their loyalty to the government. Although the author discusses cases of successful counter-insurgency, it is hard not to think of cases, such as Vietnam, where reforms were a significant part of the overall counter-insurgency effort but did not prevent defeat of the government under threat. She shows that successful counter-insurgencies were waged not on the premise that the war was a competition for the population to be won by good governance, but rather a combination of pact-making among powerful stakeholders in the government's victory, control of the population through 'brute force' and 'compellence' to break the insurgents' capacity to fight. Hazelton's scrupulous research is enhanced by her superb narrative skills, presumably honed by a pre-academic career as a journalist for the Associated Press.

Coping with Defeat: Sunni Islam, Roman Catholicism, and the Modern State
Jonathan Laurence. Princeton, NJ: Princeton University Press, 2021. £28.00/$35.00. 606 pp.

There's been an ongoing debate, certainly since 9/11, about the so-called roots of Muslim rage. The argument was personified by Bernard Lewis and absorbed, with Lewis's apparent encouragement, by the George W. Bush administration at the outset of the long 'war on terror' that followed. The crude gist of his sophisticated analysis was that Muslims had been on top of the world but, for an array of postulated reasons, had faltered, surrendering cultural and political primacy to European powers, and then their very independence. Sunni jihadism allegedly emerged from this reservoir of *ressentiment*. In the case of al-Qaeda, it was directed primarily against the outside powers that subjugated the Muslim world; the Islamic State (ISIS), on the other hand, targeted Muslim leaders seen as complicit with outside powers. A related issue pertained to the relationship between church and state. The militants framed their campaign in religious terms. Historically, the caliph was thought to have combined both temporal and

religious power in his person. Colonial rule and post-independence governments had driven a wedge between these two spheres, subordinating religion to
apostate regimes. Jonathan Laurence looks deeply into this narrative and asks,
firstly, whether it is accurate and, secondly, what it portends for the future.

To answer these questions, he compares the situation of Muslims to the
Catholic Church. Other scholars have noted that even as recently as the early
nineteenth century, the prospect of a demilitarised Catholic Church with no
temporal authority outside of Vatican City was unthinkable. Laurence advances
and refines this insight, firstly by showing that, as a practical matter, the state
and mosque were already operating as separate but unequal spheres of authority in the Ottoman era, and that the notion of a non-hierarchical Sunni clergy
is not quite true. Indeed, as both the Catholic Church and the Ottoman Empire
came under increasing pressure in the nineteenth century, they professional-
ised their respective clerical establishments and created vertical structures of
authority within them. For the Vatican, this was a path to preserving religious
authority even as its political sway shrank under pressure from secular nationalist governments. For the Ottomans, it was a way to preserve influence in parts
of the empire under the increasing pressure of Western power.

There are many valuable insights here, but perhaps the most important is
Laurence's view that Western governments facilitated the peaceful transformation of the Catholic Church by permitting the Pope and the Vatican to survive
as institutions despite the secularisation of European politics. This arrangement
was ratified, in a sense, by the Lateran Accords of 1929. Very nearly at the same
moment, the opposite decision was taken by the new Turkish state, which chose
to end the caliphate and depose the caliph. This was a profound mistake in the
author's view because it let religion slip from the grip of the state. Over time, the
post-colonial governments restored a measure of control over religious forces,
but it was too little too late. With just a couple of exceptions, most governments failed to impose an authoritative interpretation of Islam. The result was
the blooming of a thousand flowers, including violent sectarianism. This is an
ambitious but brilliant work underpinned by disciplined use of archival data.

**The Last Shah: America, Iran, and the Fall of the
Pahlavi Dynasty**
Ray Takeyh. New Haven, CT: Yale University Press, 2021.
£25.00/$32.50. 336 pp.

Ray Takeyh's fifth book combines biography and archival history to reorient
the standard perspective on US–Iranian relations in the post-Second World War
period. Takeyh is a vocal participant in the cut and thrust of the debate about

US policy towards Iran, but readers of this book should not be deterred; it is fine scholarship delivered in admirably stylish prose. Weaving original sources, contemporary reportage and a shrewd reading of the biases baked into key secondary works, Takeyh makes two important contributions to our understanding of the topic.

The first addresses the question of original sin – American culpability for the overthrow of Mohammad Mossadegh in 1953. Takeyh's reading of the record indicates that the US role was confined to the first of two coup attempts. The Eisenhower administration was divided on the wisdom of a coup, but the activists won the debate. The US role was to spread money around and to arrange, with the shah's reluctant backing, to have Mossadegh detained by the Iranian military. The plot took a farcical turn when the arresting officer was himself taken into custody and the shah fled the country. The second coup was, as Takeyh shows, a domestic affair. Mossadegh, like the shah a quarter of a century later, had alienated important constituencies, including the clergy. Demonstrations broke out. These were not in support of the shah, but they were against Mossadegh's leadership. It was this Iranian popular rejection of Mossadegh, rather than American machinations, that led to regime change. Revolutionary Iran later instrumentalised the narrative of American responsibility for the derailment of Iranian democracy to justify clerical rule by demonising the United States.

Takeyh's second argument is a defence – from his perspective – of Jimmy Carter's response to snowballing revolutionary activism in Iran in 1979. Rather than the wavering weakling that some take him for, Carter was perceptive, tough and committed to supporting the shah's control of Iran. To make his case, Takeyh mined the archives, discovering a couple of interesting things. One was that Carter had instructed the US ambassador in Tehran to reassure the shah in strong terms that the US would back whatever he had to do to stay in power. The shah's response was not encouraging: he predicted that his opponents would be galvanised by a violent response and that he risked losing the army. The other was that Carter authorised US intelligence to prepare the ground for a counter-coup and sought to have an American general familiar with Iran stage a military takeover in Tehran. Apprised that this would require 10,000 US troops, Carter dropped the idea. But these initiatives, combined with what was previously known about US intelligence contacts with Iran's intelligence service up to the seizure of the US Embassy in November 1979 and the attempt in 1980 to free the hostages, suggest that for Carter, the stakes were high and he was willing to go all the way to restore the shah to the throne.

As Takeyh shows, however, it was already too late. The time to have reassured the shah of American intentions was before the collapse of support for the government in 1978. After that, the shah was too sick and too unpopular to hold on, regardless of Washington's backing. The last word on these events will not be written until the Iranian archives become available, but until then Takeyh's account will serve both specialists and lay readers extremely well.

Escape from Rome: The Failure of Empire and the Road to Prosperity
Walter Scheidel. Princeton, NJ: Princeton University Press, 2019. £28.00/$35.00. 670 pp.

At nearly 700 pages, *Escape from Rome* is a big commitment, probably best engaged by readers no older than 40 with muscular forearms. Fortunately, it is consistently fascinating. Walter Scheidel, an eminent historian at Stanford, likes both data and big questions. The question that concerns this book is why the West beat the rest. The customary banner for this subject is 'the great divergence'. Why was there an Industrial Revolution in northern Europe and relative stagnation elsewhere? These questions have been tackled by economic historians from Douglass North to Timur Kuran, and at least touched on by Peter Turchin, Jared Diamond and others.

Scheidel's approach hinges on a point raised by earlier scholars, specifically that the fragmentation of Europe following the Reformation created conditions that fostered innovation and competition. Scheidel puts it this way:

> I wrote this book to establish ... two simple points: that interlocking forms of productive fragmentation were of paramount importance and indeed indispensable in creating the specific set of conditions that gave birth to modernity, and that the divergences that precipitated this outcome in only one part of the world but not in others were highly robust. (p. 27)

The short story is that Rome succeeded in two key things: mass mobilisation for military purposes, not to be seen again until the Napoleonic Wars; and naval dominance of the Mediterranean Sea. Political stability in the capital over long periods helped. Empires originating in the East showed how to conquer and hold territory, but stopped short of the central and eastern Mediterranean. These factors gave Rome room to roam. Taking a counterfactual approach, Scheidel concludes that there were no moments when the Roman imperial enterprise might have been staunched.

The Roman Empire eventually collapsed, but rather than ask why, Scheidel is more interested in why it was never resurrected. He contends that in Asia and the Middle East, expired empires were soon replaced by new ones. The Han empire in China disintegrated more or less at the same time as its Roman cognate, but was serially replaced for millennia afterward. Scheidel speculates on why this did not happen in Europe by examining the reasons why successive European regimes fell short of Roman-scale empires. The Franks, Mongols, Muslims and Germans all faltered. His explanations are ingenious, ranging from traditions regulating inheritance to the respective topographies of Europe and Asia.

This analysis prepares the ground for his big claim, that the permanent death of European empire fostered the Industrial Revolution. Linking events 1,000 years apart via a chain of causation is a daring manoeuvre, but Scheidel somehow makes the connection plausible. It is true that his definition of civilisational success seems to privilege wealth accumulation, but he recognises that there are other ways of looking at success. Chinese empires, he concedes, might have forgone opportunities because their elites were more concerned with the welfare of populations under their control. This is not a preoccupation one associates with the Industrial Revolution in Europe.

Asia-Pacific
Lanxin Xiang

Indo-Pacific Empire: China, America and the Contest for the World's Pivotal Region
Rory Medcalf. Manchester: Manchester University Press, 2020.
£20.00. 310 pp.

According to author Rory Medcalf, the concept of 'Indo-Pacific' is designed neither to flatter India, nor to please the United States. 'It reflects something real: a changing approach by many nations to security, economics and diplomacy.' Many concepts have already been applied to the region in question – Asia-Pacific, East Asia, South Asia, Southeast Asia – but 'nothing seems to have captured the geopolitical nature of the region today better than Indo-Pacific' (p. 3). The concept was first proposed by Japan's Abe Shinzo and embraced by India's Narendra Modi before drawing the attention of the Pentagon. It now serves as a defining concept of the United States' 'pivot to Asia 2.0'.

Medcalf stresses the critical importance of mental maps, and of the facts that support such maps, in sustaining geographic concepts of this kind. The common denominator that sustains the Indo-Pacific as a strategic system, he says, is the growing threat from China. The author admits that mental maps are 'artificial and contingent', and that the Indo-Pacific is no exception (p .6), but characterises the China threat as real and constant. Whether China's own mental map corresponds to the expansionist strategy – one aimed at controlling two oceans – that Medcalf ascribes to it is something the author has to prove. He starts with the assertion that China's mental map of the Indo-Pacific is comparable to a 'pivoted map' invented by Thomas Mitchell, a Scottish soldier based in Australia in the nineteenth century. Mitchell shifted the orientation of the traditional longitude-based world map such that 'China and the Eurasian landmass [were] dominant, with Europe diminished from the distorted greatness of traditional Mercator projections'. Little did Mitchell realise, writes Medcalf, 'that his diagonally tilted map … would foreshadow the Indo-Pacific shape of Asia that matters in the 21st century' (p. 31).

Medcalf claims that Hao Xiaoguang, a Chinese cartographic researcher, represents Mitchell's 'modern match'. According to the author, Hao's own latitude map 'powerfully reimagines the globe in the vertical frame' and is 'a stunning visualization of Chinese strategic wish-making … America is literally split and marginalized. And most curious of all, the map is centered not on China but the Indian Ocean' (p. 33). He further claims that the map was released in 2013, the year that Xi Jinping gave speeches in Indonesia and Kazakhstan announcing the

Belt and Road Initiative. Clearly, Medcalf sees a link between Hao's map and Xi's strategic thinking. Hao's map, he says, 'shows how today's China sees the world and illuminates Beijing's strategic ambitions' (p. 33).

This is a leap too far in a book that otherwise contains many good insights. The fact is, Hao's work was considered too eccentric to be accepted by China's security authorities. According to a story published by the People's Liberation Army's *Liberation Daily*, Hao's work was 'rejected off hand' when he showed it to experts and officials at numerous government agencies. To suggest that his map inspired the grand strategy unveiled by Xi in 2013 is fanciful at best.

China's Good War: How World War II Is Shaping a New Nationalism

Rana Mitter. Cambridge, MA: The Belknap Press of Harvard University Press, 2020. £22.95/$27.95. 316 pp.

Rana Mitter argues that modern China's engagement with the rest of the world is 'deeply shaped by ideas of the Second World War – both by the events and purpose of the war, and by its legacy' (p. 4). Certainly, this can be seen in China's perceptions of the Asia-Pacific region. For China, the war did not start with the Japanese attack on Pearl Harbor but, at the very latest, with the outbreak of the Second Sino-Japanese War in 1937. Indeed, official sources date the start of the war to the Manchurian Incident of 1931. Given that Western accounts of the Pacific War tend to focus on events after Pearl Harbor, China feels that its contributions to and sacrifices in the fight against Japan have been undervalued.

The question is, does China's contribution to defeating Japan justify its contemporary territorial or other legal demands? The author thinks not (p. 13). One awkward fact for China's post-war claims is that the ruling communist regime was not founded until 1949. It was the previous regime under Chiang Kai-shek that was present at the creation of the post-1945 international order, including the Bretton Woods system and the United Nations. The People's Republic was not fully admitted to this system until 1971, when it replaced the Republic of China (Taiwan) at the UN.

Under Mao Zedong's rule, the People's Republic's interpretation of China's wartime history tended to emphasise the heroic (and exaggerated) role played by the communists, and to downplay and belittle the role played by troops commanded by the Kuomintang government. When China started opening and reforming under Deng Xiaoping, the war became a major focus of official history, the better to attract investment from overseas Chinese, as well as from Taiwan's business community. As a result, the nationalist contribution during the war was restored to official narratives.

There was still tension, however, between revisionist historians who wanted to present the war in a multidimensional way, and politicians, including party historians, who were worried about the political consequences of elevating the role played by the Kuomintang government, as well as by the United States. A turning point came in 1989, the year of the Tiananmen crisis, when the leadership sought to launch a campaign of 'patriotic education' that once again stressed the communist role. The government soon discovered, however, that commemorating the war could serve its interests, not just boosting domestic nationalism but also helping to 'burnish China's global standing' (p. 86). Thus, at the suggestion of some leading party historians, the leadership began in the 1990s to engage in various official services to commemorate events such as the Marco Polo Bridge incident, the Nanjing Massacre, VJ Day and so on. The idea was to emulate American commemorations of Pearl Harbor and Allied commemorations of D-Day and VE Day.

Under Xi Jinping, study of the war against Japan has been further politicised. In 2015, Xi made it clear that the war must be re-evaluated to emphasise the link between China's wartime contributions and the idea that the country deserves a continuing role in creating the contemporary international order. Mitter concludes: 'In the future, we will hear more about China's claims to a greater role in the construction of order in Asia and globally' (p. 260).

Stronger: Adapting America's China Strategy in an Age of Competitive Interdependence
Ryan Hass. New Haven, CT: Yale University Press, 2021.
£18.99/$27.50. 240 pp.

Ryan Hass's aim in *Stronger* is to 'light a path for a more constructive approach to responding to China's rise' (p. 3). Arguing that 'managing China's rise as a peer competitor poses the most direct test of American foreign policy in decades', he seeks to present 'detailed discussion of the policy choices facing the United States and its allies, as well as an honest accounting of the trade-offs of various options' (pp. 3–4). He considers the objectives and assumptions that might underpin US policy; China's ambitions and the distribution of power between the two countries; how the US might secure its interests and retain its advantages in the face of Chinese competition; and whether there is a risk of US–China conflict.

Hass believes that the United States remains dominant and will retain the capacity to protect its vital interests even as China grows stronger. Hence, 'the United States need not – and should not – seek to block China's rise and in the process turn China into an adversary' (p. 13). Rather, the US should 'play offense' by focusing on its own strengths and enhancing its own competitiveness (p. 13).

As for China's ambitions, the prevailing view among Americans, including the current occupants of the White House, is that Beijing seeks to overtake the US and replace it in global affairs. Certainly, China has become more assertive as its power has grown, but Hass believes that the country's 'assertiveness abroad and illiberal actions at home' do not fully explain the sharp turn in American attitudes towards China (p. 19). Disappointment with China's lack of political reform has also played a role: China's economic rise has not weakened, but rather strengthened its authoritarian regime. Worse still, American businesses must now compete with China's ever-expanding state-supported trade and investment practices, leading to charges of unfair competition.

Hass contends that, until recently, competition between China and the US had been like a 'running race, where the goal is to outpace the other side' (p. 66). In this race, the US 'maintained a sizeable lead'. However, as China has narrowed the gap, the race has begun to take on the characteristics of a football-style contest, in which 'contact is rough and the objective is to prevent the other side's advance' (p. 65). The best way forward, says Hass, would be to embrace a relationship of what he calls 'competitive interdependence' (p. 67), a model that acknowledges the competition between the two sides but that also takes into account the 'dense web of financial, trade, scientific, academic, and people-to-people links that bind both countries together' (p. 67). Above all, he urges the United States to have confidence in itself. A confident America, he believes, will have the patience and discernment necessary to manage its relationship with China while boosting its own, still considerable strengths.

Hass brings a clear eye and a sober mind to his analysis of US–China relations, attributes that cannot be taken for granted among Beltway insiders (the author served as the National Security Council's China director under Barack Obama). His views should draw close attention from both Democrats and Republicans, as well as China's political elite.

Myanmar's Rohingya Genocide: Identity, History and Hate Speech
Ronan Lee. London: I.B. Tauris, 2021. £19.99. 320 pp.

The genocide against Myanmar's Rohingya community first came to global attention in 2017, when an army-led 'clearance operation' razed hundreds of Rohingya villages with fire, murdered at least 9,000 Rohingya men and unleashed a campaign of sexual violence against Rohingya women. 'These atrocities', writes Ronan Lee, 'precipitated the largest forced migration in the region since the Second World War, with more than 700,000 Rohingya fleeing Myanmar in terror for the relative safety of Bangladesh' (p. 1).

The Rohingya people, also known as Arakan Muslims, have lived in what is today Myanmar for centuries. A citizenship law proclaimed in 1948 by newly independent Burma provided a path to citizenship, but the regime that had protected the Rohingya's rights during the country's early years was swept away in a military coup in 1962 led by General Ne Win. The military, which suspended the 1948 constitution, tried to remake Burma in its own ethno-nationalistic image, enacting a discriminatory new citizenship law in 1974. Hundreds of thousands of Indian and Chinese residents were driven out of the country, and the Rohingya became the world's largest stateless people, numbering about 600,000 in 2019.

For decades, the Rohingya's statelessness was used by Myanmar's authorities to justify discrimination and human-rights violations that in some respects satisfied the UN's definition of the crime of apartheid. Myanmar's transition towards democracy – and its 2010 general election – was initially cause for optimism for the Rohingya people, but during the two terms of the quasi-civilian government, hate-speech attacks portraying the Rohingya as a threat to Myanmar's Buddhist character increased. The civilian authorities, reluctant to alienate Buddhist voters, allowed anti-Rohingya speech to proliferate, with devastating consequences. 'Key international actors, including the UN, were similarly hesitant to criticize the civilian administration's handling of the Rohingya's situation lest this undermine momentum for democratic change', writes Lee (p. 103).

For a time, the Rohingya's political leadership retained hope that the government of Aung San Suu Kyi, the Nobel laureate known the world over for her struggle for democracy, might come to their assistance. Yet her civilian government consistently failed to deal with domestic human-rights abuses, particularly by the military. These failures drew strong international criticism. A UN fact-finding mission, while acknowledging that Myanmar's civilian authorities lacked the constitutional ability to directly control the actions of the military, found that, 'through their acts and omissions, the civilian authorities have contributed to the commission of atrocity crimes' (p. 103). The military coup that toppled Aung San Suu Kyi's government in February 2021 highlighted the fragility of her own position, and stifled hopes that Myanmar might be on the way to becoming an inclusive democracy.

The Great Exodus from China: Trauma, Memory, and Identity in Modern Taiwan
Dominic Meng-Hsuan Yang. Cambridge: Cambridge University Press, 2020. £75.00. 311 pp.

This volume examines the highly consequential but understudied mass migration from China to Taiwan in the wake of the defeat of the nationalist government led by Chiang Kai-shek in the Chinese Civil War. In his account, Dominic Meng-Hsuan Yang emphasises the trauma experienced by the millions of mainlanders, soldiers and civilians alike, forced to seek refuge in an unfamiliar place, where most of the existing inhabitants called themselves Taiwanese, even though they, like the new arrivals, were ethnically Chinese. This experience created a unique feeling of loneliness, which one Taiwan-based writer has called *liuli*, or 'diasporic displacement' (p. 1). Even though mainlanders dominated Taiwan's political, economic and social systems until the end of Chiang family rule in 1988 marked the start of the island's transition to democracy, they were never able to shed the feeling of being refugees. Nor could they speak of their trauma, because Chiang's regime suppressed any discussion of its wartime defeat. When the retired mainlanders were finally able, in the late 1980s, to return to the mainland to see the homes and families they had left behind, they were in for another shock: many of their long-lost family members had suffered persecution during the Cultural Revolution because of their Taiwan connections (see chapter four, 'The Long Road Home').

The exiles were not the only people displaced. The local Taiwanese were also traumatised. The Chiang regime never trusted the locals, viewing them as semi-Japanised Chinese whose loyalty was doubtful. Japan's half-century of colonial rule had been instrumental in the industrialisation of the island: the Japanese authorities had extended the railways and other transport networks, built an extensive sanitation system and established a formal education system. When Chiang's regime took over in 1945, it acted quickly to suppress any perceived challenges. On 28 February 1947, some 30,000 locals were killed in a bid to defeat an alleged rebellion, an event that came to be known as the '228 Incident'. For the native Taiwanese, the massacre was instrumental in starting a pro-independence movement led by local politicians. It should be noted that this event took place before the great exodus of 1949, which only 'magnified and sustained' the shock the Taiwanese experienced (p. 75). The sudden appearance of large numbers of unruly soldiers and vagabonds caused crime rates to shoot up and depleted stocks of food and consumer goods, driving up prices.

Even in today's post-authoritarian age, relations between mainlanders and native Taiwanese can be sensitive and tense, affecting voting behaviour and perceptions of political identity. Yet Yang believes that mainlanders may eventually disappear as a distinct political force as the traditional division between Kuomintang and pro-independence supporters is replaced by new political alignments. The election in 2014 of a 'third force' candidate, Ko Wen-je, as mayor of Taipei may be a sign of this. But Yang warns that 'incompatible traumatic memories … will not easily go away without a proper "working through" process' (pp. 269–70).

Russia and Eurasia
Angela Stent

Russia Resurrected: Its Power and Purpose in a New Global Order
Kathryn E. Stoner. Oxford and New York: Oxford University Press, 2021. £22.99/$29.95. 344 pp.

Kathryn Stoner has produced an innovative piece of research that challenges conventional interpretations of Russia's muscular return to the world stage under Vladimir Putin. The standard belief is that Putin's Russia has played a weak hand well. But Stoner argues that 'Russia's cards may not be as weak as we in the West have thought' (p. 3). Noting that traditional measures of Russia's power – 'men, military, money' – do not explain how Russia under Putin has become so formidable internationally, she uses a variety of metrics to assess Russia's power resources. She concludes that Russia has returned to the world stage not as a conventional great power but as a great disrupter with a much higher tolerance for risk than the USSR had – or indeed, than any other great power has today. Russia may have a declining population, a raw-materials-based economy and a military that is still recovering from the Soviet collapse, but it is and has always been, in Stoner's words, a 'good enough power' (p. 18). We underestimate it at our own peril.

One way in which Russia is much more powerful than any other country is in the influence it exerts in the post-Soviet space, where it has re-established its dominance since the nadir of the 1990s. Geography and economics have enabled this: Russia is, as Stoner writes, 'a behemoth geographically, economically and demographically in comparison to its post-Soviet neighbors' (p. 35). The largest country on earth, it borders 14 other countries and can project power in Eurasia and the Middle East much more easily than, say, the United States.

The domestic drivers of Russian foreign policy include the clout it derives from being an energy superpower, its human capital and the unique authoritarian system which Putin has built. Although Russia's economy is overly dependent on hydrocarbon exports, its disciplined macroeconomic policy and its careful investment of windfall oil and gas revenues in the Stabilization Fund and National Wealth Fund have enabled it to withstand fluctuations in oil prices and the severe economic effects of the COVID-19 pandemic.

Stoner argues that Russia's disruptive foreign policy is a product neither of Russia's history, nor of mistakes made by the West. It is, she says, unique to the Putin regime, a product of a personalistic, patronal system in a country governed by a small elite that has enriched itself from oil and gas rents. Another

Survival | vol. 63 no. 4 | August–September 2021 | pp. 223–228   https://doi.org/10.1080/00396338.2021.1956204

ruler, she argues, might not have chosen to use disinformation, cyber inter-ference and other forms of hybrid warfare to project power abroad. If Putin's patronal regime does not survive him, Russia may become less disruptive.

Weak Strongman: The Limits of Power in Putin's Russia
Timothy Frye. Princeton, NJ: Princeton University Press, 2021.
£20.00/$24.95. 269 pp.

Putin's Russia is not as unique as many scholars claim, argues Timothy Frye in this wide-ranging book, but has many characteristics in common with other personalist autocracies. It often behaves like Viktor Orbán's Hungary, Nursultan Nazarbayev's Kazakhstan, Recep Tayyip Erdogan's Turkey and Hugo Chávez's Venezuela. 'Russian politics', says Frye, 'are not simply an extension of Putin's worldview, or a reflection of Russia's unique literature, history or culture, but rather involve many of the same trade-offs that all authoritarian governments face' (p. 200). Moreover, Putin is not as powerful as many assume. The same weak institutions and absence of rule of law that sustain him in the Kremlin may not protect him after he leaves office, making the stakes involved in losing power much higher than in less personalistic systems.

The Putin system is based on a complicated set of informal rules and personal relationships that seek to balance the interests of different elite networks. The members of these distinctive political 'clans' help to keep Putin in power so that they can obtain the rewards of loyalty. The system may have roots in tsarist and Soviet times, but Frye argues that its features are also present in the relationships between leaders and oligarchic groups in other personalistic autocracies. He also rejects notions of a 'Homo Sovieticus' whose acceptance of 'doublethink', passiv-ity and conformity differentiates him from citizens in other autocracies. Today's Russian citizens, says Frye, are more risk-taking, less passive and favour change.

Frye questions the findings of public-opinion polls that still show strong support for Putin. His popularity may have been boosted by the country's strong economic performance before 2014, and by the 'Crimea effect', whereby the Russian invasion gave Russians a sense that their country was once again a great power, but Putin realises that the Kremlin has to make elections look legitimate and minimise the appearance of obvious electoral fraud. He also understands that it is important to minimise the appearance of obvious and large-scale corruption.

Like other personalistic autocracies, the regime relies on autocratic legalism – that is, 'the use, abuse and nonuse of the law to promote autocratic ends' (p. 115) – to keep itself in power. Rather than ban undesirable non-governmental organisations outright (although the Kremlin has also done that), the government prosecutes them on tax violations, arguing that it is only following the law. That is how the regime treated opposition politician Alexei Navalny until he became so dangerous that he needed to be poisoned and imprisoned.

Russia is not a typical personalistic autocracy when it comes to foreign policy. Its military power, nuclear weapons, permanent seat on the United Nations Security Council, natural-resource wealth and wide geographic reach make it an 'unusual' autocracy in this realm. But, argues Frye, its unconventional foreign-policy tactics often reveal weakness rather than strength. 'Russia is a great power, albeit a diminished one' (p. 157).

The Red Mirror: Putin's Leadership and Russia's Insecure Identity
Gulnaz Sharafutdinova. Oxford and New York: Oxford University Press, 2020. £19.99/$29.95. 248 pp.

In 1996, Boris Yeltsin launched a competition for Russians to come up with a new national idea. The results were inconclusive, and the search for a post-Soviet identity continued during a very challenging decade. Vladimir Putin, says Gulnaz Sharafutdinova, has succeeded in creating a new national identity based on a blend of Soviet nostalgia, patriotic pride, feelings of exceptionalism and a sense of victimhood. This accounts for Putin's continuing popularity after more than two decades in power.

The Soviet Union succeeded in constructing a collective identity which had two key elements. The first was a sense of Soviet exceptionalism: 'the Soviet state, at the vanguard of history, was on a special path of building socialism and, eventually, communism. This path of building a socialist system was presented to the Soviet public as being morally and institutionally superior to that of the capitalist system' (p. 63). The second was the presence of enemies, both domestic and foreign. When the USSR collapsed, this identity could not be sustained – socialism had failed and there was no foreign enemy to blame. Yet it proved too difficult for many Russians to accept that the mighty Soviet Union had disintegrated solely because of its own internal weakness.

Sharafutdinova analyses how Putin, with the aid of talented 'political technologists' such as Gleb Pavlovsky and Vladislav Surkov, was able to create a new national idea and manipulate an unmoored population traumatised by the 1990s. He politicised Russia's collective identity and constructed a 'heavily propagated image of Russia as a fortress besieged by foreign enemies' (p. 27). Portraying the 1990s as a time of shame, despair, anxiety and humiliation, Putin's spin doctors have tapped into the collective trauma of modern Russia's 'time of troubles' and used it to build a new loyalty to the state. In Putin's telling, Russia is once again an exceptional country, embodying conservative social values that are superior to those of a decadent West. As in the past, it is threatened by both internal and external enemies – opposition figures and the West – but is successfully defeating them.

The author describes in detail how 'Putin-led identity politics in Russia depends on centralized media control and heavy-handed and overbearing opinion leadership by chosen media personalities who promote selected ideas and narratives about Russia's past and present' (p. 167). They depict Putin as a man of the people who really cares about their lives. The author conducted focus groups when researching the book, in which she observed the human capacity for self-deception at work in participants' willingness to reiterate the assertions of state television that there are no Russian troops in the Donbas, despite knowing that there are. By successfully harnessing Soviet-era yearning for a collective identity to modern disinformation techniques and outright political repression, Putin has been able to maintain his hold on power. Public-opinion data suggests that the younger generation is not in a hurry to challenge Russia's new self-image.

Replacing the Dead: The Politics of Reproduction in the Postwar Soviet Union
Mie Nakachi. Oxford and New York: Oxford University Press, 2021. £25.99/$39.95. 328 pp.

At the end of the Second World War, Soviet leaders faced a demographic dilemma. Having lost 27 million people, 20m of whom were male, they urgently needed to persuade women to have more children. But they also needed women to continue working because of the labour shortage caused by the massive wartime casualties. How could they reconcile the twin imperatives of production and reproduction?

In her impressive study of post-war Soviet reproductive policies, Mie Nakachi unravels the complex interaction of pro-natalist policies with changing attitudes towards out-of-wedlock births, abortion and contraception. The USSR was the first country to legalise abortion on demand in 1920. Joseph Stalin subsequently re-criminalised abortion in 1936, but in 1955 Nikita Khrushchev re-legalised it. Putin has since placed restrictions on abortion as the country once again faces a significant demographic decline. This book explains why Soviet and Russian leaders have been unable to implement successful pro-natalist policies since 1945, and why Russia today faces such a demographic challenge.

The author provides a detailed analysis of the period between 1944 and 1955, when the Soviets were focused on increasing the population. Khrushchev, as he explained to his colleague Vyacheslav Molotov, was responsible for the 'important task of replacing as quickly as possible the lost population to assure future demographic acceleration' (p. 21). Because so many men had been lost, the legislation he authored in 1944 encouraged both legal and out-of-wedlock births. The problem was that the fathers of illegitimate children were not required to take responsibility for them, leaving mothers unable to give their children their father's patronymic or to receive child support. The legislation created a social divide between married and single mothers.

Once abortion was re-legalised in 1955, it became the most common form of birth control. Nakachi asks why the USSR never invested in developing modern birth control, which would have obviated the need for multiple abortions. After all, the East Germans developed an effective birth-control pill in the 1960s. The answer lies in the flaws of Soviet central planning: 'there was no mechanism of responsive product-development based on consumer feedback and demand – Ultimately in the Soviet system political choices overruled social needs and renewed pronatalism was the most decisive factor in the fate of contraception' (p. 201).

Soviet women carried a double burden: they were expected to work full-time and to take care of the children and household in an era when shopping for groceries was a constant challenge. Nakachi reminds us that 'working mothers rarely got any help from husbands with household work or childrearing' (p. 205). No wonder most Soviet women – with the exception of those in Central Asia – never reached Khrushchev's goal of producing three children.

Putin, seeking to overcome the contradiction between production and reproduction, has offered financial incentives to encourage women to have three children. He is working with the Orthodox Church to promote family values and to discourage abortion. It remains to be seen whether he will succeed where his predecessors failed.

Is Russia Fascist? Unraveling Propaganda East and West
Marlene Laruelle. Ithaca, NY: Cornell University Press, 2021.
$39.95. 264 pp.

Putin's Russia portrays itself as the victor in the Great Patriotic War, the defender of Europe against fascism and the supreme arbiter of who is a fascist. It calls the Ukrainian government a 'fascist junta', while the Ukrainian press has nicknamed the Russian president 'Putler'. Central and Eastern European countries often equate communism with fascism, and Adolf Hitler with Stalin. Some scholars argue that Russia is now a fascist country. In the increasingly intense memory wars between Russia and Europe, the word 'fascism' is overused by both sides, raising the question of what it really means.

In *Is Russia Fascist?*, Marlene Laruelle delves into the complexity of the fascism question, arguing that the outcome of the memory wars will determine whether Russia can one day be fully included in Europe. Fascist ideas were present in tsarist Russia, the Soviet Union and post-Soviet Russia, but she concludes that Russia today is not a fascist country. Nevertheless, it uses the concept of fascism to secure the current regime:

> fascism has become one of Russia's strategic narratives, operationalized at two levels. At home it is used to generate cultural consensus in favor of the regime status quo. On the international scene it is deployed to upgrade or at least stabilize the country's status as having a legitimate say in European security, thanks to the 1945 victory. (p. 7)

The cult of the Second World War has been intensifying as veterans die – the Kremlin needs to find new ways of keeping wartime memories alive and bolstering Russia's legitimacy as the great liberator of Europe. The war is the most acceptable moment in Russia's 'usable past', since the regime prefers to downplay its communist history. Putin has ensured that Victory Day on 9 May has become 'an annual occasion for celebrating Russia in all its incarnations – "Russia as a state, a nation, a people, and Putin as the embodiment of all of them"' (p. 45). New legislation banning any questioning of the official narrative about the Second World War is designed to erase any questions about the state's legitimacy.

Central and Eastern Europeans, according to former Lithuanian president Valdas Adamkus, see 9 May as the day 'we traded Hitler for Stalin' (p. 62). As far as they are concerned, one occupier with a totalitarian ideology took over from another. The battle which ensued when a statue of a Soviet soldier was moved from the centre of Tallinn to its outskirts – a decision that was met by an extensive Russian cyber attack on Estonia – highlighted Russia's refusal to accept the narrative of occupation.

Laruelle contends that Russia is not a fascist state because it has a hybrid ideology that is not state-mandated, and governs in an ad hoc fashion, even if some elements of the regime, such as the military and intelligence branches, may support some fascist ideas. Nevertheless, she concludes that Russia's vision of a conservative, nation-state-centric 'European civilization' remains antithetical to mainstream European values and culture.

Closing Argument

Australia's 'Drums of War'

Greg Austin

I

To mark this year's Anzac Day, the anniversary of the British Empire's military invasion of Turkey on the Gallipoli Peninsula in 1915 and Australia's memorial day for war dead, Australian Home Affairs Secretary Michael Pezzullo issued a short message alerting his compatriots that we can 'hear again the beating drums' of war. He warned that Australians should not replicate the mistake of Europeans who 'did not heed the drums of war which beat through the 1930s'. It was time, he said, to brace 'again, yet again, for the curse of war'.[1] These remarks by a civil servant responsible for domestic security, but not defence or foreign affairs, echo the intensifying war rhetoric of senior politicians in the country's ruling political party and even of some senior military officers.

Pezzullo went beyond sentiments expressed by Peter Dutton, the new minister of defence, who has talked of a heightened risk of war with China, but the two statements can be read together. Pezzullo served under Dutton for seven years in related portfolios, and the two were jointly responsible for standing up the new, muscular Home Affairs Department in 2017. Pezzullo has argued that 'a nation is secure when it does not have to sacrifice or compromise on its national interests in order to avoid war or armed aggression, and is able to protect those interests by engaging if necessary in the use of force'.[2] He appears to support a potent state in which any hint

Greg Austin is IISS Senior Fellow for Cyber, Space and Future Conflict.

Survival | vol. 63 no. 4 | August–September 2021 | pp. 229–236 https://doi.org/10.1080/00396338.2021.1956205

of compromise on national interest, especially in security affairs, is seen as a weakness. In a 2015 speech, invoking Hegel, he described the state as the guardian and enforcer of the rules of civic associations and asserted that a 'properly formed and functional state … creates the space for civil society', which many liberals might contest.[3] After calling for 'nothing less than the transformation of the state itself, and the state's relationship with society', Pezzullo has suggested that Australia needs to move towards a concept of the 'extended state'.[4] While that is an ambiguous concept from political philosophy, under the leadership of Pezzullo and Dutton, Australia has introduced some of the most draconian domestic-security legislation in its history.[5] The current Australian government has imprisoned a whistle-blower who revealed war crimes and has held a secret trial of a former Australian intelligence official.

Scaremongering is well known in Australian politics, as elsewhere, as a means of diverting attention from domestic policy failings and exploiting the intuitive insecurities of the electorate. Governments can also be prone to exploiting national myths of wartime sacrifice in the name of freedom for the same political purpose. That could be happening in Australia today, as the government faces a succession of domestic crises and challenges to its credibility. One such challenge flows from a 2020 Defence Department investigation revealing 36 possible war crimes committed by soldiers in the country's Special Air Service Regiment over several years. One such soldier, Ben Roberts-Smith – a recipient of the Victoria Cross, Australia's highest military award for bravery – has brought a defamation suit against three Australian newspapers over allegations that he committed war crimes in Afghanistan.[6] The government is in open battle with the coun-try's public broadcaster, the Australian Broadcasting Commission, over its alleged bias in exposing scandals involving ministers and senior public servants. The China threat has become a contested domestic political issue, especially as Australia's confrontational positions on Huawei, Chinese political interference with domestic Australian politics and the origins of the SARS-CoV-2 virus have prompted Chinese economic coercion.

Certainly such coercion can lead to war, but it is far from clear – at least from open sources – that war with China is imminent or even particularly close. The government's provocative language is premised on the more structural, if nonetheless concerning, analysis of its Department of Defence. In its 2020 strategic update, the department observed that Australia faced a 'security environment markedly different from the relatively more benign one of the past, with greater potential for military miscalculation, including state-on-state conflict'. In the foreword to the document, the prime minister and then-defence minister Linda Reynolds noted that Australia's region was 'in the midst of the most consequential strategic realignment since the Second World War'.[7]

As the 'drums of war' metaphor implies, Pezzullo sees his mission as saving the country from dark forces as insidious as those of the 1930s that would forge a bleak new world order if the country did not radically improve its national-security posture. The prime minister's historical reference point, however, is 1945, the end of the Second World War. Is the region really witnessing the most consequential strategic realignment since then?

II

Several strategic realignments since 1945 might be considered more consequential, and in many respects more war-inducing, than current trends seem to indicate. Take 2011 as the cut-off point between the post-war period and the current period of 'consequential strategic realignment', starting with the US rebalance to Asia. Then assume the relevant region is the Indo-Pacific, spanning Northeast Asia, through Southeast Asia to South Asia and the surrounding waters.

The first major realignment following the war was the end of empire. The post-war collapse of the Asian empires of Britain, France and the Netherlands, and the political independence of former colonies such as India, Indonesia, Laos, Malaysia, Myanmar, Pakistan, the Philippines and Vietnam, were significant strategic developments that produced several regional wars and substantial death tolls through 1971. As a result of decolonisation, sovereignty over a massive amount of territory and people in the Indo-Pacific – from Pakistan and the Arabian Sea to the East Philippines Sea – changed on a scale not witnessed before in a comparably short time.

The start of the Cold War in 1948 and the global confrontation with communism, both covert and overt, was an unprecedented global shock whose repetition is not in prospect. Soviet support for global communism was very different after its victory over the Nazis than it had been before it. The Comintern controlled by Moscow had been the main external agent of Soviet communism since 1921. Suspended in 1943, the programme returned in 1947 as the rebranded Cominform, gaining considerable force as the Soviets consolidated control of their occupied territories between 1945 and 1949 – most visibly in Europe but also including the northern half of the Korean Peninsula. Between 1945 and 1948, communist parties loyal to and supported by Moscow were operating and exercising political influence in most territories of Asia, to the point where China sought permission to lead a new Asian Cominform as the vanguard of communist revolution in Asia. There is no likelihood that such networks of influence will arise in the foreseeable future.

The emergence of the military alliance between China and the Soviet Union, sealed by a treaty in February 1950, also buffeted global and regional strategic order. That was the same month that North Korea received substantial military-equipment deliveries from Stalin, who subsequently gave his political approval to launch the Korean War.[8] The communist invasion in late June 1950 shook the United Nations to its core, with the Security Council and General Assembly agreeing to defend South Korea, an action that eventually prompted China to deploy three million soldiers to fight the UN forces, which included Australian soldiers. Estimates vary, but according to the Peace Research Institute of Oslo, between 1.5 and 4.5m people lost their lives directly or indirectly due to the war.[9]

The solidarity of global communism in a bloody war in Asia emboldened armed insurgencies across the region. The Soviet Union began to sell arms to Third World liberation movements in 1955, starting with Egypt, and within a few years the Communist Party of Indonesia, on Australia's doorstep, had become one of the best organised and largest such parties outside the Sino-Soviet bloc. Moscow was supplying it with money and weapons, leading to a CIA-supported coup attempt in 1958 against the government of Sukarno, who courted communist support.[10] During that period, the United States advised Australia to consider bombing Indonesian government targets to support the rebels. That same year, during the Taiwan Strait crisis, the US military advised the American president to consider using nuclear weapons against China.[11] While these US attitudes about the global confrontation may look like historical mistakes of a high order, they were motivated in part by the mass deaths occurring in China under communist rule. Another substantial motivation was the emergence in 1955 of the Non-Aligned Movement, set up jointly by China, India and Indonesia at the Bandung Conference of 1955, which was in part an assertion of recently independent and substantially anti-Western countries' newfound power.

The next post-war realignment was the Sino-Soviet split, which broke out in full public glare in 1960 and sent tremors through the region, including Australia. The split gave some heart to anti-communist forces, again including Australia, which now hoped that the global communist movement was in decline. In fact, the split prompted the Soviet Union and China to intensify their respective efforts towards global disruption. Although national communist parties splintered between loyalty to Moscow and Beijing, a new militancy and radicalism, inspired largely by Beijing, seemed to bolster national liberation movements. While the Sino-Soviet split might have looked to many like a net gain for strategic stability, it eventually produced Asia's second nuclear crisis. In 1969, after Chinese military forces had repeatedly engaged in military provocations on the Soviet border, Moscow implicitly threatened to use nuclear weapons against China.[12] While details about nuclear forces being put on alert are sparse, both China and the United States regarded the Soviet threats as credible.

Meanwhile, the Cultural Revolution that started in 1966 had convulsed China in civil violence that led to the deaths of millions of people. Mao Zedong and his followers ruthlessly purged the leadership of the Communist Party, and the Red Guard, Mao's revolutionary agitators, rampaged through the country, leaving the armed forces in disarray. The radicals closed most universities, scientific research was suppressed, and many professors were killed or imprisoned. China's international behaviour became unpredictable, and its support to global communist parties increased. Its successful test of a nuclear device in 1964 only amplified threat perceptions. The US, supported by Australia, became mired in a ground war in Vietnam that would end in American defeat, and the genocidal Khmer Rouge regime in Cambodia emerged, killing some 2m people for lack of loyalty and revolutionary fervour. By the mid-1970s, communist parties had achieved unchallenged rule throughout Indochina.

III

The rapprochement between the United States and China in 1971, based on mutual hostility towards the Soviet Union, had a major strategic impact. It coincided with the seating of the People's Republic of China as a permanent member of the UN Security Council. Then came the drawdown of US forces in Vietnam in 1973, China's seizure of the Paracel Islands in 1974, the US announcement in 1977 that it would withdraw a large number of ground troops from South Korea, the Vietnamese invasion of Cambodia in 1978, China's retaliatory invasion of Vietnam in 1979 and the establishment of a Soviet military presence in Vietnam. By 1992, the US military withdrawal from Southeast Asia was largely complete, with the Philippines, a former US colony, demanding the closure of US bases there, in part due to US refusal to disclose the presence of American nuclear weapons in or passing through the country.

The 1970s also saw the re-emergence of Japan as a great power, albeit a mainly economic one with small and essentially defensive military forces. Japan became the second-largest global economy, a leader in global trade and investment, and a discreet player in Asia-Pacific diplomacy. It extended discounted loans to China to support its economic opening in 1979, worked for the establishment of the Pacific Economic Cooperation Council in 1980 and raised a genuine economic challenge to the United States. Japan remains an economic powerhouse, an abundant source of information and communications technology trailing only the United States and China, and a growing influence in global diplomacy.

Finally, after the Soviet invasion of Afghanistan in 1979, detente flickered out and the United States and the Soviet Union returned to pitched military confrontation, both engaging in massive military build-ups and increasing global confrontation thorough proxy activities. In the 1980s, at least one nuclear crisis arose between the two countries.[13] During this period, the Australian government secretly assessed that in a nuclear war, two US bases in Australia – both space-monitoring facilities related to nuclear missiles – would be likely targets of Soviet attack. By 1986, Ronald Reagan, the US president, and Mikhail Gorbachev, the Soviet leader, had rejected the political utility of nuclear war; by 1989 the Cold War had ended; and by 1991 the USSR had disintegrated to form 15 independent republics, five of them bordering East Asia or South Asia. These too were momentous developments.

Obviously, not all of these developments posed threats to Australian security. There was a clear peace dividend to Australia and the region from the collapse of the Soviet Union and the emergence of China as a recognised partner in the UN system and regional organisations, and a global economic power.

The pertinent question, however, is this: were any of the catalogued strategic realignments less consequential for Australia and the region than what has transpired since 2011, when the United States decided it would return to strategic competition in Asia to blunt China's growing regional assertiveness and military power? The answer has to be no, especially if judged in terms of casualties, risk of war, forward-deployed military units, hostile rhetoric and changes in territorial sovereignty. While the risks of war in Australia's region have marginally increased since 2011, they remain very low compared with those that prevailed from 1945 to 1995. Against this background, the current Australian government's assessment appears to be alarmist, and the 'drums of war' it hears artificially amplified.

Notes

1   Michael Pezzullo, 'The Drums of War Are Growing Louder', *Australian*, 27 April 2021, https://www.theaustralian.com.au/commentary/the-drums-of-war-are-growing-louder/news-story/ bf29fb3cf94b89f84eaeb22fd32d9724.

2   See Michael Pezzullo, 'Security as a Positive and Unifying Force', speech at Australian National University National Security College,

13 October 2020, https://www.
homeaffairs.gov.au/news-media/
speeches/2020/13-october-security-as-
a-positive-and-unifying-force.

3   Michael Pezzullo, 'Networked
Societies/Networked Security', speech
at the Australian Security Summit,
Canberra, 21 July 2015, https://www.
homeaffairs.gov.au/news-media/
speeches/2015/21-july-australian-
security-summit.

4   Pezzullo, 'Security as a Positive and
Unifying Force'.

5   See, for example, Damien Cave,
'Australia May Well Be the World's
Most Secretive Democracy', *New
York Times*, 5 June 2019, https://www.
nytimes.com/2019/06/05/world/
australia/journalist-raids.html.

6   See, for instance, Ben Doherty, 'Ben
Roberts-Smith Accused of Murder
and Intimidation as He Defends
Himself in Court', *Guardian*, 10 June
2021, https://www.theguardian.com/
australia-news/2021/jun/10/ben-roberts-
smith-accused-of-and-intimidation-as-
he-defends-himself-in-court.

7   Australian Department of Defence,
'2020 Defence Strategic Update', pp.
3, 17, https://www1.defence.gov.au/
strategy-policy/strategic-update-2020.

8   See, for example, Alan Cooperman,
'Stalin Approved Start of
Korean War, Documents Show',
Associated Press, 13 January
1993, https://apnews.com/article/
adf271706570fbe753e6783955675e60.

9   Peace Research Institute of Oslo, 'The
PRIO Battle Deaths Dataset, 1946–2008,
Version 3.0: Documentation of Coding
Decisions', updated September 2009,
pp. 359–62, https://files.prio.org/
ReplicationData/BattleDeathsDataset/
PRIO%20Battle%20Deaths%20
Dataset%203.0%20Documentation.pdf.

10 See, for instance, Vincent Bevins, 'What
the United States Did in Indonesia',
Atlantic, 20 October 2017, https://
www.theatlantic.com/international/
archive/2017/10/the-indonesia-
documents-and-the-us-agenda/543534/.
See also Audrey R. Kahin and George
McTurnan Kahin, *Subversion as Foreign
Policy: The Secret Eisenhower and Dulles
Debacle in Indonesia* (New York: New
Press, 1995).

11 See, for example, Charlie Savage,
'Risk of Nuclear War Over Taiwan in
1958 Said To Be Greater than Publicly
Known', *New York Times*, 22 May 2021,
https://www.nytimes.com/2021/05/22/
us/politics/nuclear-war-risk-1958-us-
china.html.

12 See, for instance, Michael S. Gerson,
'The Sino-Soviet Border Conflict:
Deterrence, Escalation, and the Threat
of Nuclear War in 1969', Center for
Naval Analyses, November 2010, pp.
28–31, https://www.cna.org/cna_files/
pdf/d0022974.a2.pdf.

13 See Gordon Barrass, '*Able Archer 83*:
What Were the Soviets Thinking?',
Survival, vol. 58, no. 6, December
2016–January 2017, pp. 7–30.